50 BEST
Girlfriends Getaways
IN NORTH AMERICA
SECOND EDITION

50 BEST
Girlfriends Getaways
IN NORTH AMERICA
SECOND EDITION

By Marybeth Bond

NATIONAL GEOGRAPHIC

WASHINGTON, D.C.

❧ ALSO BY MARYBETH BOND ❧

Best Girlfriends Getaways Worldwide

A Woman's Asia: True Stories

A Woman's Europe: True Stories

A Woman's World: True Stories of Life on the Road

Gutsy Women: More Travel Tips and Wisdom for the Road

A Woman's Passion for Travel: True Stories of World Wanderlust
(with Pamela Michael)

A Mother's World: Journeys of the Heart

Gutsy Mamas: Travel Tips and Wisdom for Mothers on the Road

For

the phenomenal women in my family: my mother, Ruth, who gave me roots and wings; my older sister, Gail, who showers me with love and encouragement; my other sister, Alice, who has taught me by example how to dream big and reinvent myself; my daughters, J.C. and Annalyse, who are my shining stars in the firmament, and for my patient husband, Gary, who always urges me to "go for it."

Contents

Go Now!

Women are stepping out with girlfriends, zooming along roads, paths and waterways with style, humor and courage. Through my own experiences and those of the women I have interviewed for *50 Best Girlfriends Getaways,* I learned that travel is one of the most powerful ways to reconnect with our deepest female soul mates—our girlfriends. And then there are reasons to travel that are unique and truly important to women: reuniting with childhood girlfriends, mother-daughter bonding, exploring every nook and cranny of a neighborhood, meandering through gardens or historic homes, being pampered at a spa, and the drive to shop 'til you drop in a retail mecca.

Flip through the table of contents and you'll see that this book is organized by themes as opposed to destinations. It addresses our different life stages: turning 40, 50, or 60; bonding with a daughter; craving adventure when the kids have left the house, coping with heartbreak, illness, or the death of loved one.

This second edition includes a new chapter describing the best places for home and garden tours, as well as new destinations: Seattle, Pasadena, Litchfield, Alexandria, Newport, Scottsdale, and Carmel.

Each chapter is set in motion with the stories of women who sought out travel with girlfriends as a means to heal, celebrate, grow, stretch, challenge themselves, or change. I also share my own stories as a travel writer, mother, daughter, and friend. These personal stories remind us that sharing a journey with our female friends is good for our self-confidence, our careers, our marriages, and other relationships.

I describe the spirit-boosting effects of a much-needed horseback riding trip with my daughters in Arizona when I was worn out and in need of a break.

Lynn recounts the joy of dancing her tail off in Louisiana's Cajun Country, defying her age and single status by two-stepping to the accordion and fiddle with girlfriends and anyone else on the dance floor. Music, dancing, and the spirit of Cajun Country always lifts her spirits.

Julie and her college roommates book a tough cross-country bike trip for a 50th birthday celebration and prove to the younger generation, as well as themselves, that they've still "got it."

Chris gets together with a circle of "best friends" from her high school days every other year. They have participated in each others' weddings, childbirths, and graduations; cooed over grandchildren, and comforted each other through chemo and the death of spouses. At their reunions they feel like sisters again, sitting around in the late evening in their nightgowns, drinking cheap wine, talking about everything under the sun, looking at old photos of themselves, nurturing each other, laughing until their faces ache, and returning home exhausted and renewed.

These stories are meant to inspire you, to give you ideas for your own travels. They are tales of ordinary women who do extraordinary things with their girlfriends by their side.

50 Best Girlfriends Getaways is geared to women visiting an area for three to six days. When you read most travel guidebooks, you are constantly sorting out what is relevant to you. In this book, I have done the filtering for you. And I have formatted the book in the same way women communicate with each other: We are storytellers, we network, we pick each other's brains, and we love to pass along the tidbits and little gems of information that we've discovered along the way.

Each and every boutique hotel, restaurant, neighborhood, garden or walking tour I recommend was carefully chosen with women in mind. We are discriminating travelers, are we not? We get a kick out of saving ourselves money, getting a good deal, but we also like to splurge on things that are truly worth our dime. Understanding how the interior design of a hotel, the mood of a jazz club, the quality of food at a café and the vista from a hike can make or break an experience, I put every destination under the microscope and pounded the pavement (or trail, as the case may be) to bring you the best itinerary for the type of trip you're seeking. Whether it's devising a plan of attack for a retail therapy spree or kicking back at a spa, I simplify your travel planning so you can focus on the most important component to the trip: quality time with your girlfriends. And it is all made easy at the conclusion of each destination with phone numbers and websites with "One Click and You're Off."

Then in the sidebars throughout the book, I have incorporated my own tips, tricks, and secrets as well as those of other experts and women travelers who have been to the destination. The sidebars offer advice on what to pack, what to expect, what to avoid, and what not to miss.

You may ask, "What exactly makes for a 'female friendly' place?" I focus on the "proximity" of hotels, dining establishments, attractions, and theaters to each other. Women want to be in the center of the action, so they are able to walk places and avoid expensive cabs or complicated public transportation. When sifting through the countless choices of accommodations, location becomes paramount, especially for a short visit. The hotels and resorts I have chosen are in safe neighborhoods, have character, and are reasonably priced. I have included some hotels that recognize women as an important market, offering unique "girlfriend packages."

For restaurants, exceptional food and a creative menu are essential. Women like to experiment. When we dine out we want to eat something we probably couldn't or wouldn't prepare at home. A restaurant should also be conversation friendly, comfortable, and a destination in itself. Good service is crucial, because many of us are usually the service provider at home, and we know good service when we see it. And at least one dining selection in each destination is an affordable option.

Why do you need a guidebook book for women only? Because most travel books are geared to the general population and don't specifically address our concerns and special interests. I believe that women travel differently than men. We look for different things in our travel experience. We're attuned to the safety of the neighborhood, the décor of the hotel room, the helpfulness of the inn owners, the softness of the pillow, the thread count of the sheets, the lighting in the bathroom, the noisy, conversation-killing atmosphere in a restaurant, and the courtesy of the waiter.

Groups of men have traditionally taken off together to fish, canoe, golf or hunt. About a decade ago, select hotel chains started offering "Girlfriend Getaway Packages" and today a few hotels are catching up with men's packages. According to their offerings, when men travel together they want penthouse rooms, poker parties, hand-rolled cigars, sport tickets, butler service and even the option to rent flashy, luxury cars such as a Porsche or a Lambourghini. Does this sound like your idea of a good time, ladies?

Women don't necessarily want the same things men do when they vacation with their female friends. We look for comfy lodging, terrific food, a variety of activities, and stunning scenery. Many women enjoy posh pampering and shopping in big cities or small artsy towns. Others thrive on adventure and lively entertainment. But what we want most of all is to be together, to catch up, unwind, laugh, have fun, and nurture ourselves and each other.

A conventional guidebook for a single destination is quickly dated, and you may toss it after the trip. *50 Best Girlfriends Getaways* is a resource women will keep on their shelves for years and refer to repeatedly for inspiration and ideas for the next girlfriends' vacation and the next and the next. *50 Best Girlfriends Getaways* grows with you. It's equally pertinent to a woman in her 30s as it is to one in her 60s. This book gives every woman the encouragement, advice, and knowledge to get out there and explore. So don't wait, call your girlfriends and go now!

—Marybeth Bond

CHAPTER ONE

Big City Getaways

⮞ MARGEE'S STORY ⮜

Margee, her sister, and a friend planned a trip to Quebec City and Montreal because they longed for French ambience and European flavor and didn't want to fly across the pond. They went on the Internet and found accommodations right in the center of the old town in Montreal and Quebec City. Several of the hotels they contacted could not accommodate three people in one room and renting two rooms would split up the group, so they rented a cozy apartment in Montreal. There they threw open the windows and looked down on the cobblestone streets, cafés, and wine bars filled with people sipping and laughing. They dined in a candlelit wine cellar and tasted fiddlehead ferns for the first time.

"The trip was really easy, a no-brainer. In Montreal we took a taxi to the train station and booked first-class tickets on the spot to go to Quebec City. During the four-and-a-half hour trip we popped open champagne and toasted each other as we watched the scenery flow by. We discovered that Quebec was even more French than Montreal. We treated ourselves (yes, yet again) to a room in the Château Frontenac," says Margee.

The highlight of traveling with her girlfriends was laughing so much, and being able to talk about any and everything. "I treasured these conversations that didn't center on husbands or kids, but focused on what was on my mind, which was adjusting to life after divorce. We laughed a lot about some of my life stories as a newly single woman. I began to see myself differently because of my trips with girlfriends. I realized I didn't need a man to feel whole and I could make my own decisions and stand on my own two feet," adds Margee.

Margee wasn't always such an independent woman with adventurous girlfriends. We met when I led an all-women's trip to France, just nine months after Margee's divorce. She got her first passport and headed for Paris because she loved all things "French" and wanted to do something daring, scary, and exciting.

She exuded a youthful energy and radiated an upbeat attitude of life, accentuated by her infectious laugh and her skill at making fun of herself. None of us knew that after a crushing divorce at age 54, she had relocated from San Diego to Seattle to live closer to her two grown daughters and started a new life. She was adjusting to the empty nest, life without a man, and living alone.

"That lighthearted trip opened a window to a new life for me. I learned that I could travel without a husband on my sleeve or in his shadow. When I was married, 99 percent of my friends were married and were people we knew through my husband's work. All my friendships were part and parcel of my marriage and they were guarded relationships. This first trip with women led to a whole new me and a new group of friends. I found out who I was. For many years I was a mother, a wife. I found I am happy without a man. I like being with myself. Now is my time to do what I want, and I love it.

"My new travel friends love me—who I am—not who I am with. I'm more open to them and I cherish them because they cherish me for being totally myself," says Margee.

After the first organized women's trip Margee decided she would plan the trips herself and found new travel friends with the same sense of adventure and spontaneity. They have gone to Montreal, Quebec, New York City, San Francisco, Spain, and all over the U.S. and Canada.

"We book our hotels in advance but let the rest unfold. We have the same inner clocks. We like to get up early and get going. We try something new and different every day, like restaurants off the beaten path. One of us will gravitate toward something unusual, something I wouldn't pick to do, like visiting an old cemetery or going to a doll museum, and I end up loving it," says Margee.

"As I get more mature, I realize travel has made me reach out to other people more. My world is not closing in around me. It's expanding. Quite simply, sharing experiences with other women is a lot of fun," sums up Margee.

❧ JUDI & LIBBY'S STORY ❧

When Judi and Libby met over 30 years ago in Midland, Michigan, they never imagined that when the kids were gone they'd leave their husbands at home for an annual blowout in the Big Apple.

"New York presents fertile ground for transcending our Midwestern, middle-class, middle-aged lives here in Michigan," says Libby. "The city is mythic to me, conjured from extravagant black-and-white musicals, romantic comedies, and *King Kong*. Long before my first visit—with Judi, by the way—I'd spent a lifetime imagining the city as experienced by Thomas Wolfe, Walt Whitman, Teddy Roosevelt, and many more writers, journalists, and theater critics."

Their first trips were pretty carefully planned—Libby and Judi were anxious newcomers—but as they came to know the place, their trips evolved into more spontaneous affairs. Now they just pick a date, make hotel and plane reservations, and see what happens. And what happens is always memorable.

"We stay for four nights and generally see a play or two," says Libby. "Part of the adventure is waiting in the TKTS line at Times Square to get discounted tickets and watch people. We also see a movie, and we try to target shows that are unlikely to make it to mid-Michigan. On our last trip we saw *Mongolian Ping Pong*, a funny, gentle story depicting the life of a young boy in Mongolia. We often take in a musical event of some kind. We check *New York* magazine and the *New York Times* for what's happening during our visit, and then engage in a sort of negotiation that has never failed to deliver a good time."

These trips were always a treat to themselves, so they did whatever they wanted to do. "When it comes out of two household budgets, it's possible to book a suite at a lovely old European-style hotel," says Judi. "We buy fancy pastries and gourmet coffee for a leisurely breakfast in our room because we both like a slow start. We get out by 11 a.m. and we're on the go until 11 p.m. With a MetroCard for the bus, we can get around easily, see a lot of New York and New Yorkers, and not worry about carrying the correct change. (You get six rides on mass transit for $10.) Fine dining isn't our priority. Entertainment is our focus. So we just stop for a meal someplace that looks interesting when we are on the fly between activities," says Judi.

They'd go the "New York's Less Visited Places" route. For instance, the Museum of Television and Radio in midtown lets visitors watch their favorite old shows. You may select up to four at a given time and go into a private carrel for viewing. Judi watched *Rin Tin Tin, McMillan and Wife,* and *Bonanza.*

"On our latest trip, Judi and I walked across the Brooklyn Bridge from lower Manhattan to Brooklyn Heights, a beautiful neighborhood of brownstone homes on streets named Cranberry and Pineapple," says Libby. "We strolled by the homes of famous authors, including Truman Capote's abode, where he wrote *Breakfast at Tiffany's.* It was a breezy, beautiful spring day, the sights were breathtaking, and we had a fantastic time.

"When I worked as a nurse in an intensive-care unit I would sometimes use guided imagery to help my patients get through a difficult or painful experience. Essentially, this amounts to revisiting a comforting and meaningful experience from the past, conjuring up as much specificity as possible. People will sometimes choose to remember the day their babies were born, a wedding day, or maybe picking blueberries with grandma. If a time comes when I need to remember an experience that I hold dear, my days with Judi in New York will do the job," says Libby.

What's great about traveling with girlfriends? You don't get grief about spending time shopping.

—Laurie Armstrong, 40s, Vice President, San Francisco Convention & Visitors Bureau, San Francisco, California

Big City Getaways

Despite its reputation for vertiginous hills, San Francisco is a town for walking. So, ladies, you'll want to lace up your comfiest walking shoes and head for its varied neighborhoods and parks, where you'll be struck by the juxtaposition of urbanity and nature. With the emerald hills of Marin County as a backdrop, San Francisco impresses with a colorful palette: from Technicolor Mexican murals to pastel Victorian homes to lush gardens to contemporary architecture. And when you tire of the pavement, retreat to the city's green spaces for rejuvenating walks: The northwest part of the city is mostly National Park land with wooded trails, gardens, and views of the bay and the majestic Golden Gate Bridge. You and the girls will find yourselves pulling out your cameras once again to get that stunning panorama or a shot of you all hoofing it up the hills. (The hills are often worth the climb—typically for the jaw-dropping vistas.) And it's also almost impossible to get a bad meal in this town of veritable foodies. You'll all gather around a large table for cheap dim sum in Chinatown, learn the proper way to unwrap the tinfoil from your Mission-style burritos, and get gussied up to hit some of the finest restaurants in the country. San Francisco has a way of rewarding you for all that walking.

BEST NEIGHBORHOOD FOR STROLLING
North Beach, the city's Italian-American quarter, a block from Chinatown, is one of my favorite places to stroll, sip house-roasted expresso, and shop. People-watch from a tiny sidewalk café filled with old Italian gents, get your carb fix with a big bowl of pasta, or have a picnic on the grass at Washington Square with fixings from a nearby gourmet food shop. Wandering through its side streets, you'll happen upon gems like the San Francisco Art Institute, a Tuscan-style villa with a Diego Rivera mural, student galleries, and a large terrace with a sweeping view of the bay. Browse the shelves of the three-story City Lights Bookstore, the legacy of the 1950s Beat poets Allen Ginsberg and Lawrence Ferlinghetti. If you love the written word, a pilgrimage to City Lights is a must.

BEST GARDEN WALK
Take a short detour from North Beach and head down the famed Filbert Steps, flanked by cascading gardens, sculptures, and benches—you'll be glad you did. You may hear or catch a glimpse of the famous wild

green parrots that soar from tree to tree, as seen in the documentary *The Wild Parrots of Telegraph Hill*. Begin your stroll at the top of the steps at the corner of Montgomery and Filbert Streets and descend to Sansome Street.

BEST CAFÉS

Take in the mix of cultures sitting outdoors or indoors at my favorite haunt in North Beach: **CAFÉ GRECO**. Locals swear it has absolutely the best cappuccino in the city, with the perfect swirl of coffee in the light foamy milk on the top. It's a mecca for expresso buffs who sip while writing next year's great novel. Located at 423 Columbus Avenue, between Green and Vallejo Streets (415-397-6261).

While in the Marina district, going into **EMPORIO RULLI GRAN CAFÉ** is like stepping into a Northern Italian café complete with Venetian chandelier, mahogany bar, and frescoed ceiling. You'll find the large selection of homemade pastries; chocolates, cookies, and gelato equally authentic and extraordinary. Italian wines are served at the bar, and you can enjoy a small plate or dinner until 10 p.m. Located at 2300 Chestnut Street (at Scott) (415-923-6464, www.rulli.com).

A block east, at 2250 Chestnut Street, the hip, yet cozy **GROVE CAFÉ** is a relaxing spot to stop for sidewalk seating and a great selection of teas, pastries, and salads (415-474-4843).

BEST DINING

ANA MANDARA means "beautiful refuge" in a Vietnamese dialect. Its dramatic interior transports you to an Asian tropical garden accented with potted palms, a koi pond, and cozy alcoves defined by dark carved wood. Ana Mandara is my favorite new Vietnamese (with French accents) restaurant because of its opulent beauty, gracious service, and fabulous cuisine. The lobster ravioli, quail with plum sauce, and clay pot of fresh-water Delta prawns in red caramel sauce are to die for. It is one of the few Asian restaurants with a full-time sommelier and an impressive list of wines that are global in scope, affordable, and well paired with the food. After dinner go up the sweeping stairs to the bar for drinks or dessert where you can often catch some very good live music. Located in the Fisherman's Wharf area, in Ghiradelli Square, across from the (free) Maritime Museum. 891 Beach Street at Polk ($30-50; 415-771-6800, www.anamandara.com).

Many locals consider **MICHAEL MINA** the finest dining experience in San Francisco. It's my favorite for a very special occasion or a dining splurge. It's expensive but worth it for the sophisticated and creative culinary extravaganza. Try the tasting menu with full wine pairing. Each food presentation consists of bite-size portions of your selection, such as scallops, lamb, or lobster accompanied by creative sauces made with Osetra Caviar, Black Truffle, Scarlet Beet, or Maine Lobster. A three-course seasonal menu is $100. Located in the Westin St. Francis Hotel on Union Square, close to the theater district, it's open until midnight and a perfect location for late-night dining. 335 Powell Street (415-397-9222, www.michaelmina.net).

You'll dine in a grand manner at the **GRAND CAFÉ**, a wonderful French restaurant with dramatic belle epoch décor. Columns, chandeliers, 30-foot-high ceilings, French murals in a Toulouse-Lautrec mode, faux finishes, bronze statues, fabulous floral pieces, and fanciful touches of art deco and art nouveau remind you of elegant Parisian restaurants. Well located near Union Square and the theater district, it delivers unpretentious service in an elegant atmosphere at a fair price. Classic entrees of generous proportion include organic duck breast, rabbit with mustard sauce, cassoulet, or fresh Hawaiian fish. You mustn't leave without dessert. My

CHEAPEST AND SAFEST WAY FROM THE AIRPORT TO YOUR HOTEL

Use the complimentary hotel shuttle van if available or take the "hotel van" that stops at numerous downtown hotels. They are less expensive and more reliable than taxis.

favorite is the flourless chocolate cake with a warm orange-chocolate and hazelnut interior served with coffee cardamom cream. The adjoining PETIT CAFÉ is also cozy, with a lamp-lit dark-wood bar and a wood-burning oven for pizzas. It's perfect for a light meal before or after the theater, or a snack when shopping. 501 Geary Street at Taylor Street. $31-50 (415-292-0101).

PAMPER YOURSELF

After a day on your feet in the big city, find tranquility and renewal at the baths of the Japanese-style Kabuki Springs & Spa, where silence is mandatory—and all for only $20 ($25 on weekends). Three days a week are for women only; massages and facials are also available. Located in Japantown, 1750 Geary Blvd. at Fillmore Street (415-922-6000, www.kabukisprings.com).

HAVE TEA

Tucked into Golden Gate Park, the four-acre, 100-year-old Japanese Tea Garden and its carp ponds, waterfalls, and bonsai trees provide the perfect respite. For a snack, enjoy a pot of jasmine tea and a bowl of Japanese cookies in its adorable tea house. Open daily 8:30 a.m. to 6 p.m. in summer; 9 a.m. to 4:45 p.m. Nov. 1-March 31 (415-752-4227).

FOR A SPIRIT BOOSTER

For a hand-clapping, foot-stomping good time, rise early on Sunday for one of Glide Memorial Church's "celebrations." 330 Ellis St. (415-674-6000, www.glide.org). The 100-plus multiethnic (and generational) choir belts out soul-warming spirituals that bring the full house to its feet.

MUST-SEE MUSEUMS

One of the largest museums dedicated to showcasing Asian art in the West, the Asian Art Museum resides in the stately former Main Library; the restoration and jade collection alone are worth the visit. 200 Larkin St. (415-581-3500, www.asianart.org).

In Golden Gate Park, the de Young Memorial Museum houses an eclectic collection (from American painting to African art) inside a newly constructed metal-and-glass building with a 114-foot observation tower offering 360-degree views (415-750-3600 for tickets, www .thinker.org/deyoung). I was a docent guide at the deYoung Museum for many years and highly recommend seeing the stellar pieces in the African, Oceania, and Mesoamerican art collections. Admission is free the first Tuesday of every month. Call ahead or go online to see when the docent tours are offered. It's well worth planning your visit around a free, informative tour. In good weather dine in the sculpture garden outside the restaurant.

The new California Academy of Sciences—ten years and $500 million in the making—opened in the fall of 2008. Don't miss this cultural icon and masterpiece in sustainable architecture. It is the only place on the planet with an aquarium, a planetarium, a natural history museum, a four-story rain forest, and 2.5 acres of live plants and flowers blanketing the roof.

Tip: To avoid lines at the door, purchase your tickets online in advance. As soon as you enter the museum, check the scheduled events for the Planetarium Shows, California Coastal Dive, Penguin Feeding, and Coral Reef Dive. Admission is free on the third Wednesday of every month. 550 Music Concourse Dr., Golden Gate Park (415-379-8000, www.calacademy.org).

THRIFT AND VINTAGE CLOTHING

At Seconds to Go in Pacific Heights you'll find name-brand, high-class clothing in good shape, no stains or holes, including women's suits with labels such as Anne Klein, DKNY, Dana Buchman, and Jones New York. Across the street is the Junior League Next-to-New Shop with equally good buys. Seconds to Go, 2252 Fillmore Street (415-563-7806); Junior League Next-to-New Shop, 2226 Fillmore Street (415-567-1627).

My favorite funky, fun place to pick up a crazy one-of-a-kind outfit or vintage clothing is Aardvarks Odd Ark on Haight Street. Aardvarks brings out the wild side of thrift shopping. And Haight Street is a great place for people watching. Yes, this is the Haight Street of 1960s notoriety, and hippies are still part of the colorful street scene. 1501 Haight Street (415- 621-3141).

For More: Keywords: Thrift Shops or Discount Shopping

FARMERS MARKETS FOR PHENOMENAL FOOD

(Marybeth Favorites) In my food-crazed city and the entire Bay Area, you'll find a dizzying selection of fresh foods for sale almost every day at local farmers markets.

My favorite in the city is located along the waterfront, in the shadow of the tall office buildings at the Ferry Terminal at the base of Market Street. Local restaurants, wine stores, cheese shops, butchers, bakers, coffeehouses, and trendy bars are located in the Ferry Building; however, on Saturdays from 8 a.m. to 2 p.m. local farmers and high-profile vendors set up tables and umbrellas on the wide sidewalk and on the waterfront with sweeping views of the Bay Bridge, water, and sky. Whether you are shopping for caviar, kiwi, olives, chocolate, or pastries, you'll find it here. Sample the ripe cheeses from Cowgirl Creamery; buy a crispy baguette from Acme Bakery, chocolates from local chocolate purveyor, Scharffenberger, peaches from Frog Hollow, and oysters from Hog Island. The prices are a bit inflated, but the location and selection can't be beat. Many of the shops inside the Ferry Building are equally fascinating. Don't miss my dream pastry shop, Boulettes Larder, to savor the flaky butter crust Apple Crosta with cinnamon and almond topping. If you're feeling like an elegant Parisian-style tasting, stop at Tsar Nicoulai's Caviar Café to sip champagne and nibble on caviar, blini, or mouth-watering smoked salmon.

TAKE A COOKING CLASS

Tante Marie's private cooking school specializes in small class size, where everyone cooks together under the guidance of the chef or cooking teacher; in other words, you participate. Some of the classes are taught by TV personalities and famous San Francisco chefs; in are demonstration classes, you'll watch the instructor cook. Don't worry, in addition to learning new dishes, you'll feast at the end of each class. There are evening classes, weekend workshops, and one-week cooking vacations. Popular weekend workshops and day classes include Sweet and Savory Pies and Tarts, Entertaining with Ease, Asian Small Plates, Classic French Bistro Menus, Go Wild with Mushrooms, and All About Lobster and Crab. It's located in North Beach, in the heart of the city. (One-day workshops $185; 415-788-6699, www.tantemarie.com)

EVENTS TO FLY IN FOR

In February, Chinatown comes alive for Chinese New Year, the largest and most extravagant celebration (think massive floats, colorful dragons, and firecrackers) of Chinese culture outside of Asia (www.chinese parade.com). And on every third Sunday in May, more than 65,000 costumed folk run across the city in the anything-goes 12K Bay to Breakers (415-359-2800, www.ingbaytobreakers.com). Spectate or get the girls to run it with you. Hear the finest country and bluegrass talent at the free Hardly Strictly Bluegrass weekend festival in Golden Gate Park each October (www.strictlybluegrass.com).

WHERE TO STAY

If it's shopping that you're looking for, you can't beat Hotel Diva just steps from Union Square, with everything from Louis Vuitton to Saks and H&M. Hotel Diva is located in a neighborhood abundant with innovative restaurants, clubs, and nightlife. The Curran and American Conservatory Theatres are conveniently located directly across the street. Hotel Diva provides ultramodern rooms and fun getaway packages. An eclectic collection of seven boutique Personality Hotels include; "Sexy" Hotel Diva, "Grand" Kensington Park Hotel, "Authentic" Hotel Union Square, "Vivid" Hotel Metropolis, "Timeless" Steinhart Hotel, and "Whimsical" Hotel Vertigo. You get the picture that each hotel has its own personality and perks. Hot Chicks or Female Frenzy are the type of girlfriend packages offered at Hotel Diva, 440 Geary Street. (Starting from $ 179 per room;, 800-553-1900, www.personalityhotels.com)

Other inexpensive, centrally located hotels, with starting prices based on season, include the Kensington Park, 450 Post Street (starting from $189 per room; 800-553-1900, kensingtonparkhotel.com); King George Hotel, 334 Mason Street at Geary (starting from $199 per room; 800-288-6005, www.kinggeorge.com); and Larkspur Hotel, 524 Sutter Street (starting from $209 per room; 800-919-9779; reservations: 415-421-2865, www.cartwright hotel.com), AAA members save 20% when you book online.

ON A BUDGET
The hostel in Fort Mason has views of the Golden Gate Bridge and Alcatraz and private rooms (starting at $75 a night; 415-771-7277, www .sfhostels.com).

ONE CLICK AND YOU'RE OFF: www.onlyinsanfrancisco.com; www .sanfrancisco.citysearch.com.

⤜ MIAMI ⤛

The Riviera of North America, Miami takes you worlds away with an international flare that can be attributed to its Latin community and chic European visitors. A visit to Miami is really two vacations in one: an exotic beach retreat mixed with a cosmopolitan getaway. There are the sultry weather, sunshine, and picture-perfect beaches, and also the classic art deco architecture and sophisticated nightlife. In Miami you can't help but feel glamorous, a little bit sexier. The hotels of South Beach drip with extravagance and style. And its international influence sparks your senses. The energy will keep you salsa dancing past midnight, make you and your girlfriends feel like millionaires as you sip fruity cocktails on a beachfront veranda, and it just may make you rent a convertible. But there's also a down-to-earth side: the natural beauty of its tropical gardens, the new flavors to be savored in its modest Cuban cafés, the accessibility and affordability of its lively music scene, and the simplicity of digging your toes in the sand. Ultimately, Miami lets you see yourself in new ways, whether as a teenager cruising South Beach on a rented bike or a socialite taking afternoon tea at the legendary Biltmore Hotel. Miami truly lets you get away.

NEIGHBORHOODS FOR STROLLING
Get a taste of Cuba in the Little Havana district. You'll encounter the domino players in Domino Park, shops with Cuban souvenirs, and the El Credito Cigar Factory, where you can watch cigars being rolled. Then sip a café con leche and feast on arroz con pollo (chicken with yellow rice) and catch an evening flamenco performance. The village-like neighborhoods of Coconut Grove and Coral Gables and their galleries, sidewalk cafes, and small boutiques are great places to spend an afternoon.

BEST SHOPPING
There's something for everyone in the open-air Lincoln Road Mall of South Beach: boutiques, big-name stores, antique shops, a Sunday morning farmers market, art galleries, and cafés. Farther north, on Collins Avenue, the Bal Harbor Shops completely transform the concept of a shopping mall. Every high-end designer imaginable, from Prada to Chanel to Gucci, has a store here.

HAVE TEA
Built in 1926, the Biltmore Hotel in Coral Gables serves a traditional afternoon tea in its elaborate lobby under a vaulted ceiling. It's great for people watching and splurging. It also has a very popular Sunday Champagne Brunch with live entertainment and sushi, carving, and pasta stations.

GARDENS
Fairchild Tropical Botanic Garden in Coral Gables boasts being the largest tropical garden in the continental United States. Set aside a full day to explore its 83 acres of blossoming trees, lakes, palms, and rare tropical rain forest plants. Located at 10901 Old Cutler Rd. (305-667-1651, www.ftg.org).

TAKE A CRUISE
See how the other half lives on the Island Queen Millionaire's Row Sightseeing Tour, a 1.5-hour cruise of the bay. You'll motor past the palatial homes of singer Gloria Estefan, NBA star Shaquille O'Neal, and Al Capone, among others, and take in a breathtaking view of downtown (305-379-5119, www.islandqueencruises.com).

MUST-SEE MUSEUMS

Wolfsonian-Florida International University in Miami Beach showcases an individual's collection of more than 70,000 objects from the modern era, including ceramics, metalwork, rare books, textiles, and propaganda (305-531-1001, www.wolfsonian.fiu.edu). In Coconut Grove, the sumptuous Italian Renaissance-style Vizcaya Museum and Gardens overlooks Biscayne Bay. Its rooms brim with paintings, sculpture, and antiques from the 15th to the 19th centuries. Located at 3251 South Miami Ave. (305-250-9133, www.vizcayamuseum.org).

A DAY AT THE BEACH

White sand, turquoise water, and beautiful people are the ingredients that have made South Beach one of the world's most famous beaches. Lavish art deco and contemporary hotels skirt the beach, but between 5th and 15th Streets, there are none: a prime spot for spreading out your towels and spending the day. And if you can't afford to be a guest at the nearby Ritz-Carlton, at least pretend you can with lunch and cocktails at its swank oceanfront DeLido Beach Club.

For more of a natural beach experience, visit the mile-long beach of Bill Baggs State Park in Key Biscayne and its 19th-century lighthouse. And on Virginia Key, a non-residential island in the bay with a large wildlife conservation area, you'll find beaches with a wilderness feel.

THRIFT AND VINTAGE CLOTHING

C. Madeleine's in North Miami Beach has outfitted celebrities and *Sex and the City* actors in their extensive collection of elegant vintage clothing and accessories. And at the Douglas Gardens Thrift Shop, a warehouse full of inexpensive stuff, you'll unearth some treasures if you're patient.

BEST DINING

One of Zagat's Top Restaurant picks in the nation, Miami Beach's NEMO is a very extravagant dining experience (in its tastes from around the world and its prices). 100 Collins Avenue, South Beach (305-532-4550).

More affordable and owned by the same person, BIG PINK is a festive, airy, modern dining room with a menu ranging from American comfort food to fancier fare. They pride themselves on serving "real food for real people" and big portions. Located at 157 Collins Avenue, South Beach. ($6-30; 305-532-4700).

If you're seeking authentic Cuban food, VERSAILLES is the real deal; it's busy, open late, bare-bones, and has an exhaustive menu of super-cheap Cuban delicacies that are enjoyed by old timers and hip young adults alike. The décor is opulent but not upscale with candelabras and gilt-framed mirrors. Average main course price is $15. Located at 3555 SW 8th Street (305-445-7614).

EVENTS TO FLY IN FOR

The most notable art galleries in the world showcase their collections of 20th- and 21st-century art in the Art Deco District each December for Art Basel, the American sister event of the renowned Art Basel in Switzerland (www.artbaselmiamibeach.com). World-class chefs descend on Miami in February for the South Beach Wine and Food Festival (877-762-3933, www.sobewineandfoodfest.com). One of the oldest, biggest, and most eclectic of its kind, the Coconut Grove Arts Festival in February is a veritable outdoor museum of work by international and local artists. Said to be the world's largest block party, the vibrant Calle Ocho Festival celebrates Hispanic heritage with dancing and cuisine each March (305-644-8888, www.carnavalmiami.com). Then in August the top restaurants in the city offer as much as 75 percent off for Miami Spice Restaurant Month (www.miamirestaurantmonth.com).

WHERE TO STAY

Sonesta Hotel & Suites Coconut Grove offers "Just Us Girls" packages that include tickets to the Fairchild Botanic Tropical Garden and a Bloomingdale's discount card (starting at $260 per room, web specials start at $139 per night; 800-766-3782, www.sonesta.com/coconut_grove).

Affordable, centrally located hotels may be found by visiting the city's official tourism website, which offers a wide selection of hotels, especially for holiday periods. You'll find an up-to-date list of accommodations based on information provided by hotels that includes room availability, location, toll-free phone numbers, and rates. Then contact the hotels directly for the most updated information, packages, and specials. For Miami Beach and South Beach hotels from $129, go to "Hotel Availability Information."

ONE CLICK AND YOU'RE OFF: www.miamiandbeaches.com.

⤳ NEW YORK CITY ⤳

You could visit New York City a hundred times in a lifetime and never see the same things twice. If you seek it out, the city will reveal discoveries at every turn. Spread over 300 square miles, the city yields incalculable secret spots to designate as "your" places, and one-of-a-kind memories to collect.

I tried to wear heels walking around New York City. I wanted to look stylish and I was miserable. A pair of low-heeled comfortable walking shoes is essential.

—Sallyann Kakas Quebec, 50s,
Management Consultant, Cohasset, Massachusetts

You'll find it a city of decadence, where treating yourself is mandatory. Really go over the top and buy handbags at Bergdorf Goodman, dine in restaurants with a celebrity chef from the Food Network preparing your meal, and see *The Producers* on Broadway. Or do New York on the cheap. The department store Century 21 offers deep discounts on major labels. Dinner could be as simple as a slice of the city's much-loved pizza. Even the finest cruise for skyline views is free: the Staten Island Ferry. But no matter your budget, the city's culture—the world's best museums, galleries, and entertainment—is rich, ubiquitous, and often inexpensive. The best way to be in the know is to pick up a copy of *Time Out New York* magazine and find out what's going on that week. There are gallery openings, tiny theatrical productions that cost next to nothing, and hole-in-the-wall ethnic eateries to be discovered. And part of the fun is seeking out those insider experiences and making them your own.

NEIGHBORHOOD FOR A STROLL
The West Village's meatpacking district is the next generation's Madison Avenue. Hip young designers, boutique hotels, galleries, and cafés serving cuisines from all over the world fill former meat wholesale warehouses that line cobblestone streets. Peruse the neighborhood's haute couture and the chic clientele.

BEST VIEW
The Metropolitan Museum of Art's renowned collection of medieval tapestry, stained glass, and manuscripts is on display at The Cloisters, which was constructed out of several European monasteries and perched in Fort Tryon Park, hovering over the Hudson River in upper Manhattan (212-923-3700, www.metmuseum.org/cloisters/general). Taking in the grandeur of the forested river valley, you'll forget you're in a city.

BEST KEPT SECRET
The palatial Metropolitan Museum of Art (212-535-7710, www.metmuseum.org) can overwhelm visitors. Where to start? Try the basement where

you will focus on the Costume Institute that houses 80,000 gorgeous costumes and accessories, some of which are on display throughout the year in special exhibitions.

WATCH THE SUNSET
The casual Boat Basin Café on West 79th Street and Riverside Park offers Hudson River views. In the warmer months, catch sundown with a strawberry daiquiri on its west-facing, open-air patio (212-496-5542, www.boatbasincafe.com).

HAVE TEA
For a splurge, take highly civilized afternoon tea in the ornate Astor Court at the St. Regis Hotel on Fifth Avenue just a few blocks from Central Park, Tiffany's, and Bergdorf Goodman (212-753-4500). Or if you prefer someplace a bit homier, lift your cups at Alice's Teacup, quaint tea salons on the Upper West and East Sides with 140 teas to choose from (212-799-3006, www.alicesteacup.com).

FREEBIES
Many museums are free at certain times of the week, and there's always music, readings, and walking tours to be enjoyed at no cost. In summer, there's also a busy calendar of free outdoor concerts and films. The New York Philharmonic, City Opera, and Shakespeare in the Park take the stage in Central Park (212-310-6600, www.centralparknyc.org). And midtown's Bryant Park, behind the grand Public Library, hosts ABC's Good Morning America summer concert series on Fridays as well as the HBO Bryant Park Summer Film Festival on Monday evenings (www.bryantpark.org).

THRIFT AND VINTAGE CLOTHING
There are six Housing Works thrift shops in Manhattan and a visit to any one of them is like attending the estate sales of New York's fashion elite: They are brimming with gently used designer labels, artwork, housewares, jewelry, and shoes. In a new home on 31st Street and Fifth Avenue, Cheap Jack's stocks wearables from every decade of the past century. As vintage shopping in New York goes, it's reasonably priced and the selection is enormous. On the east side of Ninth Street between Avenue "A" and First Avenue, you'll find a dozen small thrift and vintage shops including one for wedding dresses.

FARMERS MARKETS FOR PHENOMENAL FOOD
(Marybeth Favorites) Chelsea Market is the city's largest food mall. Housed in an old Nabisco factory, it's a one-stop-shop for New Yorkers looking for

ingredients for their dinner parties and on-the-go pastries, coffee, gelato, soups, and sandwiches. New York chefs are among the crowds shopping at the four-day-a-week Union Square Farmers Market for fresh organic produce, breads, cheeses, and flowers. It's a colorful scene with delicious cider, fruit, and fresh baked goods to grab and go. Located at 14th Street and Broadway, open throughout the year, Monday, Wednesday, Friday, and Saturday, 8 a.m. until 6 p.m.

BEST DINING

You haven't tasted Italian food until you've eaten at TV personality and Chef Mario Batali's **BABBO RISTORANTE E ENOTECA** located at 110 Waverly Place, at the northwest corner of Washington Square in the center of Greenwich Village. Its menu puts Little Italy to shame and turns pasta into delicious art. (212-777-0303).

The French-New American cuisine and sleek design of **THE MODERN**, the restaurant in the stunningly renovated Museum of Modern Art, are exquisite. The dining room overlooks works by Picasso and Matisse in the sculpture garden. You'll be tempted with dishes like seared fois gras, duck confit, charred octopus, and beignets or lemon napoleon. It's expensive but you're worth it. 9 W. 53rd Street between 5th and 6th Avenues (212-333-1220).

And don't let the line outside of **JOE'S SHANGHAI** in Chinatown deter you from eating the best dumplings you'll ever taste. (Order the pork soup dumplings, trust me.) The line moves quickly just like the service in this lively and inexpensive Chinese restaurant. 9 Pell St. between Mott Street and Bowery (212-233-8888).

FOR HISTORY BUFFS

In 1913 the Woolworth's Building was considered the tallest and most beautiful building in the world. Woodrow Wilson pushed a button in the White House and illumnated 80,000 lights throughout the skyscraper. The Woolworth Tower Kitchen, a newly opened restaurant on the first

---

I love oysters, so I never miss the Oyster Bar on the lower level of Grand Central Station because of its selection of 15 different varieties of oysters from North America. If you're in town in September don't miss the Oyster Frenzy, including a free afternoon shucking contest and slurp off.

—Carol Allen, 60s, Artist, Mill Valley, California

The East Village is my favorite neighborhood for hip, quirky, experimental, and affordable restaurants. Wander between 5th and 11th Streets spanning Avenue A, 1st and 2nd Avenues for foodie picks like Via Della Pace, Cacio e Pepe, Franks, and The Mermaid Inn. Or for a worthwhile splurge in this area go to Green Kitchen extraordinaire, Plyos.

—Lauren Kay, 20s, Dancer, Writer, New York City

---

floor, is is worth a visit for a drink at one of the two bars or a reasonably priced lunch or dinner. The high-ceilinged rooms are filled with artifacts and historic books, and every Friday evening there's live jazz. If you prefer a light meal, it's easy to share several delicious hors d'oeuvres. My favorites are seared scallops, crab sampler, steamed mussels, or a spinach salad. Located across from City Hall at 233 Broadway; enter on Barclay St. ($9-30; 212-571-2930, www.woolworthtowerkitchen.com).

TAKE A CLASS

The Institute of Culinary Education holds more than a thousand small "recreational" classes for wannabe cooks on everything from wine-and-cheese pairing to preparing an entire menu for a steakhouse (a typical four-hour class starts at $105, and has 10 to 16 students). This is *the* culinary school in New York and its facilities are outstanding, bar none. Some of their classes are taught by TV personalities and four-star restaurant chefs for an understandably higher fee; it's money well spent (around $300). You won't go home hungry. It is located right in the heart of the city at 50 W. 23rd Street (800-522-4610 www.iceculinary.com).

WHERE TO STAY

You can feel what it's like to be a New Yorker by renting a cozy furnished and fully equipped apartment or stay at a B&B. Five-night minimum for apartments and four-night minimum for a B&B (starting at $150 a night for a studio or $175 for a one bedroom; 212-533-4001).

Affordable, centrally located hotels may be found by visiting the city's official tourism website, which offers a wide selection of hotels. Search by "Location." In my experience, Times Square and the West Side are where you stand to get the best deals; the West Village has some tiny boutique hotels and it offers a quiet neighborhood; and Midtown, closer to Central Park and MoMa, are good central locations (www.nycvisit.com).

Among my favorite upscale New York hotels is the intimate 70 Park Avenue Hotel (a Kimpton boutique property), located near Grand Central Station. It is within easy walking distance of Fifth Avenue boutiques and many of the city's finest arts and cultural centers including the Museum of Modern Art, Empire State Building, United Nations, Broadway, and Times Square. The concierge is invaluable for help with last-minute theater or dining plans. I especially appreciate the quiet luxury, personal service, and the 5 p.m. wine reception. The Martinis and Manicures Package and the Pampered Pooch Package start at $279 per night. Located at 70 Park Ave, at 38th Street (877-707-2752, www.70parkave.com).

I love the old world feel (like a grandma's parlor) of the historic Algonquin, located near Times Square, which welcomed single female guests (unaccompanied by a gentleman) since it opened its doors in 1902, including Gertrude Stein and Simone de Beauvoir. For a decade between the World Wars, the Algonquin Round Table was the scene of literary lunches by celebrated writers, including Dorothy Parker. Even when I stay with friends or at another hotel, I often stop by for afternoon or after-theater drinks, sitting in the Edwardian-décor lounge, with original dark wood paneling and deep velvet chairs. The lounge and the Oak Room Bar are lively spots for locals and tourists. Rooms are small but cozy. Don't expect a view. The Algonquin was designated a Historic Hotel of America by the National Trust of Historic Preservation. Located at 59 W. 44th Street (888-304-2047, www.algonquinhotel.com).

ONE CLICK AND YOU'RE OFF: www.nycvisit.com.

☞ CHICAGO ☜

It may be labeled the country's "Second City," but Chicago has proven it's got some metropolitan chops. The Midwestern hub with its vital ethnic neighborhoods, architecture, and shopping could go head-to-head with any international city. Chicago contains both Frank Lloyd Wright homes and angular skyscrapers. Even Bloomingdale's Home Furnishings is a landmark—it's a former Shriners temple. And that brings us to the top-notch shopping. The department stores of Magnificent Mile, which runs along North Michigan Avenue, could keep you and your credit cards busy for days.

There's also the former Marshall Field's flagship store, now Macy's, on State Street, which is the second-largest department store in the world. For more one-of-a-kind items, spend some time browsing or just window shopping the trendy boutiques of Armitage Avenue, where you can refuel with a cappuccino at a charming café. Nightlife includes highly acclaimed theater companies and comedy troupes and a variety of music venues. In the warmer months, you'll want to spend time outdoors in Chicago, which takes pride in its 30-mile lakefront. Who knew Lake Michigan could be so dazzling? There are sandy beaches, sailboats riding the gusts, cyclists, sunbathers, and volleyball players. But one thing that's consistently said about this town is how friendly it is. Chicago may be cosmopolitan, but you'll find it's more like the biggest little town in America.

GO FOR A SPIN

Bike Chicago rents bicycles out of six city locations. For a true joyride, two of you should try a tandem bike! Choose from guided or self-guided tours. (888-245-3929, www.bikechicago.com).

HOTEL SAFETY TIPS

- Request a room that does not open to the outdoors onto a patio, with a sliding glass door. Avoid rooms at the end of the hall.

- If you fill out a room service order form do not tell your gender. Offer only your last name and the first initial.

- When you are alone in the room, it is not advisable to let any hotel staff member into your room. Ask the employee to come back when you have vacated the room. Confirm their identity with the front desk.

- It is not wise to use stairways where you could be alone and isolated.

- Ask bellhops and concierges about the safety of walking in the neighborhood around the hotel.

TAKE A FREE WALKING TOUR

Whether you want to see Frank Lloyd Wright's Robie House in Hyde Park or "the Loop," a guide on a free Chicago Greeter tour will enlighten you (www.chicagogreeter.com).

BEST VIEW

Skip the observation deck of the Windy City's tallest building—the Sears Tower. Instead, take the elevator at sundown to the 96th floor of the 100-story John Hancock building (more conveniently located on Michigan Avenue) where you can settle in at the Signature Lounge for a martini and views of the city below (312-787-9596, www.signatureroom.com).

BEST CAFÉS

The café in the grand Ritz-Carlton is perfect for breakfast or an afternoon pick-me-up; their pastries are mind-blowing (312-266-1000, www.foursea sons.com/chicagorc). The café is casual; the lobby is anything but. The circa-1920s Drake Hotel (312-787-2200, www.thedrakehotel.com) hosts an afternoon tea, and in the evenings serves cocktails and hors d'oeuvres accompanied by live entertainment in their Palm Court.

BEST PHOTO OP

The 110-ton, mirror-like, stainless steel, elliptical sculpture in Millennium Park is a kick to walk around. Named the Cloud Gate, the sculpture is referred to by locals as "the Bean." Photos of it make for some interesting and distorted images.

MUST-SEE MUSEUMS

The Chicago Museum Campus on South Lake Shore Drive makes it easy for you to access three world-class museums in one swoop. The Field Museum, a natural history museum, the John G. Shedd Aquarium, and the Adler Planetarium and Astronomy Museum sit on ten acres of park with views of the Chicago skyline. Also not to be missed, the Art Institute of Chicago houses one of the top art collections and gift shops in the world.

HAVE A LAUGH

Chicago is a funny city, as the alumni of the renowned Second City improvisational comedy troupe would suggest, among them Bill Murray, John Belushi, and Stephen Colbert. Fridays and Saturdays at 8 p.m. catch its famous sketch comedy performance (312-337-3992, www.secondcity .com). Or try to contain your laughter at the long-running "Too Much

Light Makes the Baby Go Blind" at the Neo-Futurists! in which actors race through 30 skits in an hour (773-275-5255, www.neofuturists.org).

THRIFT AND VINTAGE CLOTHING

Of all the Brown Elephant Resale shops around the city, the North Halsted Street location has the best selection of bargains, 3651 N. Halsted Street (773-549-5943). Think old vintage dresses, books, and funky accessories. At the Hollywood Mirror boutique, bring back a new look or buy a Halloween costume by sorting through two floors of retro furniture, kitschy toys, and wild clothes. Located at 812 W. Belmont Avenue; cross street is Clark.

BEST DINING

Lunch or dinner at the Art Institute of Chicago's **GARDEN RESTAURANT** is a real treat. Late May through early fall, weather permitting, the Garden Restaurant extends into McKinlock Court for shady alfresco dining. I usually forgo a main course and order two starters and a decadent dessert. My favorites are Raw Ahi Tuna with Summer Watermelon, Shiso, Tobiko Caviar, and Yuzu Foam, or Crispy Jonah Crab Cake with Corn Chowder and Corn Shoots. For dessert I order either the Ganache Layered Midnight Passion Fruit Torte with Chocolate Mousse, Passion Fruit Curd, and Macadamia Nuts or the Strawberry-Rhubarb Crisp topped with Toasted Pecans, Brown Sugar, Oatmeal and Vanilla Ice Cream. From Memorial Day through September 1st, there is live music from 5:30 to 9:00 p.m. Thursday and Friday evenings. Museum admission is free after 5 p.m. on Thursdays, and so is the music! Seating is on a first come, first served basis. Open daily, 11:30 a.m. to 3 p.m. (312- 553-9675).

WORTH THE SPLURGE

Forty stories above the Chicago Stock Exchange, **EVEREST** serves amazing French cuisine that is considered Chicago's best. The lavish dining room affords views of the city and a stunning sunset. Contemporary art sets the tone; bronze sculptures adorn each table, and paintings by Chicago artist Adam Siegel line the walls. An exhaustive wine list enhances the frequently changing menu, which reflects the changing seasons and available ingredients. You may order à la carte or from Chef Joho's famous seven-course degustation menu, $96, or a three-course pre-theater menu available at 5:30 p.m. on weekends and 5 p.m. on Saturday, $54. Located at 440 S. LaSalle Street, 40th Floor (312-663-8920, www.everestrestaurant.com).

TRU is a favorite Progressive French Restaurant among affluent Chicago diners who rave about the chic décor and breathtaking cuisine. Contemporary art pieces, including an original Warhol, hang from the white walls giving the feeling of a private art gallery. Each course is as delicious as it is gorgeous. Every dish is presented on visually dramatic pieces, including black marble tiles, a Versace original, and the signature Caviar Staircase. Tru is also known for its innovative and creative desserts by Gale Gand, star of the Food Network series *Sweet Dreams*. You may select a three-course Prix Fix, $95, or a Chef's selection of ten spontaneous courses, $135, designed for sensory overload. The lounge offers small bites from $16, and for $25, enjoy a five-course collection of Gale Gand's desserts (available Monday-Thursday after 9:30 p.m., Friday-Saturday after 10:30 p.m., based upon availability). 676 N. St. Clair Street (southwest corner of Huron Street) (312-202-0001, www.truerestaurant.com).

HEAR LIVE JAZZ
Many of the good jazz clubs require you to venture out of downtown. And if you're going to make the effort, you may as well go to the Green Mill in Uptown. It's been hopping since Prohibition; it was gangster Al Capone's turf. Sure, it's crowded, darkly lit, and loud, but that's what makes it the city's most legendary jazz club. Located at 4802 N. Broadway Avenue (www.greenmilljazz.com, 773-878-5552).

EVENTS TO FLY IN FOR
All summer long you can hear the Chicago Symphony Orchestra, Broadway tunes, and contemporary musicians al fresco in Highland Park at the Ravinia Festival (847-266-5100, www.ravinia.org). In Millennium Park, on Michigan Avenue, music legends converge for the Chicago Blues Festival in June (www.chicagobluesfestival.org). In June, July, and August, the Grant Park Music Festival, a free classical music series, is staged in architect Frank Gehry's remarkable stainless-steel and wood-band shell. And there's also the Chicago Jazz in Grant Park the week before Labor Day (www.chicagojazzfestival.org).

WHERE TO STAY
The city's official tourism organization (www.choosechicago.com) offers a wide selection of hotels. Try to find accommodations near or just off Michigan Avenue so you'll be in the center of town and can walk to most attractions. Chicago's hotels can be expensive, so if you're having trouble finding a moderately priced option, consider a B&B. The Flemish House is a B&B for people who don't like the B&B coziness and forced mingling at breakfast. The private studios and one-bedroom apartments have kitchens that come stocked with breakfast foods, utensils, plates, and wine glasses. It's located in a quiet neighborhood close to the Drake Hotel, less

than a block away from Rush Street and just a few blocks away from Oak Street Beach, Michigan Avenue, Old Town, River North, Lincoln Park, and the Loop. 68 East Cedar Street (starting at $155 based on season; 312-664-9981, www.innchicago.com).

ON A BUDGET

For a truly heavenly experience, take a room at the Monastery of the Holy Cross Bed and Breakfast, a Benedictine monastery located just south of the loop, in the middle of the city, where the monks prepare fresh muffins every morning. Convenient public transportation is nearby as well as Italian, Lithuanian, Greek, Chinese, and Mexican restaurants. The B&B starts at $165 a night for one or two guests. (888-539-4261, www .chicagomonk.org).

ONE CLICK AND YOU'RE OFF: www.choosechicago.com and www .chicago-bed-breakfast.com.

⮞ QUEBEC CITY ⮜

The only walled city north of Mexico, and with a history dating back 400 years, Quebec City is a delicious slice of old Europe in North America. The first settlement in Canada, Quebec City has carefully preserved its French colonial heritage; 98 percent of its residents speak French today and strict building codes have nearly frozen in time the city's 18th- and 19th-century buildings. Quebecers like to say that their capital city is like France without the jet lag or the attitude. What you'll love the most is aimlessly wandering the narrow (and safe) streets, passing boulangeries, old churches, and slate-roof granite houses with balconies dripping with flowers. The city is also full of open-air markets, quaint boutiques, sidewalk cafes, and street performers. In between all the window shopping and croissants, you'll leisurely walk along a wooden boardwalk and through the beautifully landscaped parks. And because much of the old city is on a hill (there's a funicular!), you are constantly confronted by panoramas of the St. Lawrence River below and the green peaks of the Laurentian and Appalachian mountain ranges in the distance. Winter is a long and rather cold but beautiful season that has a hold on the city from November to May. Imagine the old stone buildings covered in snow, cross-country skiing through the parks, and cozying up to a fireplace in a tiny café. The summer amounts to just July and August, which are rarely hot and welcome some extraordinary festivals.

Quebec has a touch of Europe without all the travel mess. And if you don't speak French and they don't speak English they're not impatient or angry at you. It's like being in France, only friendlier.

—Ellen Weinstein, 50s, Art Professor, San Francisco

NEIGHBORHOOD FOR A STROLL

In many ways Historic Old Quebec reminds me of Venice: You can wander its narrow labyrinthine streets, come across squares with statues and old churches, and never really get lost.

Contained within the walls of the city, it's so cute and unspoiled that you may think you're on a movie set. Two popular thoroughfares, rue Saint-Louis and rue Saint-Jean, bisect the neighborhood with boutiques, cafés, and B&Bs. The rest of the tiny streets, some barely wide enough for a truck to get through, meander up and down the hills, bedecked with immaculate stone buildings, cottage-like houses, and cafés tucked into alleys. The painted shutters, tasteful flower boxes, and new-looking bright red roofs are evidence that Quebecers clearly take pride in their city.

BEST SHOPPING

Inside the city's walls, rue Saint-Jean is lined with popular French and Canadian clothing stores—there's no Gap here. Just off this avenue you'll find a true gem, Les Dames de Soie, a porcelain doll museum, workshop, and store in one. The street then continues on the other side of the wall—this is where the locals do much of their shopping. There are specialty food shops like Jean-Alfred Moisan, which occupies an 1871 building and is brimming with chocolate, teas, prepared food, spices, oils, and preserves, mostly from Europe and Quebec. Up the street, the Musée Choco pays homage to the art of chocolate with handmade truffles and gelato that will make you swoon. At the bottom of the funicular, you can witness the traditional art of glassblowing and purchase unique glasswork at Verrerie la Mailloche on Place-Royale, the oldest retail row in North America.

BEST ANTIQUING

In Lower Town the strip of antique shops along Saint-Paul welcomes collectors with colonial era knickknacks, Victorian housewares, retro posters and tin signs, and gorgeous furniture.

During the summer season there are local festivals week after week: dance, music and art. Quebec City is an easy walking town.

—Marybeth

THRIFT AND VINTAGE CLOTHING

See what a French "friperie" (second-hand clothes shop) has to sell, in a borough called Sillery/Sainte-Foy, near the major shopping malls. It is 20 minutes by city bus from the Old City. Friperie et solderie dégriffé, 1065, route de l'Église (418-654-1054).

BEST FRENCH FOOD OUTSIDE OF FRANCE

Where do Quebecers go for duck confit or steak frites? **L'ÉCHAUDÉ RESTAURANT** is found on a side street in the Old Port district in the lower part of Quebec City near the Musée de la Civilisation. 73, rue Sault-au-Matelot (418-692-1299).

And inside the **AUBERGE SAINT ANTOINE**, a wondrous boutique hotel filled with artifacts dug up from the Old City, the stone-walled Panache dining room is in a former 1822 maritime warehouse attached to the hotel, with exposed wooden beams and exquisite light fixtures and furniture. Panache's gastronomic French Canadian cuisine has earned it recognition as one of the best restaurants in Canada. 10, rue Saint-Antoine (418- 692-1022).

At **LE GRAFFITI** you may dine al fresco under the umbrellas on the terrace along bustling Avenue Cartier, or enjoy the soft lighting, exposed red brick walls, and French country ambience inside. The Italian and French Provençal cuisine is brilliant and the service impeccable. Seasonal menus include such dishes as venison with oyster mushrooms in red wine sauce, and veal medallions with apples in a calvados sauce. 1191, av. Cartier (418-529-4949).

BEST CAFÉ

LE PETIT COCHON DINGUE in Lower Town may be crowded, but there's good reason. The sugar cake, doughnuts, and café au lait are exquisite. Chefs prepare the pastries right in front of you and there are sidewalk tables for people watching. 6, rue Cul-de-Sac (418-694-0303).

BEST DAY TRIP

The summer cottages of the Quebec bourgeoisie, old vineyards, and farms still remain on Ile d'Orleans, a short drive from the city. In the middle of the St. Lawrence, it's a bucolic island with views of the city skyline, chocolateries, old churches, wineries, and historical homes. Les Tours Du Vieux-Quebec offers bus tours of the island and there's always the option of renting a car (thankfully, you don't have to drive on the "other" side of the road).

EVENTS TO FLY IN FOR

July's Summer Festival takes over the city with a mélange of music concerts in the streets, squares, and parks. Over a long weekend in August, more than 300,000 revelers attend the New France Festival, which takes you back to when the French occupied the colony. More than 1,500 artists and performers don authentic costumes. (You can rent one of your own and join in on the fun.) The city's biggest event, Quebec Winter Carnival, is celebrated with spectacular night parades, an ice castle, ice sculptures, and dogsled races. In 2008, the city celebrated its 400th birthday with renovations to its historic landmarks and celebrations for most of the year.

WHERE TO STAY

High above the St. Lawrence River, Fairmont Le Château Frontenac dominates the skyline of Quebec City with its regal architecture. It's been the hotel of choice for presidents and royalty since it opened in 1893. (This is where Roosevelt and Churchill planned D-Day.) Now part of Fairmont Hotels & Resorts, it remains the city's premier accommodation. You could stay here 618 times and never have the same room; each comes furnished with heavenly bedding and offers views of either the river or the Old City (starting at $299 Canadian). Located at 1, rue de Carrieres, Quebec City (800-441-1414, www.fairmont.com/frontenac).

For something on a smaller scale, down the street from the Chateau you'll find Le Clos Saint-Louis, a B&B in a Victorian-era home with 18 lavish guest rooms starting at $165 Canadian from November 2-April 30; $205 from May 1-November 1. Located at 66, rue Saint-Louis, Quebec (800-461-1311). The moderately priced and charming La Place d'Armes Inn sits in the center of Old Quebec and looks onto the Chateau Frontenac (starting at $140 Canadian; 866-333-9485, www.aubergeplacedarmes.com).

ON A BUDGET

Auberge Internationale de Québec is a superlative hostel in the Old City that includes breakfast in its room rates that can run as low as $28 Canadian for bed in a dorm-style room (private rooms are available as well). Located at 19, rue Sainte-Ursule (418-694-0755, www.cisq.org).

ONE CLICK AND YOU'RE OFF: Quebec City Tourism (418-641-6654, www.quebecregion.com).

Spirit Boosters

› MARYBETH'S STORY OF HOW TO BEAT THE BLAHS ‹

I often feel like a circus act spinning eight plates at once. I try to keep all the plates spinning, but honestly, I can't do everything successfully. Beginning in childhood, I was conditioned to put my own needs last and everyone else's first. Isn't that true for most of us? I was encouraged to be a good student, good employee, good wife, good mother, good hostess, good housekeeper, and good cook. So I drive myself very hard as a mother of two daughters, a wife, and a working woman, and I've found that to keep even a few plates spinning at one time, I need a break.

When I'm running "on empty," I get the blahs and then I know it's time to take time for myself—to discover what's missing and get it back. I've learned that the fastest way to recharge my battery, to pull out of a funk and, to boost my spirits is to take a break from home and, yes, take a trip! But I do not want to travel alone; I need the companionship of my

If you obey all the rules you miss all the fun.

—Katharine Hepburn

---

girlfriends—friends from college, former co-workers, mother and daughters for adventures, laughter, and the healing power of "women talk."

Again and again I have returned to Canyon Country in the Southwest when my spirits are low. The history, wildlife, wilderness, geology, and scenic grandeur never fail to awaken and regenerate me. Due to the staggering size of the Grand Circle Loop (described below) and my limited vacation time, I have returned dozens of times for week-long trips to the stunning gorges and rocky chasms of Utah, Colorado, Arizona, and New Mexico with girlfriends. Each time, I return home uplifted and revived. I've learned that when I'm away from home I see my life very clearly. I am reminded of how much I love my family and my busy life.

In my mid-30s I began to notice how much my parents were aging and I reflected upon their mortality. Frankly, it really depressed me. My mom was in a funk too because we saw each other so rarely. I lived in California and they lived in Ohio. The physical and emotional distance from my mother, especially, weighed deeply upon me. I decided to arrange a big trip, so we could reconnect and regain our prior closeness. I knew Mom had a longstanding dream to raft through the Grand Canyon. Unfortunately Dad couldn't go due to multiple back and knee surgeries. When I called Mom to ask her if she was interested in going with me, she jumped at the opportunity. She did not give a second thought to her age (68) or the painful arthritis she suffered. Dad surprised both of us—he encouraged her to "go for it."

It was a rare gift to spend an entire week with my mom, especially without other family members. She survived the rigors of the nine-mile hike from the rim of the Grand Canyon to the Colorado River, in 100-degree-plus August heat. We paddled through swift, churning rapids by day and camped along the river at night. Mom and I spent her first nights sleeping outdoors without tents under the clear Arizona sky. We held hands until we saw the first shooting star then slipped off to sleep. In the majesty of the grandest of canyons, our spirits soared.

Several years ago, during a particularly gray February, I felt the walls were closing in and needed a boost again. I knew that a getaway would do the trick. So I organized a camping trip by horseback deep into Indian Country with a female Navajo guide, whom I found on the Internet. My 9- and 12-year-old daughters and I flew into Phoenix, rented a car, and drove on long, straight roads shimmering with heat waves, blasting the CD player and singing at the top of our voices. All my troubles were left at home, and our usual behavior and ways of relating to each other changed, too. Instead of carrots and green tea for a snack, we pigged out on potato chips and Coke. The parent-child paradigm shifted: We became girlfriends, out for a good time.

Before the pack trip started, we cruised through Canyon de Chelly and Monument Valley, which were remarkably uncrowded in mid-winter. We bought turquoise jewelry from Native Americans at the Four Corners Monument, where four states converge, and snapped contortionist pictures of ourselves with a limb in different states—Arizona, Utah, New Mexico, and Colorado.

Although the first morning of our pack trip was cold, and frost blanketed the ground, we were eager to meet our Navajo guide, mount our horses, and ride off into the Navajo Tribal Lands. Our leisurely riding during the day gave us time to absorb the magnificent landscapes. At night we camped deep in a wilderness area where there were no phones, no electricity, and no paved roads. One memorable night, cozying up to the crackling campfire, as the flickering light danced up the magenta canyon walls, our Navajo guide asked, "Stars overhead and a full belly. What more could you want?" I glanced at my two daughters, huddled close to the blazing fire, and realized she was right. We were in high spirits, life was simple again, and problems were put in perspective.

So when I'm feeling overwhelmed or down, I glance around my office and smile at my photos from the Southwest. I reflect upon these uplifting adventures and in my head begin planning the next one. My advice: When you've got the blahs, get out of town with a girlfriend!

Cajun Country

Nothing makes us feel more alive and carefree than laughing and dancing, after a feast of the tastiest food we've ever eaten. In the swamps and bayous to the west of New Orleans the opportunity to experience this lives on with a remarkable vitality. When you enter Cajun Country, the ancient cypress trees covered with Spanish moss, fields of rice and sugarcane, rundown shanties, alligators, and signs reading "Ici, on parle français" (French spoken here), let you know you're in another world. The vital

Cajun and Creole culture, local hospitality, and the delicious cuisine can lift your spirits at any time of the year. But during the days leading up to Lent, the city of Lafayette, unofficial capital of French Louisiana, erupts with unparalleled revelry during the second-largest Mardi Gras celebration in the state. Cajun Mardi Gras in Lafayette brings new meaning to the expression "melting pot." People may flock to Lafayette for the music and the food and perhaps the license to freely party each Mardi Gras season, but they end up discovering a tangible, unifying culture that is difficult to find in the U.S.

EVENT TO FLY IN FOR

Smaller than New Orleans's version of Mardi Gras, the festivities in Lafayette are tame by comparison but infused with more Cajun and Louisiana pride—minus co-eds flashing the crowds, boozing fraternity brothers, and petty crime. More than one million people annually attend Le Festival de Mardi Gras à Lafayette, and each and every one of them is in a good mood! Lafayette's official celebration typically takes place over a weekend in February. But five days prior there are parades, a carnival, costume contests, Cajun grub, and live music—this is the last hurrah before 40 days of "fasting," both from food and fun. For visitors and especially observant Catholics from the area, who constitute 90 percent of the regional population, this is a no-holds-barred party, an excuse to completely let loose. Festivalgoers don costumes that range from store-bought Halloween outfits to elaborate hand-sewn, brightly colored attire, feathered and glittered headdresses and masks. You and your girlfriends may want to dress up too; local shops sell all sorts of silly items to spice up your outfits.

During the day and at night, Lafayette's krewes—exclusive membership organizations for a parade—stage colorful processions along a seven-mile route through the city. There's a woman's krewe, a children's krewe, an African-American krewe, all with over-the-top ornate floats and marching bands. Parades can last as long as two hours. Krewe members toss out beads, stuffed animals, and other trinkets. It's okay if you get carried away trying to get the attention of float riders so you can go home with more "throws" than anyone else. The pride and solidarity of krewe members and the friendliness of the spectators is contagious.

DINNER AND DANCING

Fill up on the region's red beans and rice, po'-boys, jambalaya, chicken-and-sausage gumbo, and boiled crawfish at the area's rollicking restaurant-cum-dancehalls. They spill over with people during Mardi Gras, when you can also dance in the streets downtown to live bands cranking out infectious Cajun and Creole Zydeco music. Hear live Cajun music over a plate of crawfish enchiladas at **PREJEAN'S** anytime of the year. 3480 I-49 North Lafayette ($15-27; 337-896-3247, www.pre jeans.com). Over at Randol's the dance floor always brims with crowds dancing to the tunes of local bands. 2320 Kaliste Saloom Road (337-981-7080, www.randols.com).

BEST DAY TRIPS

To balance out all your carousing, Lafayette and the surrounding area supply you with plenty of ways to spend your downtime. Here you'll find your dollar goes much, much further than it would in New Orleans, which is a good thing because there's serious antiquing to be done in Lafayette. Comb through the textiles, jewelry, and furniture of Jefferson Street Market, a collection of shops selling folk art and antiques; or Sans Souci, a gallery featuring the works of the Louisiana Crafts Guild. Outside of the city, you'll find serenity in the bayous, swamps, splendid plantations, and tiny ramshackle settlements. On Avery Island, south of Lafayette in the Mississippi Delta, stands the McIlhenny Tabasco Company factory, home of the world-famous hot pepper sauce. In addition to its worthwhile free tour, the factory shares the island with the 200-acre Jungle Gardens, overflowing with azaleas, camellias, and bamboo, thousands of snowy egrets and the occasional alligator, deer, nutria, raccoon, and black bear.

Love to dance? No guys? For me and my like-minded girlfriends, the place I love best is Louisiana's Cajun country, where live music spills out of cafes and saloons day and night, in Lafayette and out by the bayou in Beau Bridge and any hamlet on the byways. (My favorites are the Blue Moon, Mulate's, and Prejean's.) We find a table near the dance floor, and order up some boudin, gumbo, and shrimp boil, and then go stand on the sidelines, tapping our toes. It's never long before someone asks us to dance, and we're out there, waltzing to the fine fiddle and two-stepping to the accordion. Sometimes I even ask one of the bright-eyed elderly women to whirl with me, teach me the steps, and they always seem pleased. If it's anywhere near Mardi Gras time, bands play in the streets day and night. I never fail to dance my butt off.

—Lynn Ferrin, late 60s, Writer, Lives in San Francisco
but loves to return to her birthplace, Louisiana

NEED A LIFT? VOLUNTEER!

Last July Gina and her 9-year-old daughter joined another mom and daughter on a Global Volunteers team that spent a week in the Minnesota town of Austin to help new immigrants young and old improve their English language and study skills. They taught students who ranged from children to adults and had emigrated from all over the world: Sudan, Bosnia, Vietnam, but primarily from Latin American countries. For the most part, the new arrivals were lured by jobs in Austin's main industry—meat processing. They stayed in a college dorm and spent their days instructing small groups through games, songs, and field trips.

One of the reasons Gina chose a volunteer vacation was because she had lost two close family members in the preceding year and was searching for something to do that involved giving.

> "This experience was truly the best week of the year for me. It shook me out of my sadness. I was reminded of how fulfilling it is to help others. I think it helped me to be away from home and out of my element. I had my daughter Luisa with me as an anchor, but I was with so many people I had never met before. The trip went beyond a great vacation and really lifted my spirits. I realize it was a turning point for me and a productive way to deal with grief. I was rewarded by seeing my daughter thrive in an environment of helping people of other cultures, which I so love."

—Gina Milano, 40s, Teacher, Short Hills, New Jersey

WHERE TO STAY

Taking a room in one of the area's historic B&Bs, instead of the Hilton or Holiday Inn in town, yields an authentic and out-of-the-ordinary experience. Formerly a sugar plantation, Bois des Chenes Inn keeps five suites adorned with antiques of Louisiana French origin. 338 North Sterling Street (starting at $100; 337-233-7816, http://hometown.aol.com/boisdchene/bois.htm). T'Frere's House Bed & Breakfast, run by former restaurateurs, serves up a scrumptious breakfast in their century-old bedecked inn. 1905 Verot School Road (starting at $125; 800-984-9347, www.tfreres.com).

Or consider a stay in one of the plantation cottages, located on the grounds of the antebellum mansion at Oak Alley Plantation. Enjoy leisurely strolls through the lush gardens (where scenes from *Interview with the Vampire* were filmed) or on the levee to watch the mighty Mississippi River roll by. After tourists have left the property, the grounds and your cottage are quiet with no telephone, television, or traffic. Oak Alley Plantation offers a special girlfriends package on their website. One- or two-bedroom cottages start at $182, including a full country breakfast, a pitcher of Mint Juleps, Zombie Glasses, a disposable camera, and a basket of junk food. Very casual Cajun style dining options are located within a 15-minute drive, or more upscale restaurants are 30 minutes away. (800-442-5539, www.oakalleyplantation.com).

ONE CLICK AND YOU'RE OFF: To plan your visit, contact the Lafayette Convention & Visitors Commission (800-346-1958, 337-232-3737, www.lafayette.travel).

Grand Circle Loop Road

❧ ARIZONA, UTAH ❧

When you're caught in one of life's ruts, there's nothing better than hitting the road with a few friends. You know what they say about the open road: All sorts of things happen. And there's no better pick-me-up road trip than the southwest's Grand Circle Loop, which can be taken any time of year. Here the country's most diverse and extraordinary natural wonders—red rock pinnacles and buttes, bizarre hoodoos, thick forests of Ponderosas, and enormous canyons—are within driving distance of one another. And the wide-open desert, the dry air blasting through the open car window, and the heat of the sun on your arms and shoulders are cathartic. The route links all five Utah national parks, plus Arizona's Monument Valley and the Grand Canyon and Colorado's Mesa Verde. As any road map will show you, this imaginary circle through the desert is peppered with dozens of additional "points of interest," including national monuments, overlooks, trading posts, petroglyphs, and the Navajo National Indian Reservation for on-the-fly detours.

The Grand Circle Loop can be done in a week with a short stop in each park, but it's best to take your time—at least two weeks—so you can get to know the places, keep an easy-going pace, and really detach yourself from life back home. This is a trip where you don't want to hold yourselves to a daily to-do list. The fun is in seeing where the road takes you. You'll collect all sorts of southwestern souvenirs and antiques to bring back as mementos. And your mind will be imprinted for life with images of the local characters, the one-horse towns, and otherworldly natural wonders.

ZION NATIONAL PARK

Las Vegas is the most convenient starting line for this 1,187-mile odyssey. Pick up a rental car and head for Utah's aptly named Zion National Park and its 2,000-foot sandstone cliffs and massive natural arches, etched over centuries by wind and water in all sorts of peculiar ways. Here lies a rare chance to hike a water trail: You can work your way upstream in the chilly Virgin River through the Narrows, a deeply cut canyon that gets narrower and narrower (about 20 feet wide) and the water deeper and deeper. After that you may all want to brave the hair-raising hike to Angel's Landing, a colossal rock that drops 1,200 feet on both sides with bird's eye views of the canyon floor.

TRAVEL TIP

Beat blisters as foot problems are a pain. Band-Aids can slip off toes and heels, so pack thin moleskin instead. Buy the soft self-adhesive sheets at a grocery or drugstore, cut them into small squares and keep them in your purse. If your shoe starts to rub, cover the area right away before it turns into a nasty blister.

Souvenirs and treasures. It is fun to stop at local trading posts to rummage for souvenirs. My favorite is located in Virgin, Utah, on Highway 9, just 30 miles west of Zion National Park. That's right, you can take your photo in front of the Virgin Jail and then go inside to find jewelry crafted with rattlesnake tails and heads! I had to buy the FDA-approved suckers molded over dead scorpions. I admired the Navajo Sand Paintings and largest collection of dream catchers and hot sauces I've even seen in one place.

—Marybeth

BRYCE CANYON NATIONAL PARK

Continue on to Bryce and its curious limestone spires or "hoodoos" sprouting out of fir-spruce hillsides like an aberration. Take your time wandering down through the mazes of them and catch sunset from a perch above. Back on the road again, you'll follow one of the most scenic roads in the U.S.: Route 12 was designated one of the nation's All-American Roads. A quick stop in Capital Reef National Park to marvel at the Waterpocket Fold, a 100 mile long "wrinkle" in the Earth's crust, and you're off, back on the road again.

BEST ADVENTURE HUB

The quirky town of Moab, Utah, is the gateway to two national parks—Arches and Canyonlands—and lays claim to the best mountain biking in the nation. Out of Moab, there are ATV and Jeep tours, whitewater-rafting expeditions on the Green River, and mountain biking to keep you and your group overly stimulated for as many days as you can spare.

ARCHES NATIONAL PARK

The most popular park, Arches is a specter of color, texture, and proportion. The towering rust-colored rock formations in contrast to the vividly blue sky will leave you speechless. While the park's 18-mile scenic road serves as a great sampler of the park, give yourself some time (an extra day or two) to hike to a few of its 2,000 arches.

CANYONLANDS NATIONAL PARK

To the southwest of Moab lies Utah's biggest park, where you'll peer thousands of feet down to the Green and Colorado Rivers, thousands of feet up to red rock pinnacles, cliffs, and spires, and hundreds of miles across Utah.

BEST PHOTO OP

Monument Valley Tribal Park was the backdrop for John Ford's film *Stagecoach* and remains one of the most famous sights in America. Now's the time to delete some photos from your digital cameras to make room for images of its iconic, mitten-shaped 1,000-foot-high red mesas.

BEST DETOURS

Across the Colorado border to the east, the ancient Anasazi's cliff dwellings in Mesa Verde Park are worth the extra driving. Then swing by Four Corners Monument (take turns photographing each of you with hands and feet in different states) before heading back to Las Vegas. There's one last stop that is certain to be the icing on the cake: the Grand Canyon. This 6,000-foot-deep chasm in the Earth needs no introduction.

WHERE TO STAY

Lodging on this route can be as much of an adventure as your time on the road. In addition to chain hotels along the way, there are national park lodges, campgrounds, eccentric B&Bs, and guest ranches. Highlights include the historic lodges of Zion (starting at $166; 435-772-7700, www .zionlodge.com) and Bryce Canyon (starting at $155; 435-834-5361, www .brycecanyonlodge.com); Moab's Sorrel River Ranch Resort, a hotel and spa on the banks of the Colorado (starting at $299; 877-359-2715, www .sorrelriver.com); and Goulding's Lodge, which offers sweeping views of Monument Valley (starting at $198; 435-727-3231, www.gouldings.com).

ONE CLICK AND YOU'RE OFF: Customize a trip with Utah Tourism (800-200-1160, www.utah.com).

Nashville

⤳ TENNESSEE ⤶

A remedy for a case of melancholia is a healthy dose of the country music, dancing, food, and charm only found in Nashville. Uplifting country music is the lifeblood of Nashville, home of several landmarks where the greats of the genre have played over the years—and in some cases, continue to play. In "Music City," famous musicians strut the streets, up-and-coming talent play the honky-tonk bars with dreams of becoming the next big thing, and recording studios still put out best-selling albums. Those who don't

I lived in Nashville for one year while I was in graduate school, and loved every minute of it. Las Paletas, on 12th Avenue South, was my go-to spot when I needed a pick-me-up. They make traditional Mexican popsicles fresh every day and have flavors ranging from passion fruit to hot (spicy) chocolate. I loved heading out to East Nashville to eat at Family Wash on Greenwood Avenue—a hole in the wall that has amazing pot pies and live music every night. My two top picks for barbecue are Judge Bean's (on 12th Avenue North) and Hog Heaven (on 27th Avenue North). Yep, I miss Nashville's kind but feisty atmosphere, and definitely its food.

—J. T. Leaird, 26, Teacher, Brooklyn, New York

care a lick about country music will be relieved to know that Nashville is not all BBQ food and locals in ten-gallon hats. Its eclectic music scene (think classical, jazz, and rock 'n' roll), surprising cosmopolitan ways, and entirely laid-back character appeal to everyone.

A PIECE OF HISTORY

You may have heard it on the radio or watched it on Country Music Television: The Grand Ole Opry is America's longest continuously running radio show, broadcasting since 1925. The performance now airs from the world's largest broadcast studio, which seats 4,424 people. Their list of past performers reads like the who's who of country music; both the old and new share the stage. You can't go wrong with any performance. Nearly all Grand Ole Opry shows sell out, and though it's often possible to get last-minute tickets, you should try to order tickets as far in advance as possible. Considered the "mother church" of country music, the brick Ryman Auditorium in town has showcased vocal legends including Enrico Caruso, John Philip Sousa, Sarah Bernhardt, and Charlie Chaplin. Built in 1892, it was the home of the Grand Ole Opry from 1943 to 1974. Seeing a show here is like witnessing a piece of acoustic history. And if you're visiting in summer, don't miss their bluegrass night every Thursday night late June through July. (615-889-3060, www.ryman.com)

DANCE THE NIGHT AWAY

A sign of a good vacation is when you're dancing to live music at 10 a.m. and at midnight. And downtown is the place for it. Made up of restored warehouses and historic buildings, the "District" is the beating heart of the Nashville music scene. On Lower Broadway, one honky-tonk bar after another lines the street, showcasing live bands and never charging a cover to hear them. One of the most famous is Tootsies Orchid Lounge. You and the girls can work your way through all the honky tonks—Western World, the Wildhorse Saloon, and The Stage—pairing up with new dance partners or just kicking back and sipping on Tennessee Tea. (If your moves need some polishing, Wildhorse Saloon has line-dancing lessons.)

BEST HOLES IN THE WALL
Exploring the small music joints on the block-long Printer's Alley in the District, home to the city's speakeasies back in the day, often yield big discoveries. As does the intimate Bluebird Café, unassumingly situated in a strip mall, where you can hear the work of aspiring songwriters.

MUST-SEE MUSEUM
Diehard fans of country music—or those of you fascinated by kitsch culture—can easily lose three hours in the Country Music Hall of Fame and Museum. Much of it is a study in American culture. The building itself is a homage to country music: When viewed from above, the building is in the shape of a bass clef and the northwest corner of the building juts out like the tail fin of a 1957 Chevy. Inside there's Elvis's gold Cadillac, outfits worn by legends Hank Williams and Johnny Cash, and one of Dolly's wigs. You'll all get a kick out of the gift shop, where you'll surely pick up something to bring back home with you. Besides hard-to-find country albums, who couldn't use a guitar-shaped fly swatter?

BEST BRUNCH
Worth the drive (and the wait) is the **LOVELESS CAFÉ** on the edge of town. Their classic American fare brings new meaning to comfort food. Plates come crammed with Southern-fried chicken, grits, and buttery biscuits, all to be dunked in their red-eye gravy. 8400 Highway 100 ($8-13; 615-646-9700, www.lovelesscafe.com).

SPICIEST FOOD
Hot chicken is unique to Nashville, and no one does it better than **PRINCE'S HOT CHICKEN SHACK**. Their four levels of spice, none of which are intended for the faint-hearted, will all leave you sweating, screaming, and salivating for more. Try not to miss. 123 Ewing Drive ($4-15; 615-226-9442).

BEST SURPRISES
There are also sights that one would never expect to find in the middle of Tennessee. Who knew Nashville had an exact replica of the original Parthenon in Athens, Greece, constructed in 1897? There are trendy martini bars, fine-art museums, and an up-and-coming symphony. And not all the food in Nashville comes with a side of biscuits and gravy. Its restaurant scene can stand up to any major city's. Retire the denim for a night or two and splurge at **VALENTINO'S RISTORANTE**, which has earned both the Wine Spectator Award of Excellence and an AAA Four Diamond Award. 1907 West End Avenue ($22-36; 615-327-0148, www.valentinosnashville.com).

BEST DAY TRIPS
Nine miles from downtown, the Cheekwood Botanical Garden and Museum of Art, the former mansion and botanical and sculpture gardens of the Maxwell House coffee dynasty, sits on a hill surrounded by Warner Parks. You can also slip into the age of *Gone with the Wind* at the Belle Meade Plantation, which served as a world-famous horse farm in the early 1800s and today offers tours by guides in antebellum costumes.

WHERE TO STAY
Go the fancy route and stay at Tennessee's only five-diamond hotel, The Hermitage, where six presidents have visited. 231 Sixth Avenue North (starting at $339; 888-888-9414, www.thehermitagehotel.com).

Or completely immerse yourself in the universe of the Gaylord Opryland Resort, one of the largest hotels in the country with an indoor river, tropical gardens, waterfalls, and proximity to the Grand Ole Opry and the Willie

Nelson Museum. 2800 Opryland Drive (starting at $219; 866-972-6779, 615-889-1000, www.gaylordhotels.com).

ONE CLICK AND YOU'RE OFF: For more details contact the Nashville Convention and Visitors Bureau (800-657-6910, www.visitmusiccity.com).

Tanglewood

ᴓ MASSACHUSETTS ᴒ

Tanglewood is just the thing for ladies in need of the curative effects of music, nature, relaxation, and shopping. On the golf-course-green lawns of the 500-acre Tanglewood estate, 120 miles west of Boston in Lenox, Massachusetts, you'll soak up the rejuvenating sounds of music—your very own Julie Andrews moment in the rolling hills of the Berkshires. The Boston Symphony Orchestra sets up residence in Tanglewood for the summer starting in July. And the line-up of classical and contemporary performances through Labor Day rivals Carnegie Hall's music calendar. Founded in 1934 in the tradition of the great European festivals, Tanglewood has earned itself a reputation worldwide as much for its music as for its location.

BEST STRATEGY

If you're looking for music to feed your soul, there's plenty of it here. Once Tanglewood finalizes the schedule in March, tickets can sell out quickly. The best plan of attack is to buy tickets for one of the main performances on Friday or Saturday nights or a Sunday afternoon in the Koussevitzky Music Shed (aka "the Shed"), an open-air auditorium sheltering 5,000 seats and the stage. Tickets to these shows are like a present to yourself, as they promise to be a concert of a lifetime. Superstars James Taylor, Bonnie Raitt, Bob Dylan, LeeAnn Rimes, and classical soloists Itzhak Perlman and Yo-Yo Ma have showered the Berkshires with music. James Levine, the festival's Music Director, intermittently leads the orchestra throughout the summer. Garrison Keillor broadcasts Minnesota Public Radio's "A Prairie Home Companion" live from here. And the Tanglewood Jazz Festival over Labor Day weekend lures major jazz acts such as Dizzy Gillespie All Star Big Band and Wynton Marsalis. Chamber groups and soloists appear in the smaller Seiji Ozawa Hall. There are also concerts by the students of the Tanglewood Music Center.

Music is medicine. Nothing can be finer than a picnic on the grounds at Tanglewood to hear James Taylor. Although the concert is to begin at 7 p.m., the grounds open at 3 p.m. and we roll in with our picnic packed in a little red wagon. We find a space on the immense lawn big enough for our old beach blanket and yet not touching our neighbors' tablecloths or quilts. There is total silence as James Taylor takes the stage alone with his guitar. A massive cheer erupts and refuses to be calmed until the first strum of "Sweet Baby James." The sun recedes and we are caught up in the magic of his music enhanced by the sparkle of the starry night over our heads.

—Penny Hudnut, 60s, Fund-raiser, North Egremont, Massachusetts

And open rehearsals during the weekdays can be heard at a discounted price. Now that's a lot of music.

HAVE A PICNIC

Sitting on the lawn around the Shed—tickets for which are almost always available and cheaper—is Tanglewood's greatest tradition. Audiences with beach chairs and blankets sprawl out to hear the music wafting from the stage. Before the first notes are played, sometimes hours before, groups of friends and family (as many as 8,000 people) set up their spreads for the performance: carefully packed gourmet meals, chilled wine, and sometimes flowers in glass vases, candles, crystal glasses, champagne, and tables. Planning your menu, shopping for treats at local gourmet shops, and getting creative with your picnicking is part of the experience. (Don't forget the corkscrew for your wine. Having one could also make you very popular with your neighbors.) If you don't have time to orchestrate a picnic of your own, there's also the option of ordering a Meal-To-Go from the Tanglewood Café a few days ahead of time and picking it up when you arrive ($18-50 per person; 413-637-5240). With the sun setting over the Berkshires, your shoes kicked off, a glass of wine in hand, and bathed in music, you'll feel your rundown, overworked self turning a corner (www.tanglewood.org).

BEST DAY TRIPS

Lenox has become a cultural resort with museums, music venues, and shopping coexisting with the great outdoors. Hikers can explore seven miles of trails along Lenox Mountain in the Pleasant Valley Wildlife Sanctuary.

The Mount, the grand estate and gardens of Edith Wharton, provides a wonderful lesson on the life and work of the Pulitzer Prize-winning author. Lenox and the neighboring towns are also lined with tons of bookstores, galleries, antique shops, and clothing boutiques.

PAMPER YOURSELF

When your mind and body are in need of mending, one of the yoga or fitness workshops at the esteemed Kripalu Center for Yoga and Health may be in order. Stay on the grounds, a former Jesuit seminary across the street from Tanglewood, and at night simply cross the road for the concerts. Route 183 and Richmond Mountain Road (starting at $240 for a three-night Radiant Health Weekend Retreat for Women; 866-200-5203, www.kripalu.org). Also in Lenox is the all-inclusive Canyon Ranch Health Resort, a restored mansion with an enormous spa facility and the gourmet dining that has made it famous. 165 Kemble Street ($2,270 for three nights, three meals a day, and spa treatments; 800-742-9000, www.canyonranch.com).

WHERE ELSE TO STAY

There are classic New England B&Bs and private homes for rent. Highly recommended is the immaculately decorated, luxury Stonover Farm Bed & Breakfast, which is a short walk to Tanglewood. 169 Under Mountain Road (starting at $325, based on season; 413-637-9100, www.stonover farm.com). Or visit the charming Rookwood Inn, a B&B in the village of Lenox. 11 Old Stockbridge Road (starting at $175; 413-637-9750, www.rookwoodinn.com).

ONE CLICK AND YOU'RE OFF: For schedule and tickets go to tangle-wood.org or call 888-266-1200. Find out more about the area by contacting the Berkshire Visitors Bureau (800-237-5747, www.berkshires.org).

The Grand Tetons

ஒ JACKSON, WYOMING ௸

If your frame of mind or worn-down body needs a jumpstart, the endorphins from cycling or hiking amid the grandeur of the Tetons in the summer should do the trick. In the area surrounding Jackson, Wyoming (including the legendary Jackson Hole Mountain Resort), you'll experience

Research the weather. Don't assume you'll have "summer weather" in June, July, or August in the mountains. If you are adequately prepared, with layers of fleece, a rain poncho, hat and gloves, you'll be able to make the best of any surprises from Mother Nature.

—Marybeth

luxury and adventure. There are plenty of spas, fine dining, and super fun nightlife options ranging from listening to local bands or two-stepping with a cowboy. The Teton Range, America's Alps, has more than 12 snow-capped, serrated peaks at elevations greater than 12,000 feet, morain lakes, glacier-carved canyons, and elk, moose, mule deer, osprey, and bald eagles all about. And in the center of it all sits the Western town of Jackson, the charming gateway to two iconic national parks: Grand Teton and Yellowstone. When the snow melts in June, hiking, mountain-biking and horseback-riding trails reveal themselves along the valley floor and up into the mountains. Wildflowers blanket fields. And the Snake River rages through the valley. This is the true Wild West, and simply because of the landscape's scale and splendor it's hard not to feel that anything you do here is a physical feat of sorts. Unlike a typical vacation, you'll return in better shape than when you left—in every way.

THE ROAD LESS TRAVELED

Spend a week cycling among the wildflowers and bison, with bike-tour specialists Woman Tours on their Teton Valley trip. They guide you through the less trafficked region of the Tetons in Idaho (on the other side of the mountains from Jackson). You'll have time for hiking, a yoga class, and a bicycling workshop. The trip is laid-back and ideal for first-timers who fear the hills. The group is put up in a spacious condo in Driggs, Idaho, with a chef who prepares wholesome meals to keep you fueled for all the miles you're pedaling. Or join the Yellowstone and Grand Teton trip to bike through the national parks to see herds of elk and bison, osprey and eagles, and even a coyote or moose if you're lucky. You'll stay in the classic national park lodges and take a day off pedaling to float down the Snake River. ($1,690-2,090; 800-247-1444, www.womantours.com).

If biking isn't your sport, consider a weeklong multi-activity adventure with Canyon Calling, specialists in small-group adventure trips for moderately fit women. Capture the spirit of Yellowstone and the Grand Tetons while horseback-riding, rafting, and hiking. Stay in rustic cabins; trek around geysers and boiling hot springs; view moose, elk and buffalo, and of course, Old Faithful ($1,895; 928-282-0916, www.canyoncalling.com).

DO-IT-YOURSELF BIKING
If you'd prefer to pedal at your own pace and hit the paved roads or trails on your own, Hoback Sports in town will set you up on the appropriate bike and send you on your way with maps and recommendations. 520 W. Broadway (307-733-5335, www.hobacksports.com).

BEST HIKING
More than 4,000 miles of trails stem from Jackson, varying from strolls through valleys to hair-raising technical climbs. The best day hikes can be found in Grand Teton National Park, most notably the 6.6-mile Jenny Lake loop. Despite how busy it can get, it's truly a spectacular hike—the blue lake rests at the foot of the Tetons—and is the starting point for many other trails. Take it up a notch with the 7.6-mile Death Canyon Trail (don't let the name dissuade you), which climbs up and then down to Phelps Lake, followed by a climb into the magnificent, glacier-carved Death Canyon.

CLIMB A MOUNTAIN
If you're still hungry for more, hire the services of the highly respected Exum Mountain Guides and get yourself to the top of the Grand Teton, that much photographed, 13,770-foot spire rising out of the valley. For those in decent

TRAVEL TIP

Extra security is never a bad thing. When you enter your hotel room, always engage the safety chain or the security bar to double lock the door. Some hotels don't have these safety features, so I never travel without a simple rubber door-stopper. It's inexpensive, light to pack, and gives you peace of mind. The main door may not need it, but if there is an adjoining room, it might have a fairly flimsy lock, especially at older hotels.

Music is medicine to many a soul. In fact, a Tufts University report notes that hospital patients who listen to music after surgery have less pain, and consequently need fewer painkiller medicines. They claim that music's effect is equal to a 325-mg dose of the painkiller acetaminophen. So dance away your blues to toe-tapping music and sing along with favorite tunes.

—Marybeth

shape, it's a four-day process with instruction and two days to the summit. It's an extraordinary achievement that is sure to bolster your confidence (starting at $455 for four climbers or more; 307-733-2297, www.exumguides.com).

MUST-SEE MUSEUMS

Overlooking the National Elk Refuge from a butte, the National Museum of Wildlife Art holds 4,000 works with animals as subjects. The museum stays open late for Tapas Tuesdays, which lets you enjoy the art while sampling small-plate items and cocktails. (www.wildlifeart.org) Jackson's new Center for the Arts includes state-of-the-art studios and an airy gallery space with a rotating schedule of exhibitions with works by local and national artists. Located 2.5 miles north of the town square in Jackson on the west side of the butte on Highway 89 at 2820 Rungius Road (800-313-9553, www.wildlifeart.org).

GIDDY-UP

The Spring Creek Ranch, a luxury resort that sits 1,000 feet above the town of Jackson, helps get you in the saddle. From their stables, guides help you experience a unique perspective of the Tetons on one-hour to full-day excursions (800-443-6139, www.springcreekranch.com).

RAFT

Mad River's Whitewater Combo includes a mellow scenic float down the Snake River, a lunch, and then they crank up the thrills with a run on the whitewater of Snake River Canyon. The day ends with their well-known riverside BBQ (800-458-7238, www.mad-river.com).

PAMPER YOURSELF

The Avanyu Spa at the Snake River Lodge understands that many visitors to the Tetons wear their joints out frolicking in the mountains and

There are many great "spirit boosting" outdoor programs that get you away from your everyday life and challenge you to do more than you believed you could do. You'll return home with a renewed sense of confidence, purpose, and joy. I recommend finding a course that combines activities, (hiking, biking, rock climbing, and yoga) with life coaching. The coaching follow-up is essential for long-term change. I believe the mountains are incredible teachers. What can be more inspiring than connecting your life to the mountains?

—Kim Reynolds, 40s, Founder, Mind Over Mountains, Chicks with Picks, Ridgway, Colorado

---

punish their skin in the high altitude. Among my favorite treatments, the Bending Willow massage uses the principles of Thai Massage: kneading your muscles and stretching out your limbs simultaneously (massages cost $190 for 75 minutes; 800-445-4655, www.snakeriverlodge.com).

DANCE THE NIGHT AWAY

You can literally saddle up to the Million Dollar Cowboy Bar: The bar stools are saddles. And the dance floor is always busy with locals in two-gallon hats and cowboy boots and tourists alike spinning their partners round and round. It's easy to find a dance partner out there. Located on the Town Square at 25 N. Cache Street (307-733-2207, www.milliondollarcowboybar.com).

BEST SHOPPING

All along the streets surrounding Jackson's Town Square, marked with elk antler arches, shops sell Western art and clothing, silver jewelry, T-shirts, and souvenirs. Skinny Skis and Teton Mountaineering have the best selection of outdoor wear—they're great places to pick up Patagonia clothing on sale in the off-season.

BEST DINING

The lively vibe of the RENDEZVOUS BISTRO is contagious, and their dolled-up American fare is superb. Enjoy a glass of wine and the duck confit or their popular burger. 380 South Broadway ($15-25; 307-739-1100, www.rendezvousbistro.net).

SNAKE RIVER GRILL, on the Town Square, is Jackson's premier restaurant, having won the Wine Spectator Award of Excellence. Its wood-and-stone interior provides a cozy setting to feast on its outstanding beef and fish dishes ($24-49; 307-733-0557, www.snakerivergrill.com).

Or watch the sun drop behind the Tetons from the enormous window behind the bar at the **GRANARY LOUNGE** at the Spring Creek Ranch. They have great happy hour food-and-drink specials and live jazz on Fridays. 1800 Spirit Dance Road ($7-21; 307-732-8112, www .springcreekranch.com).

PLACES TO STAY

In the center of the town of Jackson, the Scandinavian-influenced Alpine House Inn, run by two former Winter Olympians, offers a comfy (and within your means) sanctuary to return to at the end of a day in the mountains. Their chef-prepared breakfasts are incredible as are their sauna and outdoor hot tub. 285 North Glenwood Street (starting at $150, based on season; 800-753-1421, www.alpinehouse.com).

At the base of Jackson Hole Ski Resort, Alpenhof treats guests to an outdoor Jacuzzi, sauna, complimentary breakfast, on-site dining serving Swiss cuisine, and inviting Bavarian-style rooms, some with fireplaces and balconies (starting at $199, based on season; 800-732-3244, www.alpenhoflodge.com).

ONE CLICK AND YOU'RE OFF: Jackson Hole Chamber of Commerce (307-733-3316, www.jacksonholechamber.com).

CHAPTER THREE

Birthday Blowouts

∾ JULIE'S STORY ∾

For years Julie has celebrated her big birthdays with two college room-mates because they were born within a week of each other. For their 40th, they danced 'til dawn at a relative's beach cabin in Santa Cruz. Nostalgia moved them to organize a rendezvous in Madison, Wisconsin, where they all went to college together, for their 50th celebration.

Julie's most inspirational memory occurred when they celebrated another friend's 50th birthday and joined an organized bike trip through the national parks in Utah and Arizona. To keep the costs down, they selected the camping trip over the one with upscale lodging.

On the longest day of the trip they rode 120 miles from the North Rim of the Grand Canyon to Zion National Park. When the "sag wagon" passed them midway and offered a ride, they hesitated, looked at each other, and then confidently shook their heads "no." Hours later when they struggled into the campground, they were applauded by the other bikers, most of whom were in their 30s and had accepted the sag wagon lift to shorten the ride.

"We felt like hot stuff. It was really fabulous. It rocked! Age won out. To celebrate a big birthday with a physical accomplishment was especially meaningful to me," says Julie.

✿ LaDAWN'S STORY ✿

Other women, like LaDawn, opt for a comfy bed, fine food, and massages to mark the occasion of a birthday.

"We're spa girls, so to celebrate my 42nd birthday I wanted a grown-up destination where we could unwind, pamper ourselves, and go wine tasting," explains LaDawn. She selected Healdsburg because it's a small town among vineyards and less crowded than other wine districts. LaDawn, Kathy, and Tina parked their car and didn't get back into it until it was time to go home, because everything they wanted to do was within walking distance. That also meant they could have that extra glass of wine at the end of the evening.

Over the weekend they visited seven wineries, shopped, and returned to their Victorian B&B for a surprise. At 5:30 p.m., a large bookshelf in the dining room swung open to uncover a hidden staircase to a speakeasy in the wine cellar for a nightly wine-and-cheese tasting. "We got to know all the other guests in a lively, jovial atmosphere. It's a kick to let folks know it's your birthday," says LaDawn. "They do all sorts of special things for you, like insisting you try special champagne."

One afternoon they were relaxing in wicker chairs on the wraparound porch at the B&B, sipping wine. Hair mashed, faces red, yet totally relaxed, La Dawn and the girls had just ambled across the street from the spa. "I felt so peaceful, surrounded by my two close friends. No one had a phone or PDA; we had no responsibilities," says LaDawn. "I was full of love, reflecting upon everything I was grateful for."

Not all her birthday celebrations were as easygoing as the wine-country party in Healdsburg. Five of her close friends jetted off to Las Vegas for LaDawn's 40th birthday. Each friend represented a different period in her life: her college roommate, work colleagues, and a former student, 15 years her junior.

"I pulled together close friends for this milestone birthday. Not everyone knew each other, but they all had 'me' in common," explains LaDawn. "And by the end of the weekend they were a tight cohesive group."

They booked a suite at the Venetian because it could sleep five comfortably, with two queen-size beds and a spacious sunken living room with another pull-out bed. Can you imagine one bathroom having enough space for five women showering and dressing for dinner? Well the marble bathroom at the Venetian had enough sinks, showers, baths, and vanity mirrors for everyone to get ready and put on their makeup together.

Some of the girls did spa treatments and others camped out from morning 'til night at the pool area where there were cabanas, food, and drinks. LaDawn and her friends discovered there is much to do and see in Las Vegas, and much of it is free. They didn't feel the need to pre-book shows, they went to see the fountains at the Bellagio, and they visited the big hotels for art shows and live entertainment. "At one hotel there was a great Motown band," says LaDawn "and we just started to dance with each other, then we'd twirl around and be dancing with someone else."

Whether you sip wine in the vineyards, raft through the Grand Canyon, bike through Zion National Park, or shake your bootie in a big city, the place you go sets the stage for your celebration. The most lasting birthday gift of all is the deep commitment you have to each other.

Las Vegas

◈ NEVADA ◈

A hedonistic retreat in the middle of the desert, Las Vegas takes you so far from your everyday life that you may just forget after a day or two what birthday you're there to celebrate. Was it 60 or 20? It's hard to tell when you're lounging on a sandy beach with a Mai Tai in hand, laughing and squealing like a teen, and dancing in discos. You've likely heard the overused adage "what happens in Vegas stays in Vegas"? Well, use it as your excuse to find out for yourself how it earned the name Sin City.

WHEN TO GO

The spring-fall shoulder months tend to be the busiest times; mid-summer grills Vegas over coals, and winter tends to be mild with the infrequent chill. Holidays make it impossible to get a room, but are known to be wickedly fun. And then there's the random convention, which can make any day in Vegas seem like a holiday. My last trip to Las Vegas, with my 18-year-old daughter, was in August, when the thermostat hovered above 100°F; however it didn't dampen our spirits. You can spend days in Las

Vegas and not leave air conditioning. We limited our time roasting by the pool and spent more time shopping and going to shows.

BEST SITES

A theme park for adults, Las Vegas mixes Disney-like amusement with panache. Walk across the miniaturized version of the Brooklyn Bridge at New York-New York, visit the Eiffel Tower at the Paris, a ten-story Sphinx at Luxor, the canals of the Venetian, the sculptures of ancient Romans at Caesars Palace, and the pirates of Treasure Island.

MUST-SEE MUSEUMS

The Venetian's Guggenheim Hermitage, through a partnership with the State Hermitage Museum of St. Petersburg, Russia, exhibits masterworks from the museum's immense collection of impressionist, postimpressionist, and early modernist works. On entirely the other end of the cultural spectrum, you'll be bowled over by the outrageous sequined capes, rhinestone jewelry, flashy cars, and fabulous candelabra inside the Liberace Museum.

NEIGHBORHOOD FOR STROLLING

When sun sets on the Strip, the millions of twinkling and flashing lights, huge fiber-optic signs, and thousands of people create a sensation that borders on ecstasy. Get out there with the gals and stroll down the Strip. Stretch limos, luxury sports cars, women draped in jewels, debonair men resembling characters in *The Godfather* all fill the street under the glow of the lights.

GAMBLING

You don't have to be a high roller to get a kick out of gambling in Las Vegas. Even if you just play the nickel slot machines or sit down for a hand at a blackjack table, where players have the best odds, experiencing the casinos is a form of entertainment. You and the girls should make a casino crawl, popping into as many of them as you can, to overload on the sounds, people, and glitz. It's a thrill to get dressed up and make a night of it, drinking fancy cocktails along the way. The serious gamblers among you may want to head off the Strip; downtown there's less pretension and the stakes are lower. Those of you whose only experience with Lady Luck is bingo may want to polish your gambling skills with a free lesson at the Excalibur and Aladdin casinos, among others.

BEST BIRTHDAY MEAL

The self-indulgence of Sin City doesn't stop at gambling. The spas in Vegas are perhaps its greatest extravagance—and greatest birthday present to yourself. For your big birthday dinner, make reservations at Wolfgang Puck's POSTRIO at the Venetian, or SPAGO at Caesars Palace. There's also the PICASSO at the Bellagio, which has the painter's masterpieces on the walls. Las Vegas also redefines the buffet as most of us know it. You'll get your fill of lobster tail and clams at the VILLAGE SEAFOOD buffet at the Rio. The Bellagio buffet serves wild duck breast, venison, crab legs, and wild boar. And there's always the 99-cent shrimp cocktail at the Golden Gate Hotel and Casino served in the SAN FRANCISCO BAR AND DELI.

CATCH A SHOW

To top off your celebration, buy tickets for at least one of Vegas's larger-than-life shows. The Cirque du Soleil's *Mystere* and the "O" performances will leave you all speechless (www.cirquedesoleil.com). There are the antics of the Blue Man Group and Broadway hits such as *Phantom* or *Mamma Mia*. And there's always some famous singer performing somewhere in town.

FREEBIES

There's no need to pay for much of the entertainment in Las Vegas, as this city is a 24-hour show. The people here put on some of the most memorable performances, if not the best stories to retell for years to come. And you'll pull your cameras out for the choreography of the Bellagio fountains, the erupting volcano at the Mirage, the Pirate Show in front of Treasure Island, and the singing gondoliers at the Venetian.

SHOPPERTAINMENT

While not all of us can procure Giorgio Armani, Hermès, and Prada, here we all can pretend we can. Even if you leave your credit cards back in the room, there's people watching and browsing the boutiques of major

European labels, not to mention the amusement-park environs of each mall. The Forum Shops at Caesars, a 560,000-square-foot mini-metropolis, features animatronic Bacchus and Venus sculptures, giant fountains, and a spiral-shaped escalator. The Grand Canal Shop at the Venetian includes a canal running up the center of the shopping area. Resembling Madison Avenue, the Wynn Esplanade holds Chanel, Giorgio Armani, Hermès, and Prada, including the first Jean-Paul Gaultier designer store in the nation. Over at the Fashion Show Mall you'll find the largest department stores in the country under one roof: Neiman-Marcus, Saks Fifth Avenue, Bloomingdale's Home, Macy's, and Nordstrom. There are outlet shops galore. But if all you really want is a "Welcome to Fabulous Las Vegas, Nevada" magnet, you're sure to find it at Bonanza Gifts, the world's largest gift shop.

WHERE TO STAY

If you're going to do Las Vegas right, stay in one of the big theme hotels—the Bellagio, the Venetian, Aladdin, Mandalay Bay, or Paris. One alternative for a group is a one-bedroom suite at the Hilton Grand Vacations Club on the Strip. Four of you can comfortably stay in this mini-apartment with a king-size bed, full sofa sleeper, kitchen, and washer and dryer. If you'd rather save your nickels for the slot machines, cook a meal or two in your suite. In the summer, a hotel with a pool scene may be your preference (Hard Rock, the Palms, Mandalay Bay, Wynn, or Bellagio). Cabana rentals around the pool are a fabulous way to turn a visit to the desert into a beach vacation.

ONE CLICK AND YOU'RE OFF: Las Vegas Convention and Visitors Authority (877-847-4858, www.visitlasvegas.com).

Biking Through Wine Country

≈ SONOMA VALLEY ≈

Sonoma Valley is North America's answer to Tuscany. And just like its Italian counterpart, this fertile valley in Northern California, with its dedication to winemaking and fresh food, picturesque rolling hills, and Mediterranean climate make for a gourmand's ideal birthday getaway. And there's no better way to experience Sonoma Valley than by bike. In many ways, this valley surpasses its neighbor, Napa Valley, for best bike touring. Its roads see less traffic and there are more back roads, which wind through

Last summer I discovered that Las Vegas is ground zero for weekend bachelorette parties. Clusters of girlfriends sunbathed by the large pools, wearing visors with glitter letters identifying each person: bride, sister-of-the-bride, or college roommate. Many women prefer the Venetian because of the spacious suites (750 square feet) with two queen beds, a separate living room, and huge marble bathrooms. When you share a large suite and divide the cost by four, comfort and luxury are affordable. Look for off-season specials and low rates on websites like Travelocity, Expedia, Orbitz, and Hotels.com

—Marybeth

the Russian River area to remote vineyards and farms. The occasional tractor and truck carrying the harvest pass by on the quiet, gently rolling roads. The honey light of Sonoma Valley gilds the stone farmhouses.

A bike allows you to experience the sights, sounds, and smells of this world-famous wine country. You notice details you'd otherwise miss from a car: Around one corner a stand of towering redwoods, around another turn majestic oaks, then palm trees and cactus, and next a meadow of bright yellow mustard. You'll be enveloped by the scents of eucalyptus groves, the fecund earth, blossoms from gardens, and fields of lavender.

BEST TOWN
The country town of Healdsburg conveniently sits at the confluence of the Russian River, Alexander, and Dry Creek valleys in Northern Sonoma County. Its Spanish-style plaza hosts a Summer Concert Series and antique fairs, and the streets are lined with historic homes and quaint storefronts.

RENT A BIKE
Wine Country Bikes in Healdsburg will set each of you up with a comfy bike (equipped with a lock and a handlebar bag); they also arrange both guided and self-guided day trips. Or ride the 25-mile loop of Dry Valley on your own. Get a map from the Chamber of Commerce and plot out your route (866-922-4537 or 707-473-0610, www.winecountrybikes.com).

WINE TASTING
Across the three valleys there are a hundred or so wineries scattered about, ranging from huge, world-famous facilities and grand chateaus to modest

family-owned vineyards. Many of them offer complimentary tastings; some charge a nominal fee that is typically deducted from a wine purchase. There's something festive about wine tasting, even though it's not wise to drink and pedal (remember you don't actually have to swallow). You and your girlfriends will have fun discerning the different tastes (Berries? Oak? Butter? Manure?) and picking up some vino knowledge. In no time you'll be chatting about tannins, aromas, and the body of a wine amongst yourselves, if only half jokingly. The tasting rooms are also cool oases from the sun and an opportunity to browse locally made items for your kitchen or gift giving. At some of the larger wineries, you may be curious enough to take a tour of their grounds and barrel cellars to sample wines directly from barrels for a deeper understanding of their winemaking techniques. In the afternoons, you can always return by car or access with a car some wineries that you missed that day by bike. This is when you can load up on bottles or cases to bring back home.

FOR GARDEN LOVERS
The crown jewel of the Dry Creek Valley—and a must-see for the gardeners among you—would have to be the Ferrari-Carano Vineyards and Winery. A magnificent Florentine estate, it is surrounded by streams, waterfalls, and five acres of immaculately designed gardens with 30 species of trees (both exotic and dwarf varieties), gazebos, benches, and footpaths. Each spring more than 10,000 tulips and daffodils take center stage. Tulip fans can call the Tulip Hotline, 707-433-5349, in the late winter or early spring months to find out when the tulips will be in full bloom. 8761 Dry Creek Road (707-433-6700, www.ferrari-carano.com).

FOR ART LOVERS
The newest addition to Healdsburg's wine country is the modern Roshambo Winery & Gallery. It's worth hopping off your bike to sample their award-winning Chardonnay, take in views of the vineyards, and check out an art exhibit. 3000 Westside Road (888-525-9463 or 707-431-2051, www.roshambowinery.com).

FOR FOODIES
With a Sonoma County Farm Trails map, found in local shops and at the visitors bureau, you can intersperse your visits to vineyards on your bikes with stops at local farms with sheep, llamas, honeybees, orchards, and gardens. Farmers markets set up every Saturday morning behind the Dry Creek Hotel in Healdsburg and on Tuesdays from 4 to 6 p.m. near the plaza. Be sure to try the succulent locally grown Dry Creek Peaches.

We've lived in Healdsburg for 25 years, and for many years there wasn't even a cappuccino machine in town. Now Healdsburg has become very chic, but we still have a small-town atmosphere. There are no parking meters in town and we don't get the big tourist buses. In the morning the hot spot for locals is the Flying Goat coffee house, where they roast their own beans. The Newstand next to the Dry Creek Hotel serves the best cappuccino and every conceivable newspaper and magazine. Grown-ups enjoy Powell's Old Fashion Candy Shop just as much as the children do. They sell everything under the sun: blocks of rainbow-colored popcorn, gummy bears, jelly beans, big chunks of toffee, creamy gelatos, fresh made fruit sorbets. We're like kids when we go in there.

—Nancy Wells, Vinter, Healdsburg, California

BIRTHDAY DINING

RAVENOUS offers large portions of American bistro food, freshly prepared with the local farmers market ingredients. Locals recommend the grilled spear fish with mango salsa. Desserts and breads are made in-house. The bustling bar is open late and serves beer on tap from local micro breweries and a nice selection of wines by the glass. Closed Monday and Tuesday. 420 Center Street ($22-35; 707-431-1302).

WILLI'S SEAFOOD AND RAW BAR gets rave reviews from local women because they serve a variety of delicious small plates—perfect for sharing. The décor inside is warm and vibrant, or you may choose to dine al fresco. Heat lamps will keep you cozy on cooler evenings. They're known for their fresh seafood bar featuring tuna tartare and ceviches and specialty cocktails: Mojitos, Raspberry Lemon Drops, and Pomatinis. Closed Tuesday. 403 Healdsburg Avenue (small plates $7-15; 707-433-9191, www.williswinebar.net).

BEST PLACE TO BLOW YOUR DIET

A true celebration for your birthday is dining at chef Charlie Palmer's DRY CREEK KITCHEN in the Hotel Healdsburg. The freshest ingredients from Wine Country are transformed into scrumptious plates paired with selections from their notable all-Sonoma wine list. Don't miss the warm fois gras with a passion fruit-and-prune garnish or the lamb, Liberty Duck, or artisan cheeses from REDWOOD HILLS and COWGIRL CREAMERY. Indulge in the decadent desserts like the Valrhona Bombe of chocolate and caramel mousse with vanilla bean Bavarian or the warm pear-cranberry crisp.

Charlie Palmer, one of America's leading chefs, also has restaurants in New York and Las Vegas. A meal here is an epicurean experience and it's not overpriced for the value of the food. I recommend you "go for it" and order the six-course tasting menu. Located on the square at 317 Healdsburg Avenue, $28-39 à la carte or a six-course tasting menu at $74 per person, or $119 with paired wines (707-431-0330, www.charliepalmer.com/dry_creek).

MAKE YOUR OWN PICNIC
At the DRY CREEK GENERAL STORE, founded in 1881 and considered the best deli in the area, you can pick up made-to-order sandwiches, toss them in a pack, and have yourselves a feast at a winery picnic area overlooking vineyards. 3495 Dry Creek Road (707-433-4171).

BEST PLACE TO HEAL IN A STRESS-FREE ZONE
To revitalize your body, visit the Spa at Hotel Healdsburg on the square. Although you may choose from many treatments, the massages are exceptional.

BEST WINERY MAP
Call or email the Russian River Wine Road organization for a fabulous, detailed free map listing more than a hundred wineries. It will help you plan your bike rides and wine tasting. This invaluable map, which folds out to 16 by 16 inches, covers Alexander Valley, Dry Creek Valley, and the Russian River appellations of Northwest Sonoma County. Contact www.wineroad.com to request the free map (800-723-6336).

Very detailed maps are also available online at www.visit-wineroad .com/daytrips.htm. These maps show all the wineries, restaurants, roads, and tasting hours.

My favorite bike trip (or by car) is detailed on Day Trip Number Two, (on the above mentioned website) through Dry Creek, visiting these wineries: Lambert Bridge, Dry Creek, Passalacqua, Mauritson, Mazzocca, and Ridge Vineyards, returning on Lytton Springs Road.

WHERE TO STAY

Dozens of B&Bs and cottages can be found in Healdsburg and tucked in between vineyards. Standouts include the frilly Victorian Grape Leaf Inn near the plaza and the Hotel Healdsburg, located right on the plaza. Your group may choose the privacy of a vacation home: a chalet-style farmhouse or a bungalow. Grape Leaf Inn, 539 Johnson Street (starting at $200; 866-433-8140, www.grapeleafinn.com). Check the website for Internet specials. Hotel Healdsburg (starting at $260 based on season, better rates online; 800-889-7188, www.hotelhealdsburg.com); Best Western Dry Creek Inn, 198 Dry Creek Road (starting at $89, 800-222-5784, www.drycreekinn.com); or the Travelodge, Healdsburg, 178 Dry Creek Road (800-499-0103, www .winecountrytravelodge.com). Check their website for Internet specials.

ONE CLICK AND YOU'RE OFF: Contact the Healdsburg Chamber of Commerce and Visitors Bureau for more information. (707-433-6935, www.healdsburg.org).

New Orleans

ᘒ LOUISIANA ᘓ

From the jazz streaming out of nightclubs to the crowds on Bourbon Street to the parades of Mardi Gras, there's always a party going on in the Big Easy. Even Hurricane Katrina couldn't extinguish the liveliness of this city for long. New Orleans supplies all the components of a memorable birthday: food, music, and dancing...and more food. The vibrant culture, found nowhere else in the world, is the pride and joy of New Orleans; the locals truly want you to have the time of your life. So it's guaranteed you'll do just that.

EVENT TO FLY IN FOR

Since 1970, The New Orleans Jazz & Heritage Festival, a.k.a. Jazz Fest, has been one of the premier music festivals in the world. Thousands of musicians, cooks, and craftspeople welcome as many as 500,000 visitors each May to this ten-day celebration of all genres of music and Louisiana culture. In the infield of the Fair Grounds Race Course, the third-oldest racetrack in America, you'll find the friendliest celebration you're ever likely to be a part of. Jazz Fest attracts a more mature crowd than Mardi Gras—there's never been a brawl in the 40 years of Jazz Fest. Here, everybody's your friend.

The name Jazz Fest does this event a grave disservice. From 11 a.m. to 7 p.m. on any day you can hear almost any genre of music: gospel, Cajun, zydeco, blues, R&B, rock, funk, rap, bluegrass, folk, African, and Caribbean. Through the years, its specialty remains Louisiana music. The city's best exports come back year after year to perform, from the Neville Brothers to the Marsalis family to Harry Connick, Jr. Others who have also graced its stages are Jimmy Buffet, Ani Difranco, Herbie Hancock, Dave Matthew's Band, Lionel Ritchie, and Bruce Springsteen.

It's the bands you've never heard of that leave the deepest impressions. At Economy Hall you're sure to make some discoveries. And you're bound to see at least one revelation at the Gospel Tent, which can hold up to 1,500 people. That it's consistently full to capacity is proof of the inescapable magnetism of the music. All faiths share in the experience, holding hands and swaying.

What helps keep you all going from morning until night is the variety. It's likely you'll do more dancing here than you ever have in your lives. You'll get carried away and join the second line parade, a rollicking entourage behind the main line musicians that roll through the Fair Grounds a few times a day. Louisiana's finest restaurants dish up their specialties. And artisans from around the country display their wares at a prestigious crafts fair where you may find a voodoo priestess or an artist in action. Each of you is sure to come home with a memento of the occasion, maybe some jewelry, photography, sculpture, clothing, a quilt, or a painting. Groups of friends who are repeat festivalgoers hold their own traditions here year after year. They'll meet for a special toast or orchestrate a watermelon sacrifice ceremony. Celebrate your birthday by starting a ritual of your own.

BEST STREET FOR BROWSING
Magazine Street is the city's shopping thoroughfare for specialty boutique shops for all ages, offering baby clothing, shoes, evening wear, and plus sizes. (www.magazinestreet.com).

THRIFT AND VINTAGE CLOTHING
You'll find a remarkable collection of retro and vintage dresses, jewelry, handbags, shoes, hats, velvet capes, corsets, and lingerie on Magazine Street.

Whether you're window shopping or hunting for costumes, check out Trashy Diva and the House of Lounge where you'll find all styles of retro lingerie and costume items such as feather wings, fans, marabou slippers, and cigarette holders. Trashy Diva, 2024 Magazine Street. Open seven days a week (www.trashydiva.com). Also: House of Lounge, 2044 Magazine Street (www.houseoflounge.com).

In the same block, there's an elegant gentlemen's shop called Aidan Gill where you can buy the man in your life handmade shaving gear, a badger shave brush, a well-made necktie, soaps, cufflinks, and other Old World accessories. Aidan Gill for Men, 2026 Magazine Street. Closed Sunday (www.aidangill.com).

Further up Magazine Street from the French Quarter, Miss Claudia's Vintage Clothing and Costumes is filled with original styles and costume ideas from decades past—Flapper to Mod to Disco from the 1920s through the 1980s. Miss Claudia's, 4204 Magazine Street (504-897-6310).

BIRTHDAY DINING

Now is not the time to abide by a diet: Eating a lot in New Orleans is mandatory. My favorite dishes include andouille gumbo, po-boy sandwiches, soft shell crabs, and a must—boiled crawfish. Upscale dining experiences are equally diverse: You'll slurp raw oysters with the crowds inside the informal FELIX'S, and then indulge on haute-Creole cuisine under the chandeliers of the famous (and high-priced but worth it) ARNAUD'S, a block-long 18th- and 19th-century building in the French Quarter.

If you're looking for the birthday restaurant in New Orleans, then GALATOIRE'S is a must-visit. Located in the 200 block of Bourbon Street

For the past 20 years six high school girlfriends and I have met for a yearly reunion. New Orleans is not like any other city we've ever been to, so we travel there every other year. We've gone at least ten times. There is just so much to do. We find new restaurants, galleries, and theaters. Of course we like to eat a lot. We dine at our favorites, Irene's and Napoleon House, but every visit we discover a new place. We always shop Magazine and Royal Streets and we take the street car to eat in Uptown. We've lived with hurricanes all our lives, so Katrina won't keep us away. Next year we plan to go during the Jazz Festival.

—Marcie Jarratt, 50s, Volunteer, Avid Traveler, Austin, Texas

One of my most memorable shopping adventures was in New Orleans on Magazine Street. At Trashy Diva and the House of Lounge, my daughters, their girlfriends, and I tried on sexy silk corsets, leopard camisoles, bustiers, lacey baby doll nighties, and other unmentionables. We modeled our "fantasy finds" to each other both in and out of the dressing rooms. Now we're all set for Halloween and costume parties and who knows what else.

—Marybeth

---

in the French Quarter since 1905, this James Beard Foundation "Most Outstanding Restaurant" winner is one of the city's finest traditional French Creole restaurants. You'll dine with a diverse cross section of the New Orleans' society scene as well as a sprinkling of tourists. It's upscale but also lively and interactive. The waiters will get the entire restaurant in on your birthday celebration. Locals say the shrimp remoulade is to die for—don't worry about the calories. An insider's tip: Go early on Friday for lunch and sit downstairs for the action. No one goes back to work after the lunch extravaganza. Closed Monday. 209 Bourbon Street ($22-34; 504-525-2021, www.galatoires.com).

As for other great restaurants, among the city's best are **LILETTE**, featuring French, Eclectic, and International cuisine. 3637 Magazine Street between Louisiana and Napoleon. Closed Sunday and Monday. ($21-28; 504-895-1636, www.liletterestaurant.com). **BAYONA** is an equally fabulous restaurant, serving eclectic world cuisine with Louisiana influences, located in the heart of the French Quarter. 430 rue Dauphine ($25-35; 504-525-4455, www.bayona.com).

MUST-SEE MUSEUM
The Ogden Museum of Southern Art, a fairly new institution in the Warehouse District, boasts the largest collection of Southern art in the world and has a fantastic gift shop.

RETREAT
Find solitude in the gardens of Audubon Park, once a colonial plantation. The oak trees and the banks of the Mississippi are prime locations for a midday snooze. Admission to the 400-acre park is free. You may also enjoy the zoo, a golf course, tennis courts, horseback riding, and jogging and cycling tracks. It is located in uptown New

Orleans between St. Charles Avenue and the Mississippi River, near Tulane University.

LEARN TO COOK

Some of you may want to learn the basics of Cajun cooking. At the Cookin' Cajun Cooking School, maybe you can figure out how to make that insanely tasty crawfish etouffée that you ate at Jazz Fest—and that you can't stop thinking about.

WHERE TO STAY

In the French Quarter, the Soniat House, considered to be the most beautiful hotel in town, and the Victorian-style Melrose Mansion Hotel are top picks. Soniat House, 1133 Chartes Street (starting at $311, with seasonal specials as low as $145; 800-544-8808, www.soniathouse.com). Melrose Mansion, 937 Esplanade Avenue (starting at $225; 800-650-3323, www.melrosegroup.com).

Close to the Jazz Fest Fair Grounds, you have your pick of B&Bs such as the Benachi House Bed & Breakfast Inn, a former 19th-century mansion, or the Degas House, where the French Impressionist painter once lived. Benachi House Inn, 2257 Bayou Road (starting at $115 (800-308-7040, www.bbonline.com). The Degas House, 2306 Esplanade Avenue (starting at $140; 800-755-6730, www.degashouse.com).

Other options, if you're willing to commute into the city, are plantations in the area that offer accommodations, such as the Oak Alley Plantation and Houmas House, (see Chapter 2, Cajun Country for details).

ONE CLICK AND YOU'RE OFF: New Orleans Convention and Visitors Bureau can help you book lodging and plan your visit (800-672-6124, www.neworleanscvb.com). For ticket and general information for Jazz Fest, visit www.nojazzfest.com.

Take a Cruise

☞ CARIBBEAN OR MEXICO ☜

There's something celebratory about cruise ships. Perhaps it's the gorgeous tropical destinations, around-the-clock eating, or their seeming defiance of the principles of buoyancy. The beauty of taking a cruise for a celebration is that you can focus on the celebrating: Once you book your reservations and find your way to the ship, there's no need to think past that. It's just peaceful intervals on the open sea and then mornings when you wake up to a new seaside town.

With ships leaving from more North American departure cities each year, it's an easier ride then ever to paradise. There are one-night dinner cruises to 14-day journeys to fit your budget. And cruise lines have evolved ships into incredible next-generation floating resorts (so get that image of shuffleboard out of your head). There are now climbing walls, surf-simulator pools, yoga studios, and movies under the stars. You can expect to get one of the best massages you've ever gotten from their enhanced spas.

Where cruises differ from your typical resort is they actually move. In addition to a healthy dose of relaxation, you'll explore the scenery and culture of the islands. Months in advance of when you set sail, you can prereserve onshore excursions, which include horseback riding, kayaking, scuba diving, and bus tours to famous attractions. And there's always striking out by cab or public transportation on your own.

WHERE TO SPEND THE MOST TIME

Up on the top decks you'll experience an extraordinary version of a day at the beach, minus the sand and lugging beach chairs and coolers. Girlfriends find this scene to be the highest form of decadence: You'll stake out lounge chairs for the day and let the cute waiters fetch you frozen drinks.

TRAVEL TIP

All ships have fine-dining rooms where you pay a surcharge of $20-25 per person for your dinner. The food is an upgrade from what's available in the ship's dining rooms: top quality beef, a variety of fresh shellfish, seafood, cheeses, patés, and even escargot. You'll relax, dine for two to three hours and luxuriate in the white-glove service. Reservations cannot be made before you board the ship, but book a table on your first day aboard if you wish to celebrate a special occasion.

MAKE IT SPECIAL

Cruise lines love to make a big deal out of your occasion. When you book your reservations, let them know how you'd like to celebrate the big day: A cake with singing waiters at dinner, champagne in your room, or a private cocktail reception for your group.

NIGHTLIFE

At night you may find it difficult to act your age: What better pick-me-up for a birthday is there? There are magic shows, comedians, karaoke, gambling, Broadway-quality performances, discos, and movies. After a cardio workout on the dance floor or a few hours at the slot machines, there's late-night snacking to be done. Depending on the ship, this can vary from 24-hour restaurants, to midnight buffets, to cookies coming out of the oven.

CRUISE LINE PICKS

Holland America, Royal Caribbean, Carnival, Princess, and Crystal are the cream of the crop when considering itineraries and ships to the Caribbean and Mexico. All have their strengths and weaknesses and versions of itineraries. But you can rarely go wrong with any of them as they have the youngest and biggest fleets to choose from.

BEST SHIP FOR THRILL-SEEKERS

Experience the world's largest ship on Royal Caribbean's new *Independence of the Seas*. With the first ever onboard surf-simulator at sea, whirlpools cantilevering 200 feet beyond the sides of the ship, an ice-skating rink, and their largest rock-climbing wall yet, it's a big draw for adventurers. Departing from Fort Lauderdale, it sails to the eastern and western Caribbean on four-, six-, and eight-night cruises.

BEST OF THE EAST

If you've dreamt of the rugged mountains and dense rain forest of Dominica, the world-famous multicolor coral reefs of Turks & Caicos, visiting a deserted island, spying flamingoes, playing a round of golf in Bermuda, or snorkeling with stingrays, a cruise off the East Coast is your cup of tea. Now departing from more cities along the eastern seaboard, cruise lines offer the most choices with itineraries to the Caribbean all-year round.

Routes for this region are typically divided into the Bahamas, Bermuda, and the southern, eastern and western Caribbean. This is where you'll find postcard-perfect clear turquoise water and white-sand beaches. Highlights of these tours include private islands in the Bahamas—for example, Royal Caribbean's Coco Cay. In the western Caribbean, ports of call typically include the Grand Cayman; Belize; Cozumel, Mexico; and Jamaica. Southern Caribbean places of interest consist of Puerto Rico, Aruba, Curacao, St. Maarten, St. Thomas, Dominica, and Tortola. The islands of St. Lucia, Antigua, and Martinique are part of eastern Caribbean itineraries.

BEST OF THE WEST

A West Coast itinerary comprises the cliff-hanging seaside towns of Mexico; migrating humpback, gray and blue whales; horseback riding in the Sierra Madre; and people-watching in a zocalo (town square). Los Angeles is the main departure city for year-round West Coast routes, followed by San Francisco, Seattle, and Vancouver. Stops include Catalina Island, Baja, Acapulco, Ensenada, Ixtapa, Vallarta, and Cabo San Lucas. A few ships venture farther down the coast to Guatemala, Panama, and Coast Rica. Via the world-famous Gatun Locks of the Panama Canal, you can also pass through to the islands of the Caribbean Sea. Cruises range from 7 to 11 days.

ONE CLICK AND YOU'RE OFF: Holland America (877-932-4259, www.hollandamerica.com); Royal Caribbean (866-562-7625, www.royal caribbean.com); Carnival Cruise Lines (888-227-6482, www.carnival.com); Princess Cruises (800-774-6237, www.princess.com); Celebrity Cruises (800-760-0654, www.celebritycruises.com).

Hilton Head

⊱ SOUTH CAROLINA ⊰

Hilton Head is a prime example of utopian planning; the island was built in 1956 as a residential and vacation oasis that blends with nature. The island is divided into four plantation-like resorts, each with thousands of acres of pine and palmetto-tree woods and stands of Spanish moss-draped oaks. On Hilton Head every room has a view of the Atlantic, a golf course, or a lagoon, and no building is over five stories or taller than the trees. Here everything is within reach—the beach, bicycling, golf; you can even rent a condo and party as a group. It is also the perfect place to watch the sunrise after a real birthday blowout.

BACK TO NATURE

The surprisingly uncrowned white-sand, dune-lined beaches of Hilton Head are special in that they're hard-packed: just right for a long bike ride in the sea air along its 12 miles of shoreline, spying the occasional bottlenose dolphin offshore. Horseback riding, surf casting, and kayaking can also be arranged.

PERFECT FOR PLAY
The island takes tennis as seriously as golf; there are 300 tennis courts and seven golf courses on the island.

BEST DAY TRIP
Take a ferry to Daufuskie Island (home to descendants of African slaves freed after the Civil War) where the population is a staggering 429. This is a good place to bike ride, shop for artisan crafts, and observe local wildlife. There are two resorts, three golf courses, and three lighthouses here. The island is rich in beauty and history.

GALLERY GAZING
The art galleries on Calhoun Street in Bluffton's Old Town, just over the bridge on the mainland, are the most impressive. Make sure you visit A Guild of Bluffton Artists, 20 Calhoun Street (843-757-5590, www.bluffton1.com).

NIGHTLIFE
Broadway shows visit the island's Arts Center of Coastal Carolina. The best place to listen to live music is The Jazz Corner. There's always a crowd and the food is pretty good too. 1000 William Hilton Parkway (843-842-8620, www.thejazzcorner.com).

EVENTS TO FLY IN FOR
During peak season, in spring, temperatures are typically in the mid-70s and several worthwhile events take place. In March, the largest outdoor wine tasting on the East Coast sets up on Hilton Head: WineFest (843-686-4944, www.hiltonheadhospitality.org/sections/wine-fest).

BEST BIRTHDAY MEAL
Locals recommend the fresh seafood at **ALEXANDER'S** at Palmetto Dunes. You have a choice of dining in the enclosed veranda that overlooks a lagoon, at the wine bar, or in the main dining room decorated with vintage Harley-Davidsons. Try the fresh oysters, raw on the half shell or Rockefeller or Savannah style, $20-30 (843-785-4999, www.alexanders restaurant.com).

And if any of you are foodies, you'll want to dine at the **OLD FORT PUB** at Hilton Head Plantation, which has been featured on the Food Network.

With one of the best waterfront views on the island to catch the sunset, the restaurant blends southern specialties with international flair. Don't let the word "pub" fool you, it's a very high-end restaurant. It's pricey, but worth it. The menu reflects a New Southern cuisine with specials like Sea Island bouillabaisse or Cajun Carolina trout. Check out the reasonable three-course tasting menu for the first seating. Be sure to visit the historical Civil War–era fort next door (first seating: $14-21, dinner, $25-35; 843-681-2386, www.oldfortpub.com).

The OCEAN GRILL, located at the entrance of Palmetto Dunes' Shelter Cove Marina, offers an American-style menu and excellent views from its second-floor dining room of the marina and bay. Enjoy live piano entertainment every night and fireworks on Tuesday in the summer (early dining $15-24, dinner $25-35; 843-785-3030, www.oceangrillrestaurant.com).

WHERE TO STAY

The toughest choice you'll have to make when booking your lodging is what view you want. There's the 60-room Inn at Harbour Town in the Sea Pines Resort, which presents you with the choice of seeing a tennis court or a golf course out your window. This boutique hotel knows how to indulge you: Their kilted British butlers take care of your every need 24 hours a day. And a few steps from its doors, is the first tee box to the Harbour Town course. Bike around the golf course at dusk on one of the complimentary bicycles or relax on the rocking chairs on the back patio. Rated AAA Four Diamond, 32 Greenwood Drive (starting at $159 in low season; 866-561-8802, www.seapines.com).

If your group has four or more women, consider renting a villa at one of the plantations where you may get golf privileges or discounts. Always ask for the discounts! Remember that larger resorts often cater to conference business and have kids' camps. Consider the AAA Four Diamond Crowne Plaza at Shipyard Plantation, set in 800 private acres with tropical gardens on the oceanfront. Try booking online (starting at $129 in low season; 800-334-1881, www.cphiltonhead.com).

Hilton Oceanfront Resort at Palmetto Dunes is located on three spectacular miles of white-sand South Carolina beaches. There are 324 guestrooms and 20 ocean front suites or studio suites with kitchenettes, living, dining, and bedroom areas, and large private balconies with ocean views (starting at $139 in low season; 843-842-8000, www.hilton.com).

Another option for vacationing girlfriends is to rent a villa, typically a short walk to golf courses, tennis courts, and the beach, which are often more affordable for a group (www.hiltonhead.com).

The best time to go to Hilton Head is in early fall or late spring. The busiest times of the year for the town are Easter, the Fourth of July, first week in August, and Labor Day. During these times, as well as the summer months, the town can be crowded, which means long lines and traffic; there are also summer storms to watch out for. Avoid going between Thanksgiving and mid-February as many businesses close. The seven miles from Hilton Head Island Airport to downtown Hilton Head is a 15-minute drive. From the Savannah/Hilton Head International Airport to downtown Hilton Head it's 45 miles, a one-hour drive.

ON A BUDGET

If you're looking to save some pennies, many hotels offer packages in the off-season, November to February, at much lower prices. In May the Beaufort County Arts Society hosts free concerts, aptly titled the Arts in the Parks. There are both lunchtime concerts at noon and early evening concerts at 5:30. Admission is free (843-379-2787, www.beaufortcountyarts.com).

ONE CLICK AND YOU'RE OFF: For a free vacation guide, contact the Hilton Head-Bluffton Chamber of Commerce (800-523-3373, www .hiltonheadisland.com). Another useful website to find activities, lodging, or directions to all the restaurants: www.hiltonhead.com.

CHAPTER FOUR

Family Bonding

᷐ **GINNY'S STORY** ᷑

Every summer of her childhood Ginny, her brother, and her sister hopped into the back seat of the family Chrysler sedan and set off for a camping trip in the mountains. Her single mom would pack up the car with pillows, teddy bears, books, and lots of old sheets for the kids to use to make tents in the back seat. That was before the days of mandatory seat belts, in-car TV screens, or entertainment systems. They'd drive from their home in Northern California to somewhere far away, usually to Colorado or Utah. Ginny says, "These long road trips were a time for family bonding."

Ginny believes that one of the best ways to catch up with her mom, daughter, or sister is burning up the pavement on a road trip. So every summer she and her mom, her teenage daughter, and her sister, Ann, who lives in Southern California, drive six hours north to attend the Ashland,

Oregon, Shakespeare Festival. "It's great," says Ginny. "We get a lot of catching up done in the car."

Although they look forward to fine dining, shopping, and theatrical performances, they all agree that the confined time in the car leads to the most intense bonding between the three generations of women. The sisters tease each other and joke about their teen years. "We talk about our careers, volunteer work, relationships, and people," adds Ginny. "The intimate group size and six hours of 'talk' time gives Kari, my 15-year-old, an opportunity to express herself and interact as 'one of the girls.' Of course Grandma reverts to her role as parent and offers lots of advice on all topics." They've discovered that in the car they communicate on a deeper level than possible at many family get-togethers where there are many guests and numerous interruptions to conversations. And the guys? "They really aren't interested," says Ginny. "My husband takes our son camping while we enjoy the theater and female time."

Helen, Ginny's 78-year-old mother, has taken over the role of trip planner. And she starts a year in advance selecting the plays and ordering tickets early to get good seats for everyone. She compares all the hotel and B&B choices before making her selection and looks for new restaurants in town. Meanwhile Ann, Kari, and Ginny read synopses of the plays to better understand the plots, symbolism, and Shakespearean language because, as Ginny says, "it's easy to get bogged down in all the Old English."

They're on the go the whole time they're in Ashland, walking around town admiring the quaint Victorian homes and seeing two shows a

---

I've been traveling with my daughters for more than 15 years. We began right after Paul died. Now I invite each daughter on a trip with me every year. We have the time to tell each other everything we're doing. It brings out memories from their childhood and it makes us so much closer. I now include two daughters on a trip. With five daughters I always have several travel companions. I am proud of my relationship with them. We love active trips where we can hike, kayak, and do nature walks. Our favorite North American adventures have been to Alaska and Baja—where we kayaked among the whales.

—Evelyn Woelz, 80s, Retired Teacher, Volunteer for the Blind,
Santa Rosa, California

day, one in the afternoon and one in the evening—half Shakespeare, comedy or tragedy, and half famous American playwrights. The highlight for them is the Shakespeare plays under the stars in the outdoor Elizabethan theater.

"My mom is loosing her sight to macular degeneration, but I know even when she's blind she'll still want to go to hear the plays and to be with her daughters and granddaughter, and we'll want to be with her," says Ginny. "We would never pass up the six hours of talk time driving both ways."

࿊ JULIE'S STORY ࿊

"Mom always wanted to see the 'Big Apple' and the best time to go was before the holidays when she could see all the lights and decorations. So when she turned 80 my two sisters and my sister-in-law took her to New York. Through a cyber agency, we rented a flat on 58th Street between 6th and 7th with two bedrooms, a pull-out couch and a tiny kitchen," says Julie.

"We wanted a pied-a-terre, not a hotel, because we thought Mom would want to go back to the apartment for afternoon rests, but we were wrong. She was on the go all the time," adds Julie.

Long before the departure date in early December, Julie and her siblings, nieces, and nephews were making plans. At a family reunion the summer prior to her 80th birthday, everyone gave grandma apples with gift certificates for her trip to the Big Apple. One of her sons gave her a carriage ride in Central Park. Her vegetarian grandson gave her a lunch at his favorite vegetarian restaurant. Everyone had a chance to get involved and to chip in on the cost of the trip.

They scheduled events in advance, buying tickets to the Rockettes' Holiday Special at Radio City Music Hall, but also left free time to peek into windows along Madison Avenue, browse through the Museum of Modern Art, take in a late-afternoon mass at St. Patrick's Cathedral, wander through a Christmas fair in Central Park, eat in an Indian restaurant, and settle into a leather banquette at the sophisticated bar to sip martinis at the Carlyle Hotel. Julie adds, "Mom loved the live soft jazz in the Bemelmans' Bar and the attention of the dashing doormen wearing bowler hats and white gloves."

"It is such a gift to have a mom so open, physically and mentally in shape, and so much fun to be with," explained Julie. "We laughed a lot."

"Mom forgot to bring a warm hat and it was chilly when we were walking around Washington Square, so we visited all the street vendors and

Mom tried on stacks of hats. We have hilarious 80th birthday photos of her in the final selection—a pink cloche."

One chilly night the ladies took a carriage ride in the park. "The horse was trotting along in line behind the other carriages until we told the driver that we were celebrating my mom's 80th birthday," says Julie. "Then the horse sped up like crazy, passing the other carriages and tearing back to the start. We laughed and laughed, because the driver acted like he better get through this ride quickly before she dies."

For their mother's Christmas gift the next holiday they created a scrapbook with ticket stubs and photos. "It was a nice way to capture the experience for family members who weren't there and for her to show to her friends," adds Julie. "Mom says she'll never go back to New York because she feels another visit could never top the perfect experience she had for her 80th birthday."

❧ VALERIE'S STORY ❧

Valerie's family embarked on the legendary *Queen Mary* ocean liner when she was five-years old, on a Thanksgiving cruise between New York and Nassau, Bahamas. Three years ago she took her mom on a nostalgic visit to the *Queen Mary*, whose sailing days are over. (She's now a floating hotel, in dry dock in Long Beach, California.) Thirty-eight years after their first voyage, they slept in the same cabin (A112 in first class), surrounded by the same wood veneer walls.

As a travel agent, Valerie's mother introduced her to the world, "and now it's my turn to reciprocate," says Valerie. "Our return to the *Queen Mary* allowed me to help her during a painful time in her life. It was her first big trip since she lost her lifelong traveling partner. Mom's so easy to be with. We've traveled from Hong Kong to Athens, to spas, many times to Newport, Rhode Island, and across the country. We share lots of laughs and tears on all our travels."

In their familiar cabin aboard the *Queen Mary* (Hotel), they reminisced about their sail to the Bahamas. "I looked in the mirror above the dresser and thought of the five-year old girl who stared back at me when I was with my family on our very first cruise," says Valerie. "Did my mother hang my fancy little clothes in these narrow closets? Did my tiny hands tug at this chest of drawers? Back then, I needed a parental boost to press my nose against the glass and watch the whitecaps of the Atlantic Ocean float by. Waves of nostalgia washed over me."

CRUISE ADVICE

- The most popular East Coast cruise is from Miami to the Caribbean on the Royal Caribbean Line. Their ships have lots of lounges where you can enjoy a variety of entertainment day and night, and women love their spas.

- My advice for first-time cruisers is to use the services of a cruise specialist to select the correct cruise for their taste and budget as well as getting the most desirable cabin at the best rate available. A cruise specialist can also make all the proper airline connections, which can be complex when dealing with a cruise. Also, a cruise specialist can be called on to resolve any issues or offer advice on subjects such as wardrobe, shore excursions, or passport requirements.

- Inexperienced cruisers who book online may have no clue as to where their cabin is located or what their view may be. For example, a cabin in the forward part of the ship may cause sea sickness from the roll of the ship. Or a cabin that's listed as having an ocean view may be partially obstructed by a lifeboat.

—Rose Staadt, early 50s, AAA Cruise Specialist,
Vallejo, California

Valerie's mother fondly recalled dancing her way through the ship. She took advantage of the time her children were in the playroom to kick up her heels with her husband, moving to the music of John Collins and his orchestra in the Lounge, or the Serenaders in the Observation Bar. During her return trip to the *Queen Mary*, Valerie says, "She confessed that after dinner they tucked us in, sashayed up to the dance floor, and never looked back. As Mom and I revisited our past and viewed the nicks in the original yellow linoleum floor on the Promenade Deck, I couldn't help but wonder if a few of those scuff marks were made by the high heels of my young raven-haired mother." On their return trip, the roles were reversed and Valerie was leading the way. Life-size photographs lined the Promenade Deck featuring old-timers such as Fred Astaire, Bob Hope, Loretta Young, even Liberace.

Before debarking they toured an historical exhibit onboard from World War II depicting the *Queen Mary* as a troop carrier from 1940 through 1946. From ceiling speakers, Bing Crosby serenaded them with "Million Dollar Baby." "Mom hummed along and a soft shuffle developed in her step. This way, cha, cha, cha, that way, cha, cha, cha," says Valerie. "I smiled and sighed. There's my mother, dancing onboard the *Queen Mary* again."

Boston

☞ MASSACHUSETTS ☜

For families in want of big-city choices and small-town attractiveness, Boston makes for a wonderful long-weekend getaway. What I love most about Boston is it gives you time: Time to talk, time for contemplating, and time for wandering. It's a self-guided urban museum that allows you to set your own pace. The city has more sites pertaining to the American Revolution than any other. You'll enjoy walking its old streets, some cobble-stone and just wide enough to get a horse and carriage through. Do your best to get lost on these historic streets of brownstone buildings: You'll end up somewhere incredible and likely learn a thing or two. Make your way to the clapboard home of Paul Revere. Or meander the backstreets of Beacon Hill where most of the homes are redbrick federal, Victorian, or Georgian styles until you find my favorite square: Louisburg Square, modeled after Georgian homes in London and reputed to be the most expensive real estate in Boston. University crew teams practice their rowing on the Charles River, which you should all walk along at least once. On the grass of Boston Public Garden, you may be tempted to find some shade and just relax while watching the swan boats. And as you near the waterfront, the salt air and fishing boats in the harbor remind you that you're on the Atlantic coast.

You'll appreciate how easy it is to get around; nearly all of its subway (or "T") lines will get you to where you need to go and many of its best sights are within walking distance. And the food, well, the food is delicious. You may all simply agree to eat every meal at Quincy Market, the famous 535-

foot colonnade that is a reconstructed version of the city's old meat fish and produce market. There's also fun in gathering around a large table to feast on pasta in the Italian North End or in wearing lobster bibs over a meal of freshly caught seafood with a bowl of creamy clam chowder.

BEST NEIGHBORHOOD FOR STROLLING

The South End has a special spot on the National Register of Historic Places: It has the largest Victorian brick-row-house district in the country. Meandering its streets, while taking in these landmarks and the many parks in this area, is something all of you are sure to enjoy. The SoWa (south of Washington Street) gallery district attracts art buffs on the first Friday of every month. And Sundays from May to October, the vibrant South End Open Market is a fun bazaar of art, antiques, organic produce and people-watching.

BEST SHOPPING

Tree-lined Newbury Street in the Back Bay is a shopper's delight. In brownstone buildings business is stacked on top of business: a café may be at street level, while a boutique may be upstairs and a gallery may be above that. All the big clothing stores can be found here as well as some one-of-a-kind, locally owned businesses such as Knit & Needlepoint and Trident Booksellers & Café. And once only a Massachusetts phenom-enon, Filene's Basement's "off-prices" mean deep discounts on any and everything. A new one recently opened on Boylston Street.

BEST ANTIQUING

On Beacon Hill's Charles Street you'll find a cobblestone, gaslit street with historic brick buildings occupied by numerous boutiques, cafés, ice cream shops, and restaurants. This is the heart of Boston's antiquing: You can browse through porcelain, jewelry, metalwork, and furniture. And don't be afraid to wander some of the side streets; you're bound to find more treasures.

BEST THRIFT SHOP

The Closet, located on posh Newbury Street, sells current and vintage "gently worn" designer clothing and is considered to be one of Boston's best consignment shops. Open daily. Call for store hours. 175 Newbury Street (617-536-1919).

HAVE TEA

Teatime has been a custom in Boston since the 18th century, when it was also mired in protest. Take part in the tradition and sit for English afternoon tea at the wood-paneled Bristol room in the Four Seasons. They serve an exquisite arrangement of delicate tea sandwiches and buttery scones. 200 Boylston Street (617-351-2037, www.fourseasons.com/boston).

MUST SEE MUSEUMS

The Isabella Stewart Gardner Museum houses the work of Old Masters and Italian Renaissance artists in a 15th-century Venetian palazzo, once home to its wealthy namesake. Gardner's private collection of illuminated manuscripts, paintings, and sculptures and flower-filled courtyard will keep you occupied for hours. Very close by, the Museum of Fine Arts is heralded for its Egyptian mummies, a muraled ceiling by John Singer Sargent, a Buddhist Temple Room, and a notable collection of 19th-century French painters and Asian art. The Boston Tea Party Ship and Museum includes a docked replica of one of the British East India Company's ships in the harbor, and a mock town-hall meeting that includes the dumping of tea overboard. And the Institute of Contemporary Art's new home in an ultramodern glass box on the waterfront is a wonderful way to experience art and the Boston harbor simultaneously.

BEST TOURS

The self-guided three-mile Freedom Trail, easily walked by following red blazes on the sidewalks and signposts, starts at Boston Common and brings you past 16 sites and eventually to Bunker Hill in Charlestown. Along the way you'll see the gold-domed State House, the graves of patriots John Hancock and Paul Revere, the first public school, the old State House, the site of the Boston Massacre, the home of Revere and the Bunker Hill Monument. For the quickest and most fun narrated tour of Boston, hop on one of the amphibious vehicles in the Duck Tours fleet. You'll cruise the streets and then plunge into the Charles River to complete the exploration of the city.

BEST DINING

A neighborhood favorite, THE DISH, a very affordable bistro, lets you soak up the South End scene and feast on wood-oven pizzas and pan-seared beef tenderloin with cognac sauce. 253 Shawmut Avenue ($30-40; 617-426-7866, www.southenddish.com).

But when Bostonians want the freshest fish, they still head to LEGAL SEAFOOD after all these years (despite its growth into a 30-restaurant operation). The family-run landmark started out in 1968 in Cambridge and their motto remains: "If it isn't fresh. It isn't legal." They have the best clam chowder in the city and an exhaustive list of straight-from-the-sea items. I prefer the Copley Plaza location for its view of the South End ($20-45; 800-343-5804, www.legalseafoods.com).

EVENTS TO FLY IN FOR

Beginning at the end of June and culminating with the Fourth of July, Harborfest includes concerts, fireworks, a reenactment of the Boston Tea Party, and a Chowderfest. The Fourth of July is also marked by a Boston Pops performance in the iconic Hatch band shell on the Charles River Esplanade with a spectacular fireworks show. Fondly referred to as "ahts" ("arts" with a Boston accent), the growing Boston Arts Festival invites artists and craftspeople to take over the waterfront and sell their wares over a weekend in September. And in October, spend the day along the banks of the Charles River cheering on the championship races in the Head of the Charles Regatta, one the world's largest and most festive rowing events.

PLACES TO STAY

The modern Onyx Hotel's downtown location puts it steps away from Beacon Hill and the Italian North End. Their "GO Boston" package includes a two-night stay, a guidebook to the city, shopping coupons, and admission to countless attractions, including a whale-watch harbor cruise and museums, from $299 a room. Plus the hotel has a complimentary wine hour each night. 155 Portland Street (866-660-6699, www.onyxhotel.com).

Located in the heart of Back Bay, the Lenox Hotel, a Kimpton Boutique property, offers good value and spacious rooms and suites, all beautifully restored. Family owned and operated. B&B packages from $269. Located at the corner of Boylston and Exeter (617-536-5300, www.lenoxhotel.com).

On a side street in the trendy South End (a hop, skip, and a jump from Newbury Street), the Clarendon Square Bed and Breakfast is in a 19th-century, six-story townhouse with flawlessly decorated rooms. 198 West Brookline Street (starting at $155-165 per room in winter or spring season; 617-536-2229, www.clarendonsquare.com).

ONE CLICK AND YOU'RE OFF: Greater Boston Convention & Visitors Bureau (888-733-2678, www.bostonusa.com).

Seattle

☞ WASHINGTON ☜

Seattle is a great city to explore by foot—its neighborhoods, restaurants, shops, and scenery are some of North America's very, very best. It also has a fascinating history, weaving through lumber, shipbuilding, jet planes, Microsoft, and Starbucks. Seattle's neighborhoods, particularly Pioneer Square and Central Downtown, will arrest all of your senses (in a good way!); their architecture, flowers, shops, and restaurants are like something that's stepped out of an Impressionist painting. All of this is framed by the majestic beauty of Puget Sound; it's enough to make you think you've found a new kind of paradise.

BEST NEIGHBORHOODS FOR STROLLING
Pioneer Square is the heartbeat of Seattle with striking architecture and underground tours of the original city. Just north of the city center is Fremont, a bohemian neighborhood, with a contemporary art scene and great outdoor cinema. Belltown, directly north from Pike Place Market, is the best area for trendy restaurants and small shops; and Central Downtown is where you'll find all the sizzle—Pike Place, the public library and the art museum.

BEST SIGHTS
Pike Place Market has been going since 1907; it's huge—contained within 16 multilevel buildings with over 600 hundred vendors. Here you'll find an array of entertaining fishmongers and not-to-be-missed jargon. It gives you a real flavor for the city, and the fresh fish is some of the best in the nation. You can also find extremely fresh fruits, veggies, and flowers. Plenty of great restaurants too. 1501 Pike Place (206-622-6198, www.pikeplacemarket.org).

BEST PARKS/MUSEUMS
The Olympic Sculpture Park hosts contemporary sculptures installed by the Seattle Art Museum. It's a fusion of indoor and outdoor beauty, each complimenting the other. This is a good attraction on a sunny day and it's free. 2901 Western Avenue (206-654-3100; www.seattleartmuseum.org). The Washington Park Arboretum is 230 acres big. It's home to

well-maintained gardens, and interesting exhibits. 2300 Arboretum Dr. East (206-543-8800, www.depts.washington.edu/wpa).

BEST DAY TRIP

Yakima Valley is a very scenic destination for wine tasting. It's 140 miles southeast of Seattle but worth every mile of the drive. It grows some of the best grapes in Washington and will reward you with some of the best views too. Visit Chandler Reach Vineyard and feel as if you've traveled to Tuscany. 9506 West Chandler Road (509-588-880, www.chandlerreach.com).

BEST FERRY RIDE

The trip from Seattle is to Bainbridge Island gives you the best of the best of views: the Seattle skyline, Olympic and Cascade Mountains, and of course breathtaking Puget Sound. This ferry ride will mark your memory—forever. Remember to arrive 20 minutes in advance during non-commute hours. The 35-minute one-way journey costs $6.70. 801 Alaskan Way, Pier 52 (306-705-7000, www.wsdot.wa.gov).

BEST TOUR

The Savor Seattle Food Tours are two and a half hours of pure tasting bliss. You are guided through selected Seattle neighborhoods to savor the best food in the city. 8521 B Interlake Ave. North (800-838-3006, www.savorseattletours.com).

BEST SHOPPING

Nordstrom's shoe department is sensational! This is the chain's flagship store and its most interesting too. The service is excellent. 500 Pine Street (206-628-2111, www.nordstrom.com). Across the street from Nordstrom is

TRAVEL TIP

It rains a lot in Seattle, so remember to bring the appropriate attire—even in the summer. The distance from Seattle Tacoma International Airport to downtown Seattle is 13.9 miles, a 19-minute drive.

Barneys. Upstairs on the 2nd floor is great wearable sportswear. It's fun to go and look. They also have great sales. 600 Pine Street (206-622-6300, www .barneys.com). Seattle's Premium Outlets offer a wide variety of designer stores (including Burberry, Coach, and Calvin Klein) at discount prices. 10600 Quil Ceda Blvd., Tulalip (360-654-3000, www.premiumoutlets.com/seattle).

EVENTS TO FLY IN FOR

Seattle International Film Festival (May-June) hosts a wide range of cutting edge international films. (400 9th Ave. North 206-324-9996, www. siff.net). Pike Place Market Street Festival (June) is a great party with art, music, food, wine—even a dog show! (206-774-5249, www.pikeplacemarketstreetfestival .com). Bite of Seattle at the Seattle Center is a massive (free) festival where you can taste the best of what the Northwest has to offer in the food department. Seattle Center (425-283-5050, www.biteofseattle.com).

BEST MEAL

UNION is a good choice if you want something local, beautiful, and delicious. The menu changes daily; although it's coined a "unique culinary adventure," it's really just a great place if you want something elegant but casual at the same time. The bluenose bass is excellent as is the chilled beet soup and potato gnocchi. Don't get me started on their dessert menu! Dinner only. 1400 First Avenue ($16-18; 206-838-8000, www.unionseattle.com). MATT'S IN THE MARKET is a local favorite. This place is tiny but eclectic with great downtown views; it overlooks Pike Place's red neon sign. Try the sea scallops or Alaskan halibut—they come fresh from Pike Place's market. Closed Sundays. 94 Pike Street, Suite 32 ($25-38; 206-467-7909, www.mattsinthe market.com). MACRINA BAKERY is the perfect place for a midmorning pick-me-up. The lemon lavender coffeecake is full of love. Owner Leslie Macay is famous and quoted in all of the big cookbooks. This is also a good place for a light lunch. Choose three of their half dozen fresh salads for the day; all come with a pastry or bread. 2408 First Ave. ($5-12; 206-448-4032, www.macrinabakery.com).

WHERE TO STAY

The Inn at the Market is an exceptional hotel with the best location—just across the street from Pike Place Market. The rooms have views and are a reasonable size; the bellman at the front door welcomes you warmly. 86 Pine Street (starting at $195; 206-443-3600, www.innatthemarket.com). The Fairmont Olympic Hotel has everything and then some. It is the definition of decadence; the lobby is gorgeous, the pool is tranquil (you can even have breakfast or lunch beside it) and the rooms leave nothing to be desired—pure and total bliss. 411 University Street (starting at $349; 206-621-1700, www.fairmont.com/seattle).

ONE CLICK AND YOU'RE OFF: The two best websites are www .seattle.gov and www.visitseattle.org

Aspen

⤳ COLORADO ⤶

If you're in search of fun in the mountains and don't want to give up the finer things in life, the ski town of Aspen, Colorado, should be the site of your next family get-together. Nothing can bring you and the women in your family closer than sharing an adventure in the wilderness of the Rockies—and pampering yourselves in world-class spas, hotels, and restaurants. This former silver-mining community 200 miles southwest of Denver still hints at its Old West roots with century-old sandstone and brick buildings that today house big-name shops that you'll all enjoy perusing. Renowned for its A-list residents and visitors, Aspen knows how to indulge its guests. Despite its ritzy reputation, it's not unusual to see CEOs and ski instructors rubbing elbows in restaurants, music-school students walking down the streets with instruments, and ski bums hailing from as far away as Brazil. The town has not abandoned its enthusiasm for simply having a good time in the outdoors. If you love to ski, Aspen is likely already on your life list. The area's four ski resorts—Aspen Mountain, Aspen Highlands, Buttermilk, and Snowmass—attract skiers from all over the planet. Or maybe all of you just like the look of a mountain village under the snow. If so, January and February are the months to go because they see the biggest snowfalls. Do you all like hiking, biking, golfing, rafting, and music festivals? Then plan to visit June through August. Bargains can be had on hotels in the fall, which is best time to come take advantage of discounted rooms and witness the aspens changing to golden yellow.

BEST DAY HIKES
Right in town, Smuggler Hunter Creek Loop starts off via switchbacks before dropping down into splendid Hunter Valley. It should take you about three hours roundtrip.

For a serious workout, take the two-mile Ute Trail from town: The bird's eye view of Aspen is well worth the steep, 1,700-foot climb up.

BEST PHOTO OP
Maroon Bells is perhaps the most photographed spot in Colorado. You've probably seen the spectacular jagged snow-covered peaks of Maroon Bells reflected in clear Maroon Lake on Colorado postcards and calendars. It's well worth the effort to take a shuttle to the wilderness area for fabulous photo ops, a walk, a hike, or a picnic. The easy hiking Scenic Loop Trail around the lake is 2.2 miles.

Maroon Lake is set in a spectacular U-shaped alpine valley dotted with aspen groves and meadows of wildflowers. Take it easy if it's your first day in the area—the elevation is 9,000 feet. During the summer months you won't find solitude. There will be crowds, especially on weekends. The shuttles operate from Memorial Day until Labor Day, daily. The first bus leaves Aspen at 8:30 a.m. and the last bus leaves Maroon Lake at 5 p.m. (970-925-8484, or the Aspen Ranger Station at 970-925-3445). The cost is $5 per person round trip. Off season the road is open on weekdays. I drove to Maroon Bells at dinnertime—after 5 p.m. when the road re-opens for private vehicles. We met very few other hikers and were rewarded with a rosy alpenglow sunset and glimpses of mule deer and elk on the return trip to Aspen.

GO FOR A RIDE

In summer bikers hit the Rio Grande Trail, a mostly flat path that begins in town as a paved road and then turns into a dirt trail that follows the Roaring Fork River northwest to Woody Creek. Never been on a mountain bike? This is the perfect beginner route: it's mellow and rewards with views, ribs, and fresh-squeezed lime margaritas at Woody Creek Tavern, the eccentric hangout of the late Hunter S. Thompson. Ute City Cycles, 555 E. Durant Avenue (970-920-3325) can set you up with mountain bike rentals.

WINTER WONDERLAND

Aspen's four ski resorts range from expert to beginner, all of which can be accessed with a single ticket (800-525-6200, www.aspensnow mass.com). For the cross-country skiers in your group, Aspen/Snowmass Nordic Council maintains a free Nordic trail system with nearly 40 miles of groomed trails (www.aspennordic.com).

BEST SHOPPING

Of the 225 boutiques in Aspen, there are high-end (Pitkin Country Dry Goods) and higher-end (Prada) options. If even just to window shop, don't miss Aspen Antiques for collectibles and the custom-made cowboy hats at

I discovered a fabulous, funky bookstore, crammed from floor to ceiling with everything from the latest best sellers to classical literature. If you're an avid reader you'll appreciate the breadth of knowledge of the friendly Explore Bookstore staff, much like the wonderful Tattered Cover bookstore in Denver. It is located in an old brown-and-white Victorian house on Main Street (between Monarch and South Aspen). Stop by and check the program for evening speakers. The Aspen Institute attracts big names, and many of them are old friends of the owner and drop by for a short talk. Unfortunately I missed Madeleine Albright, who spoke before I arrived. Upstairs the Bistro serves high quality organic, mostly vegetarian fare.

—Marybeth

Assume you'll take twice as many photos as you think you will. If you bring your digital camera, bring an extra or bigger memory card. Otherwise, you'll find yourself running out to find a disposable camera.

—Marybeth

Kemo Sabe. Your best chance of finding bargains is on Saturdays from June through October at the outdoor market downtown, where Aspenites comb through the goods of local artisans, antique dealers, and organic farmers.

PAMPER YOURSELF

During your treatments at the Reméde Spa at the St. Regis, the champagne and truffles they serve will take your mind off what you're spending. Fully customized massages and facials follow their extensive consultation process, addressing your specific needs and getting you your money's worth. Or choose from a menu of specialty treatments: Their hot stone massage is very popular (60 minutes for $165; 970-920-6783 www.remede.com).

BEST DINING

Eating at PINE CREEK COOKHOUSE is an event. Guests leave their cars in the old mining town of Ashcroft and cross-country ski, snowshoe, or ride a horse-drawn sleigh to this log-cabin restaurant 11 miles outside Aspen. If it's summer, they hike or bike. All this effort is made for the delicious "mountain gourmet" menu of seafood and game. The experience is worth the splurge, but be prepared for a pricey meal. Dinner and sleigh ride are $90, before tax, tip, and wine (970-925-1044, www .pinecreekcookhouse.com).

When you think of mountains, raw fish may not be a food you'd think you'd see too much of, but ski towns have a reputation for having the yummiest sushi joints. Of the three in Aspen, TAKAH SUSHI is the locals' pick with creative rolls and fresher than fresh fish ($18-50; 907-925-8588, www.takahsushi.com).

HALF THE PRICE

Experiment with bar menus at places like CACHE CACHE, OLIVES, and L'HOSTARIA, where you can enjoy the fabulous ambiance and food from the same kitchen as the restaurant—but at a fraction of the price (generally less than half price). All three of these places have nice tables in the bar areas. It's what the locals do. Cache Cache, 205 South Mill Street (970-925-3835 www.cachecache.com). Olives, 315 East Dean Street (888-454-9005 www.stregisaspen.com). L'Hostaria, 620 East Hyman Avenue (970-925-9022).

BEST NIGHTLIFE

A place everyone in the family will enjoy (regardless of any generation gaps), the J-Bar at the circa 1888 Hotel Jerome is a sophisticated but lively establishment with pigskin-covered barstools, tin ceilings, marble floors, moneyed clientele, and a unique take on the Manhattan cocktail, the Manhaspen. If your budget permits, staying at the hotel is the ultimate splurge (800-331-7213, www.hoteljerome.com).

EVENTS TO FLY IN FOR

Recent Grammy winners and music legends of yore are invited to the stage at the Jazz Aspen Snowmass, held over two weekends, one at the beginning and one at the end of the summer. One of the country's top summer music festivals, Aspen Music Festival lasts nine weeks from June through August with performances by the Aspen Chamber Symphony and Aspen Festival Orchestra in the futuristic Benedict Music Tent or a concert hall. A ride on the gondola up to the top of Aspen Mountain delivers you to the festival's free Saturday concerts performed in the glory of the Elk Mountains. And if the names Batali, Puck, and Flay get your heart rate up, you should schedule your visit around June's Food and Wine Classic, a weekend-long tribute to taste buds.

WHERE TO STAY

Avoiding the holiday season and the height of summer (June through August) can earn you some big discounts on accommodations, including the lavish St. Regis Resort, which at the base of Aspen Mountain is the premier hotel in town (starting at $495 based on season; 888-454-9005,www.stregisaspen.com).

Contemporary design lovers and those young at heart should reserve rooms at the trendy Sky Hotel, which offers packages for women that include spa products and a yoga class (special packages starting at $179 per room; 800-882-2582, www.theskyhotel.com).

Equally convenient but cheaper alternatives are the simple rooms at the Limelite Lodge right in downtown (starting at $130; 800-433-0832, www.limelite-lodge.com).

Large groups may prefer to rent a condo (starting at $170 in summer, $330 in winter; 888-649-5982, www.stayaspensnowmass.com).

ONE CLICK AND YOU'RE OFF: Aspen Chamber Resort Association (800-670-0792, www.aspenchamber.org).

Ashland

⁂ OREGON ⁂

The theater lovers, foodies, and nature enthusiasts in your family can all agree on a visit to Ashland, Oregon. Looking at a map, you'd never suspect that this hamlet north of the California border is a cultural epicenter with a half-century-old tradition of staging Shakespeare's plays, new stylish cocktail bars, and restaurants, art galleries, vineyards, and 30 B&Bs. Nearly 360,000 people a year find their seats at the Tony Award-winning Oregon Shakespeare Festival, one of the oldest and largest professional non-profit theaters in the nation. There are only about four months when there are no performances at all. Eleven plays are staged a year and not all of them are Shakespeare. In the summer, you're treated to performances at the outdoor Elizabethan Theatre, modeled after the venue where 17th-century audiences in England enjoyed their beloved playwright. This multicultural, liberal, laid-back town of pioneer-era buildings and Victorian houses doesn't have a single neon sign or chain restaurant; you'll find locally owned boutiques and cafés instead. The advantage of being a small town six hours by car from the nearest city is the beauty of Ashland's location in the foothills of the Cascade and Siskiyou Mountain ranges. Mount Ashland looms in the distance at 7,533 feet and the Rogue River rushes through town, constant reminders of the hiking and rafting to be done. Temperatures are mild in this region with highs in the 80s and lows in the 50s; therefore, deciding when to go depends on which plays you want to see.

FOR ART LOVERS
The art center in town, located on A Street, is the Railroad District. It's newest residents are a dozen or so galleries and studios (displaying creations from handmade quilts to West Coast contemporary art). Make sure to visit the glassblowing studio with live demonstrations.

FOR GARDEN LOVERS
Now a 93-acre sanctuary with a Japanese garden, duck ponds, a rose garden, and lawns, Lithia Park started out in 1892 as an eight-acre recreational area with a band shell that today still hosts concerts. Situated downtown, it's the perfect setting for a picnic or walk between shopping or plays.

GO FOR A SPIN

Take advantage of Oregon's bicycle-friendly culture and cruise Ashland's streets or access the Bear Creek Greenway running through 600 acres of woodlands and various communities. The Adventure Center on the plaza in town rents bikes and maps; helmets and locks are included. 40 N. Main Street (541-488-2819, www.raftingtours.com).

PAMPER YOURSELF

Waterstone Spa will soothe your weary bodies with warm therapeutic waters from its own natural mineral spring. You'll find the massages reasonably priced for its impeccable service and facilities. A pre-soak in their mineral tub has been known to cure all types of ailments. 236 E. Main Street ($85 gets you a 60-minute massage; 541-488-0325, www.waterstonespa.com). For more on the inn, see below in "Where to Stay."

BEST DINING

That fresh California cuisine seeped over the border and onto the menu of the casual DRAGONFLY restaurant. Organic produce and Latin and Asian foods are whipped up into clever creations that delight vegetarians and foodies alike. Open for breakfast, lunch, and dinner daily. Located below the Cabaret Theater at 241 Hargadine Street ($5-20; 541-488-4855).

CHATEAULIN has been highly regarded as one of the Pacific Northwest's premier French Restaurants since opening in 1973. The atmosphere is romantically French, the service is polished, and the portions of fine French cuisine are just right. Try the popular three-course prix-fixe menu, an excellent value for $40 that includes two glasses of wine. After the theater, drop by for strong coffee, fresh desserts, a glass of wine, and good conversation; it's open until after midnight. Located near the theaters at 50 E. Main Street (541-482-2264, www.chateaulin.com).

For a special occasion, dine at the top-notch WINCHESTER INN RESTAURANT AND WINE BAR. The dining rooms overlook the Victorian inn's English gardens. In the summer you may dine on the porch or deck. During the

---

The full-price season extends from June until early October. You can save 25 percent from mid-February to June and for most of October.

—Marybeth

holidays there are festive Dickens feasts. Located at 35 South Second Street ($22-45; 800-972-4991, www.winchesterinn.com).

WHERE TO STAY

The Winchester Inn is regularly ranked in the top echelon of Best Places in the World to Stay because of the service and attention to detail, the gardens, and the ambience in the rooms and suites. If you prefer to keep your group together, you may rent all seven Victorian rooms in the Main Guesthouse, or both suites at the Carriage House or Larkspur Cottage (starting at $135 in low season and $175 in high season). It is located in the heart of Ashland within walking distance of the Oregon Shakespeare Festival, Lithia Park, restaurants, and shopping. 35 South Second Street (800-972-4991, www.winchesterinn.com).

Historic B&Bs such as McCall House and Arden Forest Inn are a short walk from the festival. But if you prefer to get out into the countryside, the Lithia Springs Inn, which owns Waterstone Mineral Springs Spa, will gladly accommodate your small group in their suites overlooking the surrounding vineyards. Their hot breakfast and afternoon hors d'oeuvres are delicious. McCall House, 153 Oak Street (541-482-9296, www.mccallhouse.com). Arden Forest Inn, 261 West Hersey Street, (541-488-1496, www.afinn.com). Lithia Springs Inn, 2165 W. Jackson Road (541-482-7128, www.ashlandinn.com).

BEYOND THE BARD

In addition to the Oregon Shakespeare Festival, check out Oregon Stageworks and Camelot Community Theater. The Oregon Cabaret Dinner show (for light musical performances) is an excellent option for Monday nights during the season because Monday is the Shakespeare Festival's dark day.

ONE CLICK AND YOU'RE OFF: Oregon Shakespeare Festival (541-482-4331, www.osfashland.org). Ashland Oregon Chamber of Commerce (541-482-3486, www.ashlandchamber.com).

Gore-Tex! It's a highly breathable, waterproof fabric found in jackets that is imperative on a trip to Alaska. It's likely you'll wear a Gore-Tex jacket every day and it'll be worth the investment ($100 plus). A windbreaker or a raincoat will leave you either soggy or sweaty or both. And it's not a bad idea to buy shoes made with the fabric too.

—Gwen Kilvert, 20's, Writer, New York

The 49th State

In the company of family, a trip to Alaska becomes an epic journey with shared discoveries, moments of exhilaration, and laughter. Experiencing Alaska is tantamount to a religious experience. Everything about it is gigantic: the mountains, the glaciers, the wildlife, the portions of food, and the size of it (Alaska is two and half times the size of Texas). The best introduction to the 49th state is a cruise to the glacier-studded Southeast. On the water is exactly where you want to be to witness natural spectacles such as Glacier Bay National Park and Preserve, the apex of any trip to the Southeast with 11 glaciers blanketing mountains, spilling chunks of crystal-blue icebergs into the sea. From the deck, watch 50-foot humpback whales come up for air, the shiny dorsal fins of Orcas slice the surface of the water, and sea otters float on their backs. The colossal snow-capped peaks and deep fjords tower all around you with mountain goats clinging to their walls and the occasional black bear and moose along the shoreline. Much of this region is a puzzle of lush islands, which ships navigate via the Inside Passage. A cruise takes the pressure off of planning which towns to visit and how to get there. Instead, you just focus on enjoying each other's company. You'll disembark in small towns to explore historic main streets, learn about Native Alaskan (Tlingit) culture, warm yourselves up with seafood chowder, and experience local adventures on the water or in the Tongass National Forest—the world's largest temperate rain forest. Cruises run from May to September. Summer in the Southeast may be more like fall where you come from with chilly evenings and periods of drizzle. Remember, you're in a rain forest.

BEST OF THE BIG SHIPS

Princess Cruises operates three ships in the Inside Passage accommodating up to 1,950 passengers and loaded with features such as spas and specialty restaurants (starting at $750 in May, interior cabin; 800-774-6237, www.princess.com). Celebrity Cruises also runs three ships in the Southeast, holding as many as 2,046 guests; the cruise line is best known for its world-class nightly entertainment and elegant interiors (starting at $800 in May, interior cabin; 800-647-2251, www.celebritycruises.com). Onshore excursions with both cruise lines are extra, and cruises average seven days in length.

- SHOP
  Teens expect shopping to be part of every trip. Set a limit for the amount of time and dollars.

- NEGOTIATE
  Trade activities and interests. "Mom really wants to view the Matisse exhibit so in exchange I'll take you to the East Village to shop. After we shop, let's do something for someone else; write a postcard to Grandma, call a sick aunt."

- LET THEM SLEEP
  Give them slack. At times let them stay up really late to watch a movie or read, then sleep until noon. Pack your silicon ear plugs and eye shield so they can whisper on their cell phones, text message, or watch TV while you fall asleep. You can take a walk or do some sightseeing while your teen sleeps in. Carry your cell phone so you're reachable, and plan to meet at noon.

- GIVE THEM AMPLE BATHROOM TIME
  Girls need lots of privacy in the bathroom, so schedule your own shower time so you aren't on top of each other.

- EXPECT MOODINESS
  Like PMS, it's a given. Don't engage. Just keep quiet and take a walk. That's why having "time outs" for everyone is so important...to refuel and enjoy some solitude.

- BURN CALORIES
  Boisterous, hormone-driven kids thrive on daily physical activity. Sports-oriented vacations channel your teens' abundant energy, and provide opportunities to acquire outdoor skills, make new friends, and build self-confidence.

BEST OF THE SMALL SHIPS

On a Cruise West boat there are no more than 38 guests, compared to traditional big ships carrying 1,300 to 3,000 passengers. You won't find evening entertainment or casinos on them—instead you'll have daily lectures and slide shows by interpretive guides and you'll cruise up close to the tidewater glaciers, pup seals on floating ice slabs, humpback whales, calving glaciers, and even bears along the coastline.

Their small size enables the ships to edge closer to the shore and make their way into fjords that big ships cannot access. Itineraries of the Southeast start at four days and can be as many as 25 days long; you can choose trips that include nights on land in hotels. Most onshore excursions are included in the price (starting at $6,549; 888-851-8133, www.cruisewest.com).

DO-IT-YOURSELF CRUISE

Alaska's Marine Highway is a network of ferries throughout the state. The beauty of it is that you can drive a car or RV onto the ferries, or simply use them just like any other cruise but with the option of deciding how long you want to stay in each port. The ships have dining, tons of windows for incredible sightseeing, and cabins with a private bath on overnight ferries. The senior citizens in your family will appreciate the generous discount on fares. You can also roll out a sleeping bag in the common area to save money (the See Alaska Pass allows you three stops for $160; 800-642-0066, www.dot.state.ak.us/amhs).

BEST SHOPPING

It takes a little bit of effort to get beyond the fortress of jewelry stores (diamonds anyone?) and T-shirt emporiums in every town. But once you do, there are some truly amazing locally owned shops to discover. In particular, the Dockside Gallery in Ketchikan showcases the work of Alaskan artists and has a wide array of pottery, beads, jewelry, and gorgeous yarns. Visit the studio of artist Brenda Schwartz in Wrangell—her paintings of coastal scenes on nautical maps you'll be seeing everywhere you go. At Dejon

---

If you're looking to do Alaska on the cheap(er), visit in September. For many locals, early autumn is their favorite time of year: the crowds dwindle, the air is crisp and cool, and prices for many attractions, accommodations, and tours fall with the leaves.

—Marybeth

Delights in Haines and Skagway, load up on smoked wild salmon or halibut from their small custom smokehouse to bring back home with you. All the honey, syrups, jams, and mustards they sell are from Alaska.

BEST THRILL

Fly through the rain forest canopy with Alaska Zipline Adventures, located outside of Juneau at the Eaglecrest Ski Area. Ziplining involves a harness that attaches you to a sturdy line strung between platforms perched nearly 100 feet up spruce trees. You'll yelp and laugh as you fly through the woods taking in views of snow-covered peaks and the streams below. It's exhilarating and the guides are very professional, enthusiastic, and knowledgeable about the ecosystem they work in. It's a great confidence booster. Heck, they have had a woman in her 90s zip with them ($138; 907-790-2547, www.alaskazip.com).

MUST-SEE MUSEUMS

Sitka National Historical Park preserves the site where the Tlingits were defeated by the Russians in 1804. A mile-long coastal trail guides you past 18 magnificent totems. Indoors there are exhibits on Native Alaskan culture, and Tlingit artists demonstrating their craft. Wrangell is a small town not often visited by major cruise ships. The Wrangell Museum is a diamond in the rough; opened in 2004, the museum pieces together the vibrant past typical of the villages of the Southeast, from its Tlingit presence to the gold rush. The gift shop is equally superlative and where you'll likely stock up on Alaskan gifts.

BEST VANTAGE POINT

Nothing can get you closer to a glacier than a helicopter; they can drop you right onto one. Temsco Helicopters Inc., out of Juneau and Skagway, flies over forests and peaks to their dogsledding camp on the Mendenhall Glacier. They also offer guided hiking tours on glaciers. Located on the waterfront at 901 Terminal Way (glacier tours start at $249; 866-683-2900, www.temscoair.com).

I never wore the shorts I packed. I was in pants and layers the entire time. The umbrella that I thought I really wouldn't need, I used. And my binoculars were around my neck practically the entire time.

—Elsie Kilvert, 60s, Retired Teacher, New York City

BEST WAY TO SEE WHALES

Not seeing a whale in Alaska is like not having a bagel on a visit to New York. To ensure you spy one of nature's most amazing creatures (and have a blast while doing so) acquire the services of two fun-loving Juneau locals known as Harv and Marv. No more than six passengers go out in one of their boats—it beats the standing-room only, large whale-watching boats typical of the area. Harv and Marv's Outback Alaska tailors trips to what you want to do (perhaps hook a king salmon?) and when you want to go—and guarantees you'll see a whale (starting at $149 per person; 866-909-7288, www.harvandmarvs.com).

PLACES TO STAY

If you decide to work the ferry system and will be staying in hotels, don't expect too much from the accommodations in Alaska: This way you'll be pleasantly surprised. Hotels are very basic. As quaint B&Bs go, there are some cute places to stay run by very friendly innkeepers. Among the finest: At the White House, in Skagway (starting at $125; 907-983-9000, www.atthewhitehouse.com); Wrangell's Rooney's Roost (starting at $75; 907-874-2026, www.rooneysroost.com); and Alaska's Capital Inn, in Juneau (starting at $249; 907-586-6507, www.alaskacapitalinn.com).

ONE CLICK AND YOU'RE OFF: Alaska Travel Industry Association (www.travelalaska.com).

CHAPTER FIVE

Adventure Escapes

~ ELLEN'S STORY ~

Visitors come from all over the globe to the rim of the Grand Canyon simply to gaze into the mile-deep gorge accented with pink granite spires, black schist layers, and purple mesas. They drink in the sublime grandeur of one of the world's natural wonders. And many find their eyes drawn deep into the rose-tinted depths, searching for a glimpse of the mighty Colorado River that snakes its way through the canyon for 200 miles.

But there are some women who challenge themselves to move beyond the edge of the Grand Canyon, to hike into its mysterious depths and ride the rapids of the Colorado at the bottom. When my mother was 68 and I was 33, we fulfilled her childhood dream. Despite misgivings and unfounded fear, we hiked nine miles down the Bright Angel Trail to the river, and rafted through the ever-changing landscape for a week. Other

On our outdoor trips we leave the girly stuff, like makeup, behind and take the essentials: bug juice, Kleenex, chapstick, sunscreen, and After Bite. Winning the "Fashion Award" takes a different twist when you leave professional clothes and makeup at home. Decked out in my bug suit and a mesh mosquito hat I took all honors on the river.

—Sue Blouch, 50s, Consultant in Organizational Change, Cleveland, Ohio

---

gutsy women, such as Ellen, are seduced by the siren's call of the surging Colorado and must "once more."

The floor of the Grand Canyon is a far cry from Ellen's day-to-day life in the urban canyons of New York City. As Vice President and CIO of the Carnegie Corporation, she's up at the crack of dawn, works out at the gym, and then walks down Madison Avenue to her high-rise office building where she keeps up a frenetic pace until well after dark. Why has this city girl braved the raging rapids of the Colorado River three times in the past 15 years?

"The beauty of the canyon draws me back again and again. To sleep on the sand listening to the roaring river and look up at the bright stars in the pitch-black sky has a profound effect on me. There is no pressure to do anything. So few experiences are like rafting the Colorado, where you don't care what time it is, where you don't wear a watch. I believe being in nature puts things in perspective. It fosters a lot of very confidential personal conversations about life and relationships," Ellen confides.

When she was 35 Ellen accompanied her dad down the Colorado River in an oar boat with guides doing the paddling. She expected a sedate float trip, sitting in the boat all day, reading, improving her tan, and admiring the steep spectacular walls above her. Instead, she bobbed through long stretches of swirling, muddy water and rapids, where boiling cauldrons of whitewater plunged into deep holes that made for a wild rollercoaster ride. She laced up her hiking boots and climbed up precipitous side canyons to crystalline waterfalls, forded rivers, and explored caves and cliffs painted with ancient Indian petroglyphs.

Inspired by the magnificent canyon, she vowed to come back again, and five years later she returned with more family members and several girlfriends. Looking ahead to her 50th birthday, she made a vow to celebrate the big day at the bottom of the Grand Canyon with lots of friends.

She invited her husband and several girlfriends and their partners. The husbands either didn't want to go, or couldn't, so she planned a chick trip for her 50th birthday.

Ellen's adventurous gal pals included her sister and five tennis partners she'd met on the courts a decade earlier in New Haven, Connecticut, where she was living at the time. Jean, who was married with two sons in their 30s, had recently retired as Head Mistress of a private East Coast school, and was ready for an adventure to jumpstart the transition into the next phase of her life. She joined the group to celebrate her own sweet 60th birthday at the foot of the magnificent Grand Canyon.

But it wasn't going to be that easy. Jean struggles with vertigo. "In the Atlanta airport on the trip to Phoenix, Jean went to great trouble to use the elevator because she suffers from torturous vertigo on escalators," Ellen recalls. In the depths of the canyon, Jean faced her fears and did every hike. In order to see the ancient Indian paintings of tiny handprints under a rock ledge, she climbed the steep cliffs high above Deer Creek and inched her way along a narrow, exposed path. "Jean was mentally tough and concentrated through the vertigo with amazing power. Women are tough and we're supportive of each other, which helps us accomplish our goals."

Organizing the 13-day, oar-boat trip was easy. A year in advance, Ellen booked it with a tour company specializing in rafting the canyon. They provided all the food, cooked all the meals, did the dishes, took care of all the logistics, and provided four (40-year-old) women guides.

For two weeks they floated downstream, braving the thunderous rapids for drenching, high-adrenaline thrills three, four, sometimes five times a day. They hiked up side canyons, swam and plunged into pools below waterfalls and at night they slept on the sand, looking up at the stars.

"It's so fun being with my girlfriends. When I'm with my family or my husband, I always worry about them," says Ellen. "It's a different dynamic with girlfriends. It's very supportive, emotionally easy, and relaxing. We could have had fun with our husbands, but it would have been a very different trip."

◦ JANET'S STORY ◦

Like many women of the baby-boom generation, Janet grew up with Westerns on TV and horses on the brain. She might live in suburbia, but her inner Annie Oakley gallops happily along in the dust of yesteryear with the equine stars of "Rawhide" and "Bonanza."

Take trekking poles on hikes. My sister and I swear by them. They collapse and can be lashed to a pack and they're really helpful on descents: They help with balance and keep you from putting too much weight on one leg.

—Elsie Kilvert, 60s, Retired Teacher, New York City

A love for horses and the cowboy culture never left her. The challenge of riding for days at a time, rounding up cattle and sleeping on the ground, as well as the contrast between the open range and the urban environment in which she works are exactly what spurs adventurous women like Janet, a journalist, to sign on to a cattle drive.

Cattle drives have traditionally been a macho activity that intimidates many women, but not Janet and her friends, who twice in recent years have played out their cowgirl fantasies as participants in the Reno Rodeo Cattle Drive. Held each June in conjunction with "the wildest, richest rodeo in the West," the four-day drive serves the dual purpose of honoring Western tradition and delivering 300 head of roping stock to the rodeo grounds. Long hair flowing from their cowboy hats, Janet and her friends sat tall and confident in their saddles and kept up with the guys just fine.

"For four days, you ride with the cattle across beautiful high-desert country," Janet says. "It can be hot, and it can be windy. The terrain is rough, and the saddle starts to feel like a torture device after six hours or so. Even for most of the dudes, it's a trip way outside the comfort zone."

There's also the matter of working the cattle. "You learn how to string out the herd and bunch it up and how to chase steers that squirt from the pack," she explains. "There's a real sense of teamwork and accomplishment that comes with that."

"It's a wonderful experience to share with woman friends," she says. "We'd sit around the campfire at night, listening to the cowboy poets, watching the stars come out, and feeling a part of a vanishing tradition. It was deeply moving in ways we couldn't have anticipated beforehand."

It was also good for some laughs: "We'll giggle for the rest of our days about the dirt in our teeth and the woman trail boss who found a snake in camp, picked it up and threw it out in the sagebrush," Janet says. "And the sight of horses and cows moving over the open range... it's all so visual, so picturesque. I couldn't shake the feeling I'd stumbled into a movie set—just like one of those TV Westerns we watched when we were little girls."

Raft the Grand Canyon

❧ COLORADO RIVER ❧

Nothing can put life into perspective better than a whitewater adventure a mile deep inside a two-billion-year-old canyon. Whatever is causing you anxiety in life will likely seem trivial at the end of a rafting trip through northern Arizona's Grand Canyon, one of the seven natural wonders of the world. After hectic days of managing a family and career, it will do you good to simply allow the Colorado River to take you where it will.

Rafting season here spans from April to October. And while summer temperatures can peak at over 100 degrees, the river remains around 50 degrees so there are ways to cool off. Most tours put in at Lees Ferry, upstream from the national park, concluding either 226 miles down the Colorado River at Diamond Creek, or 54 miles later at Lake Mead. There are roughly 160 rapids along the way, but while you're likely to white-knuckle it through a few of its bigger rapids, much of the trip is flat water. Full canyon tours typically take 12-18 days. But there are partial trips of either the Upper Canyon (five to six days) or the Lower Canyon (eight to nine days). If you choose a partial trip, consider whether you'd rather hike up or down the nine-mile Bright Angel Trail. That may help you determine which segment to select.

And you have some choice in conveyance. A few outfitters offer motorized trips, but it's best if you're in a boat with oars: It's a slower ride (read: more time on the river), and a much more tranquil experience. Motorless you can hear the sounds of the canyon, the growing roar of rapids around the next bend, raptors overhead, and the best sound of all: silence. Choose

---

Grand Canyon rafting outfitters provide all meals, non-alcoholic beverages, dry bags, life jackets, eating utensils, sleeping bag, pad, liner, tent, waterproof bag, geological explanations, historical narratives, and more.

—Marybeth

from a dory boat—a hard-shelled, flat-bottomed rowboat with seats—or an inflatable raft, which sits lower in the water. The latter are particularly fun, especially when you have the opportunity to paddle along with the guide, which some outfitters permit clients to do.

Hiking should also be a large component of any trip you sign up for. You're likely to spend about five hours in the boat; the rest of the time is left for guided walks to tucked-away side canyons, clear pools and waterfalls for swimming, past caverns, fossils, and the remnants of the ancient Anasazi.

The guides make these trips so memorable. Some have as many as 30 years experience on the river and even hold PhDs in geology. But the female guides are the ones that will leave the deepest impression on you with their inspirational strength, spirit, and leadership. They'll have you convinced that the fun is in roughing it. The guides pack out everything (including human waste), you sleep outside or in a tent, bathe in the river, pee in a bucket and eat dinner made on a camp stove. But you'll be shocked by how this will seem luxurious over time. You'll opt to sleep out under the stars, and savor sipping coffee in the chill of dawn by the river. Laughs will be had over the portable toilet situation, learning how to pitch your tent the first night, and screaming at the top of your lungs like a kid as the rapids splash into the boat. And the teamwork aspect cultivates bonding: Unloading and loading the boats, paddling, and even helping out with dinner will make you truly feel part of the trip. You'll feel adventurous, capable, and rewarded with a renewed sense of self.

ON THE CHEAP
Unless you're a certified rafting guide, you should expect to invest a chunk of change into this kind of trip. It's worth it.

PACKING TIP

Pack ample products for skin care. Rafters often underestimate the power of the wind, water, sun, and sand in the Canyon. Bring a heavy-duty moisturizer, sunscreen, and chapstick.

Once you decide what type of Colorado River trip you would want to take, expect to book it a year in advance as trips sell out.

—Marybeth

ONE CLICK AND YOU'RE OFF: O.A.R.S. offers 6- to 19-day trips (starting at $2,345; 800-346-6277, www.oars.com). Arizona Raft Adventures leads 6- to 16-day trips (starting at $1,870; 800-786-7238, www.azraft.com).

Heli-Hiking

∞ THE CANADIAN ROCKIES ∞

Heli-hiking might sound like an extravagance reserved only for millionaires, but in the Canadian Rockies helicopters and hiking are synonymous. For nearly 50 years, choppers have been delivering all types of folk to spots they'd have to otherwise bushwhack over 10,000-foot serrated peaks for a week to get to. And if helicopters sound like something only guys can get excited about, think again. Flying in a chopper can make anyone feel like a kid. You and your girlfriends will find it thrilling, from the dramatic take-offs to the jaw-dropping views to the cute pilots. After all, how many people come home from their vacation with photos of themselves getting out of a helicopter? Now those are bragging rights.

Canadian Mountain Holidays is a pioneer in the realm of summer heli-hiking: They invented it in 1978, 13 years after beginning their heli-skiing program in the Canadian Rockies region. While they know loads about safety and the mountains, they also could also write the book on wilderness luxury. When you arrive at one of their six cozy lodges (five of which you can only get to via helicopter), you'll see they haven't skimped on anything. It's all taken care of: tasty meals, creature comforts—they even outfit you in boots, rainproof jackets, backpacks, and walking sticks. You're also divided into groups of about six people based on hiking ability so there's no need to fret that you'll be stuck playing catch up with a bunch of teenagers.

Each morning starts off with a stretch class and the scent of croissants in the oven wafting through the lodge. Then you're off in the helicopter. With an expert guide leading the way, you'll be dropped off in meadows

I needed to do something that broke me away from the routine of home, buying groceries and brushing the kids' teeth before bed. Lisa and I were only gone for five days, so it wasn't too hard on our families. This is the first time either of us has been away on our own since our children were born. But our husbands encouraged us to go. Wow, think of it … today we rode in a helicopter and made snow angels on a glacier. We feel young again.

—Sandra Dagelman, on her 40th birthday, Toronto, Canada

---

peppered with wildflowers, by turquoise lakes as flat as glass and cupped in by saw-toothed peaks with colossal glaciers blanketing their flanks. You stand on what feels like the top of the world. Maybe you'll eye a bear or a herd of mountain goats through the binoculars or start a snowball fight. And if given the opportunity, consider learning mountaineering (with ropes, helmets, the whole nine yards). Whenever you hear that "clatter, clatter" from somewhere beyond, you know it's time to be whisked away to another locale or to dinner. Darn, is it that time already?

Welcomed by hors d'oeuvres and cocktails at the end of every day, you'll sit around and chat with your fellow lodge-mates, have a soak in the outdoor hot tub, get a massage (be sure to book it the day before), or retreat to a comfy corner of the lodge to read. Dinner is almost as extraordinary as the scenery you took in that day. While you and friends can all sit together, dinner is served communally. And that's part of the fun. Over decadent meals with Canadian wines, friendships are made, stories told, and laughs shared. After dinner there's often the choice of a slide show, a bonfire to toast marshmallows, or sometimes the guides and guests get dolled up in costumes and perform silly skits. And as you make your way back to your snug bed, milk and warm cookies await you. After such stimulating days, it's no wonder the rooms don't have televisions: Nothing could compare.

ON THE CHEAP
Many heli-hiking operators in Alberta run day trips for around $200. Visit www.travelalberta.com for a list of outfitters, or call 800-252-3782.

ONE CLICK AND YOU'RE OFF: Canadian Mountain Holidays offers three- and six-day heli-hiking trips from July to September (starting at $2,318; 800-661-0252, www.canadianmountainholidays.com).

Paddling

There are people who have kayaked all over the world—Vietnam, Baja, Fiji—and they still favor Maine. Its 228 miles of coastline expand to 3,478 miles of shoreline once you factor in all of its coves, harbors, and 6,000 or so islands. Paddling gives you access to many lighthouses, dilapidated but charming fishing shacks, hidden islands, copious amounts of wildlife, and enviable waterfront homes you otherwise would never see. You'll trace the jagged granite coastline fringed with spiky spruce trees, pull your boats up onto the shores of untouched islands, and hunt for blueberries or lie on slabs of sun-warmed rocks. There are towns with art galleries and cafés to stop for, clusters of harbor seals sunbathing on rocks to spy on, and salty lobsterman on the water to wave to. Frequently, the song of loons, the chirp of bald eagles, the dip of your paddle in water or the splash of a porpoise is the only sound to be heard. And when the tendrils of fog wind their way between islands and the deep bass of a distant foghorn sounds, you'll swear you're not on Earth.

Really the only way to get to know the Maine coast is with a certified kayak or canoe guide in July or August. With mercurial weather (fog has a large presence here even in the summer) and with the countless islands, it's easy to get disoriented. If you've never kayaked or canoed before, there are tons of outfitters offering lessons as well as day and half-day trips. An experienced guide can also teach you new paddling skills, local folklore,

---

The first year eight friends and I tried camping and canoeing in Northern Maine, we were really novices. One brought her stuff in a plastic garbage bag. Another came with a hard suitcase. We helped each other get outfitted with hats, gloves—the works. The first night we left our food out and raccoons got into it. The second night we thought we got smart and hung it from a tree. I will never forget the sound of Octavia as she woke us up at 3 a.m. screeching and screaming at the raccoons as they clawed into our bags. Who won? It was a draw. She deserved to win with the noise she made.

—Sue Blouch, 50s, Consultant in Organizational Change, Cleveland, Ohio

The fun part of these trips is to be together, singing, telling stories, enjoying the campfire, doing yoga when we get stiff, and just being outside. The work seems to divide itself up. One woman who loves to do the dishes begins and then we all chip in. We all have our areas of strength, like one who is good with directions and maps There is just good energy. I really love seeing the stars and being away from all the technology of cell phones and computers. On the river we get close to wildlife. One time we followed a mother and two teen moose. We were within 30 feet of them. It was just magical.

—Sue Blouch, 50s, Consultant in Organizational Change, Cleveland, Ohio

geology, and biology. And if you really want to spend some time on the water, overnight trips from inn to inn or to campsites on uninhabited islands are also available.

With so much coastline to choose from it can be daunting to pick an area to focus on. The best way to start is to select a bay. The middle coast offers some of the most pristine shoreline (minus the resorts and crowded beaches of the southern coast). Look to Penobscot, Casco, Frenchman's, or Muscongus Bays. In particular, the 60 islands of Deer Isle in Penobscot Bay, almost smack-dab in the middle of the Maine coast, are ideal for paddlers. If you really know what you're doing, head farther north to Down East Maine. The rugged coastline there offers the most dramatic coastline in the country—and with it more risk, including rocky shoreline and rough water.

Paddling lets you be part of a team and still be an individual. You'll all drift together as a group at times for lengthy discussion and then disperse as you cruise at your own pace and lose yourself in thought. After a kayaking trip here, you'll be convinced it's the most deluxe and enjoyable mode of travel. You can pack a boat with gear (instead of shouldering it) and just glide to your next destination without extreme exertion. Perhaps the greatest aspect to paddling is that you can always sit back, look up, take it all in, and let the tide transport you. You'll find it doesn't take long to acclimate to the pace of life in Maine: slow.

ON THE CHEAP
The Maine Office of Tourism website helps you plan your own trip with a directory of kayaking outfitters, B&Bs, and maps (www.visitmaine.com).

ONE CLICK AND YOU'RE OFF: Visit www.maineseakayakguides .com for a list of outfitters and guides.

Hiking Inn-to-Inn

➣ VERMONT ➣

One of the most rural and the smallest of the 50 states, Vermont is a hikers' paradise. And like a game of connect the dots, one can hike from inn to inn around the state's Green Mountain National Forest. The B&Bs here are some of the most famous and quintessential country inns in the nation—what most B&Bs try to be. This is why hiking in Vermont can be so decadent. From June to October (with the first two weeks in October being the window for prime leaf-peeping), outfitters will shuttle your luggage from inn to inn, where you're fueled by a restorative night's sleep in quiet inns and extravagant four-course dinners then sent on your way each morning with scrumptious packed lunches.

The hikes between inns, which can be done with a group or customized just for you and your friends, are a doable six to twelve miles a day through densely wooded forests of sugar maples and yellow birch with waterfalls and mountain lakes, moose, white-tailed deer, wild turkeys, rabbits, and the occasional black bear. If you're looking for a bit of challenge, you can choose to follow the ridgeline of the Green Mountains along the famed Long Trail, the country's oldest long-distance trail, about 100 miles of which it shares with the Appalachian Trail. Or choose a mellower stroll through the woods without too much elevation gain.

So far from your everyday life, you'll find yourself focused on more primitive concerns, such as eating lunch. And there's the quaintness of the towns you'll pass with their New England charm: You can't take enough photos of the whitewashed chapels, Victorian cottages, and covered bridges.

Beat blisters. Long walks on trails or on uneven surfaces can lead to blisters. Band-Aids often slip off toes and heels. Pack thin moleskin in your purse or backpack. Leave new shoes at home. Old shoes that are broken-in are the most comfortable.

—Marybeth

The inns are the exclamation point of each day. The state's finest include the Blueberry Hill Inn, a 19th-century clapboard inn at the end of a 5.5-mile dirt road. Its antique furniture and snugly quilts, fine dining, and a wood-fired sauna will be a welcome extravagance after a day on the trail. Or there's the homey Churchill House Inn, where you can all sit down to a meal prepared with veggies from their garden. In operation for nearly 200 years, the Waybury Inn is a historic landmark. It posed for the opening scene of the TV show "Newhart."

Since this journey is self-powered you'll feel a sense of accomplishment as you walk up to the inn each afternoon. And at dinner when fellow guests ask how you got to the inn, you can all say you walked, containing your giggles at your pride.

DOING IT ON THE CHEAP

Most outfitters offer self-guided tours for less money. The Vermont Outdoor Guide Association website (www.voga.org) assists you in planning a trip of your own.

ONE CLICK AND YOU'RE OFF: Country Inns Along the Trail offers guided group tours (starting at $125 per day; 800-838-3301, www.inntoinn.com). Wonder Walks customizes tours (starting at $100 per day, not including lodging and meals; 877-897-7175).

Discovering Your Inner Cowgirl

THE WILD WEST

A dude ranch vacation takes you back to an age of horses, cowboys, and the Wild West: the simple life. Experiencing it is an exercise for the senses: the smell of horses and hay, the sounds of hooves and mealtime bells, and the feeling of dust and sun on your skin. It's an escape where you can forget about a manicure lasting. There's no need to pack little more than jeans, a shirt, boots, and a hat. And you won't be concerned with spiffing yourself up, just with focusing on your connection with the land and animals. It's physical, challenging, and galaxies away from your everyday life. And you don't even have to know how to ride a horse.

While horses are always at the heart of dude ranches, there are a few different kinds of ranches to choose from. A resort dude ranch takes care to provide the Western experience with plenty of vacation amenities. There

Eleven essentials for women in the outdoors: bandanna, headlamp, water bottle, energy bar, sunscreen, sunglasses, blister kit, hat, gloves, spare batteries, girlfriends.

—Marybeth

---

may be a spa, tennis courts, a pool, and maybe an 18-hole golf course. While a traditional dude ranch will offer other activities such as hiking and fishing, the main focus is on the horses and less on the amenities. Then there are working dude ranches, which make a living off their livestock. Guests have an opportunity to play a role in many aspects of their everyday business, such as escorting cattle from one pasture to another, feeding the livestock, and grooming the horses. Adventure Women offers a week at a family-owned working cattle ranch in Montana, see below. A final option, particularly for more experienced riders, are cattle drives, on which you travel for a few days on horseback and camp out at night. Equitours, out of Dubois, Wyoming, offers a cattle drive in Montana, see below.

There's no best time to visit a ranch: They're year-round. But if you want to go in winter, consider Arizona. Meanwhile in the summer, Wyoming and Montana are thawed and gorgeous settings for horseback riding. You can find ranches in the dusty desert or in the thin air of the Rockies, ranging from high-end resorts that accommodate up to 125 people a week to more rustic cabins that sleep only eight. Many ranches also offer packages just for gals. These are days when women can take part in the ranch's activities without any testosterone, any intimidation. With female wranglers in charge, it's a chance for women to bond and to try new things in a supportive group.

Ranches are generally all-inclusive and host guests from Sunday to Sunday. On the first day, you are paired up with a horse based on your skill level. You'll care for that horse all week, feed it, groom it, spend hours on top of it. (Don't be alarmed if you cry at the end of the week when you have to part ways with Mr. Ed. Almost every guest does). The week might consist of full- or half-day lopes through prairies and on mountain trails (or lessons if necessary). There's the opportunity to learn how to properly toss a lasso. Sometimes there are penning competitions and mini-rodeos for guests to participate in. On hand are wranglers, some female, to guide and instruct. Meals vary from sit-down, eight-course affairs to ribs from a mesquite grill. A breakfast of eggs, sausage, biscuits, and gravy might be served from the chuck wagon. And in the evenings, the

A FEW WORDS OF ADVICE

- DUCT TAPE TO THE RESCUE
  Duct tape comes to the rescue if a strap on a sandal snaps, a purse handle or backpack strap breaks, or luggage gets ripped. Wrap a foot of duct tape around an unsharpened pencil and tuck it in your luggage.

- ZIPLOC BAGS WORK WONDERS
  Freezer-weight re-sealable plastic bags are indispensable. They keep a wet bathing suit separate from clean clothes. If something should leak, a zipped plastic bags keeps it contained. If you pack socks in one bag, clean underwear in other, they help keep your clothing organized. And, everything is in clear view.

- INSECT REPELLENT
  The ingredient Deet offers effective protection but is a known eye irritant and can cause skin problems. Go for lower concentrations (10 percent) and spray sparingly. Wash it off thoroughly when you come indoors.

- BAD HAIR DAYS
  Beat bad hair days in the wild. A fashionable hat or scarf will save the day. Hats with too loose a weave will let the sun in and don't do much to protect your skin. Pick a hat that has a wide brim and save the baseball cap for baseball. Add a scarf, a pin, or a flower for a splash of color and pizzazz. If you have long hair, pack a few colorful, inexpensive elastic bands that don't damage your hair. Then put your hair in a flattering ponytail or in braids.

Bandanna Fashion. Pack colorful bandannas. They can serve as a dust mask, sun hat, napkin, sweatband, handkerchief, washcloth, sling, or tourniquet. Wrap it around your neck, it conserves heat. Wet it and wear it around your neck, it helps keep you cool.

—Marybeth

Western tradition lives on typically with square dancing and cowboy songs around the campfire. It's not unusual for guests to use cowboy lingo or to wear cowboy boots long after returning home. It can't be helped; it's a way of life that gets into you.

Adventure Women's Montana Cattle Ranch Ride offers a horseback-riding vacation on a family-owned working cattle ranch, encircled by seven mountain ranges. Riding options are unlimited at no additional cost ($2,595; 800-804-8686, www.adventurewomen.com).

Equitours, out of Dubois, Wyoming, is America's largest and oldest horseback-riding company. They offer horse trips in the Badlands and Big Horn Mountains in Wyoming, and from April to October you may join a cattle drive in Montana, where you'll experience branding, vaccinating, roping, wrangling calves, trailing the pastures, fencing, and bull gathering. Their broad range of riding vacations include horse trips, pack trips, classical dressage, in Arizona, Utah, California, Texas, Vermont, and Massachusetts and foliage tours in Quebec, Canada (800-545-0019, www.ridingtours.com).

ON THE CHEAP

From October to May Rancho de los Caballeros, outside of Phoenix, hosts a two-night "Giddy-up Gals Getaway" every month for those who just want a taste of the cowboy life (starting at $820 per person; 800-684-5030, or 928-684-5484, www.sunc.com).

ONE CLICK AND YOU'RE OFF: The Dude Ranchers' Association works with 108 of the best ranches in the West and will help you select the right one for your vacation (866-399-2339, www.duderanch.org).

CHAPTER SIX

Friends Reunions

~ LISA'S STORY ~

There are some moments in life that foment lifelong friendships. It seems the highest highs and lowest lows tend to bring women together...forever. Lisa, a 36-year-old physics teacher from Santa Rosa, California, made her two closest friendships during graduate school, an intense time when they slaved day and night studying for engineering PhDs. "It was one of those agonizing life experiences when you work hard and need to play hard, too," says Lisa. "Those tough years were a course in survival and we really bonded." Together they created diversions to endure the grind. As an escape from the campus, they drove to big cities to visit museums and to dine in good restaurants.

But after graduate school, they found themselves scattered around the country and felt a genuine void in their lives. "So," Lisa explains, "we've made the effort to travel together every year, weddings and childbirth notwithstanding."

They select a travel destination based upon their interests, not proximity. Someone always winds up coming from farther away and paying more for her plane ticket. So they add up the cost of all the tickets, then divide it by three, and thus share the airfare cost equally.

Lisa recounts one of their most memorable trips—to Savannah: "It was the perfect Southern romantic destination. We are nostalgia hounds and had read and loved Ann Rice's books and others set in Savannah. We walked to all the historical sites during the day and we drank and talked 'till all hours of the night. After we explored all the touristy places we got out into the swamps and took graveyard tours that creeped us out. The transvestite character Lady Chablis from *Midnight in the Garden of Good and Evil* really fascinated us, so we went to see a drag queen show. Of course, we loved gawking at the men in drag: They are extremely convincing."

David, Lisa's husband, understands and appreciates her close female friendships. He recognizes that the time she spends with them refreshes and invigorates her. He's learned that when she returns from a trip with her best friends, she's missed him, appreciates him more, and is able to communicate more clearly. "It's like therapy to be with my girlfriends," says Lisa. "David also knows that when I have problems, I have someone else to dump them on. It makes our marriage stronger."

Lisa explains that she loves to travel with her husband, but that it's a different experience. "I feel a little bit like I'm not on vacation because part of my job as a wife is to be responsible in some ways for him. My concern is always, 'what does he want to do?' and 'what can I do to make our vacation be perfect.' With my girlfriends there is a lot less pressure. Things happen that are going to happen. We don't plan everything. We go where the wind blows us. We're driving, and someone says, 'Hey, that looks interesting, let's stop.' And we do. Our goal is to be together, and enjoy each other."

"The power that we have as women to connect is remarkable," she continues. "It's as if my two best friends and I are sisters, particularly because of our experiences in the past. When we get together it feels like going home. It's that warm feeling you get from a soft, old blanket. We talk about everything. All of us attempt to psychoanalyze each other—that's always fun. We celebrate by eating, dancing, and drinking the most exotic concoctions on the menu, usually those served with decorative umbrellas."

These annual reunions also help them get their lives on track again. "All three of us get so wrapped up in our darn routines," she explains. "We're all professionals and working our butts off—all the time. When we get together we take ourselves out of that environment and go back to a time when it was just us against the world."

"It's very likely that 50 years from now," Lisa predicts, "we'll be little old ladies cruising around a new city. And we'll tell each other, 'stop drinking so much, you're going to choke on your umbrella.' " Lisa and her friends will still be taking annual holidays together and sipping tropical drinks with the fancy paper umbrellas.

✧ CHRIS'S STORY ✧

Chris met several of her best friends playing jump rope in first grade. When they graduated to bobby socks and saddle shoes in high school, their circle of "best friends" expanded until they graduated in the Class of 1960 at Birmingham High School in Birmingham, Michigan.

Since then they have participated in each other's weddings, childbirths, and graduations; cooed over grandchildren; and comforted each other through chemo and the death of spouses. Today, Chris lives in Southport, Connecticut, and her 20-plus girlfriends are scattered from the shores of the Atlantic to the Pacific Coast.

After marriages and motherhood, the first big reunion of the best friends was a 40th birthday party at one of their vacation condos in northern Michigan. Since then, they've met every two to three years for a weekend or a week. They've been to Palm Springs, Santa Barbara, St. Martin, Chicago, and Charleston. The girls discovered that renting a big house or condo at the beach, or in the mountains, works best for their group size.

"We like to stay under the same roof so we can be like sisters again, sitting around in the late evening in our nightgowns, drinking cheap wine," says Priscilla, from Los Angeles, who has attended 11 of the reunions. They fix meals together, visit local attractions, bike, and shop during the day, but their most important activity is talking to each other.

One gal brings memorabilia to every reunion: letters they sent each other from summer camp and photos taken at their high school proms and homecoming dances. They flip through hundreds of photos of past reunions and watch hours of videos, of themselves, of course.

One or two women volunteer to organize the next reunion. They scout the location, (a lot is done on the Internet) and then drive or fly to check out rental homes before they book one. They present a selection of three houses and everyone gets to vote. Next, a non-refundable $100 check reserves a spot. This money pays the down payment for the rental home, which can be pricey in a choice tourist area. The remainder of each woman's share is due one month before the reunion.

Everyone puts $50 into a kitty and one person is in charge of paying for everything. When funds run low, everyone pitches in again. If there is anything left in the kitty at the end, there's a refund. "When we have a rental house, the reunion can be a lot of work for the organizers, who set it up, buy and haul in the wine and breakfast supplies and often end up doing a lot of cooking," explains Priscilla. "So we organize ourselves into groups. Everyone prepares her own breakfast and lunch and gets some kind of kitchen duty. Three women prepare dinner each night. We always have a cocktail hour before dinner to regroup after golfing, shopping, beach combing, biking."

There's a small gift to represent each trip they've taken—it could be a sweatshirt or a tote bag with something specific to that year's location on it. "For example, when we went to Charleston we had a white tote bag with ribbon trim, and palm trees were woven into the ribbon. The palm tree is symbol of Charleston. We even have a crest, shield, and motto from the eighth grade," says Chris. "It says, 'Joci Causa,' which in Latin means 'For the sake of a joke, or anything for a laugh." And they do get wild. Priscilla says, "Not tacky wild, just crazy wild. There was that the year we were cited by the condo committee for excessive noise."

For this year's reunion, they're planning a "white elephant" gift exchange: anything old, left over, unwanted, or even an attic item. Everyone is urged to be creative and remember that items from the fifties and sixties are in again. Priscilla plans to bring her high school prom dress for the swap.

"We all feel like we are 18 again," reveals Chris. "We laugh until our faces ache. Of course, the stories get better each year. We're such a nurturing group and yet very diversified. We've been through all the big life experiences together. Aging mothers are a concern at present, as are grandchildren. A big topic is how to deal with retiring husbands, and of course health issues and politics. We learn so much from each other and we come home exhausted and renewed."

Seize the moment. If you get an offer to travel with a friend, take it! I've passed up so many opportunities because I thought I couldn't get away, for many reasons. In retrospect, I could have made it happen.

—Karen Foss, 60's, Neophyte Sailor, Northern California

Asheville

For a girlfriend gathering replete with shopping in locally owned craft stores, nature, and a superior selection of lovely accommodations and restaurants, look to Asheville, North Carolina. Regarded as the Boulder, Colorado, of the East, Asheville is a mountain town that's been attracting a motley assortment of well-off vacationers, bohemians, and athletes. You'll love the carefully preserved culture of the Blue Ridge Mountains from which bluegrass music and earthenware crafts and quilts emerged, and appreciate the down-home spirit and warmth of the people here. It's the perfect compromise for those seeking nature and an elegant small city. And in classy shops, resorts, and restaurants, you'll have the opportunity to treat yourselves over and over again. Asheville's mild year-round weather has always served as a respite from the humidity in the South, and its cool evenings are a welcome end to the daytime. October sees the most visitors because of the fall colors, so it's best to visit at the end of September or in early November to witness the foliage; April and May then pick up again for the blossoming rhododendron and wildflowers.

BEST NEIGHBORHOOD FOR STROLLING

Asheville's historic downtown brims with hundreds of unique stores, including antique shops, restaurants, and 30 or so galleries. One of its biggest draws is the architecture; downtown claims more art deco architecture than any southeastern city other than Miami Beach. There's an eclectic mix of styles mixed in too, from Neoclassical to Romanesque Revival to Beaux Arts to Spanish Renaissance. Over at Chocolate Fetish, pay your respects to the cocoa gods at this custom truffle shop, which uses peculiar ingredients such as wasabi. And you can find some wonderful mountain crafts in the shops of the circa-1929 Grove Arcade, which also houses Bath Junkie, where you can concoct your own lotions and body washes.

BEST ANTIQUE SHOP

An interesting place to rummage for all kinds of antiques and one-of-a-kind pieces is the Antique Tobacco Barn, a 70,000-square-feet warehouse with hundreds of booths. You'll uncover treasures—from vintage clothing to hand-blown perfume bottles, Parisian hats to books dating from the

1800s. Located on Highway 81 near the Biltmore Estate. Open seven days a week. 75 Swannanoa River Road (828-252-7291).

HAVE A PICNIC

Spend at least a day at George Vanderbilt's 250-room Biltmore House. The French Renaissance chateau, which was completed in 1895, is America's largest private home with 75 acres of gardens designed by Frederick Law Olmsted (of Central Park fame), a winery, and a village. After a self-guided house tour of its 60 rooms filled with art and antiques, stroll through gardens and the conservatory. (You can hike trails and ride horseback, too). Then enjoy a picnic by the lake. If it's summer, stay around for their concert series with acts such as Tony Bennett and The Temptations.

BEST DINING

To mark the occasion of your gathering, dine at the world-class **MARKET PLACE**, which cooks with fresh local ingredients hand selected from community markets. Try the pan-seared crabcakes and the porcini-crusted North Carolina sea scallops. It's worth blowing your diet for a dessert like the dark chocolate cherry bread pudding with pistachio ice cream and Port wine cherry sauce. If you dine early, consider the three-course dinner for $26, available nightly for seatings until 6:30 p.m. 20 Wall Street ($15-27; 828-252-4162, www.marketplace-restaurant.com).

For elegant food in a chic atmosphere try **VINCENZO'S RISTORANTE & BISTRO**. Choose between the more formal and elegant dining room upstairs or the casual bistro downstairs, which offers nightly live entertainment from jazz to blues to rock and roll or soul. Best of all, there is no cover charge. The northern Italian cuisine highlights specialties of Veneto, Lombardy, Tuscany, and Piedmont. Don't miss the oysters Rockefeller or the rich ossobuco. Small servings of pasta are available if you prefer a lighter meal. 10 N. Market Street ($8-30; 828-254-4698, www.vincenzos.com).

Don't miss Asheville's beloved **TUPELO HONEY CAFÉ**. Locals rave about the friendly staff, fun atmosphere, moderate prices, large portions, and superb southern comfort food (with a creative twist). If you feel like breakfast anytime of the day or evening, order fluffy omelets or sweet potato pancakes topped with peach butter and spiced pecans. For dinner try the fried green tomatoes over goat cheese grits with basil, or the blackened Cajun Catfish topped with green tomato salsa. Select seating outside on the patio during warm months or inside among the potted plants and original artwork. Closed on Mondays. 12 College Street ($12-19; 828-255-4863, www.tupelohoneycafe.com).

SORORITY SISTERS

Last year 41 of my Sigma Delta Tau Sorority sisters and I met in New Mexico for a four-day reunion. At Ohio State, Sigem Delta Tau girls were often nicknamed: "Seldom Dated Twice." We came from 13 states to lounge by the pool, catch up with each other, enjoy spa treatments, shop in Santa Fe, and sing familiar pledge songs. I was washed by waves of memories. One sister said she came to this reunion because she was so happy when she was 18 and lived in the sorority house and she wanted to find that person again.

We all wrote our bios and everyone had the opportunity to read them along with responses to a questionnaire: What was your most daring feat? What are you most proud of? It was hard to impose the word limit! Unlike a family reunion where you are catching up on what has been happening, we spent the major portion of our time together looking at photos and slide shows reminiscing and marveling at the silly and serious young women that we were.

Our biggest topics of conversation were: weight loss, children, grandchildren, and marriages—everyone was very open about their marriages, present and past. There was a feeling of being safe with old sorority sisters. After all, we know all the old boyfriends. What made the success of this reunion? Only people who are very happy with themselves attended, so all participants were upbeat. I am convinced that friendship is an underrated component of good health.

—Ruth Stotter, 70's, Storyteller, Northern California

BEST DAY TRIPS

The 469-mile Blue Ridge Parkway runs through the Asheville area. Allot at least a day to tour the road's highlights. Drive to the top of the tallest mountain east of the Mississippi, Mount Mitchell, at 6,684 feet, and get 85-mile views from the observation tower. Pull over at the Folk Art

Center to shop for crafts made by Southern Appalachia artists: ceramics, textiles, baskets, and jewelry. They often have artists demonstrating their trade right on the premises. Then tool around on a Segway—those futuristic stand-up scooters—on a Glide Through Nature tour of the 434-acre North Carolina Arboretum. Hikers may want to summit Mount Pisgah farther down the road. And you can view the real Cold Mountain from an overlook along the parkway.

Penland Arts & Crafts College, the national center for craft education, is located an hour from Asheville and is well worth a visit. Find a unique gift or add to your own craft collection. In its Gallery you'll find work by instructors, residents, artists, students, and neighbors. It sells functional and sculptural work in books, clay, drawing, glass, iron, metals, painting, papermaking, photography, printmaking, textiles, and wood. There are also ongoing art shows. Or visit the school's resident-artist studios and dozens of working studios in the area. On Tuesdays and Thursdays from mid-April to early December, you can join a tour of the campus (reservations required). The school offers one- and two-week classes in the summer. Closed Mondays (828-765-6211, www.penland.org).

BEST SUNSET
The Grove Park Inn Resort and Spa, built in 1913, sits perched in the Blue Ridge Mountains above Asheville. From their Sunset Terrace, gaze out over the skyline of the city backlit by the setting sun. Take dinner there or simply sip a cocktail.

PAMPER YOURSELF
The spa at the Grove Park Inn Resort and Spa is a sight to be seen; it's subterranean and lined with stone. The 80-minute Sanctuary of the Senses Body Treatment for Women is a treat albeit high-priced: Rose essential oils are first applied; then exfoliation and wrap are followed by a massage. A basic massage will set you back $170, but it's worth it to gain entry to their pools—a tranquil hideaway that rejuvenates weary bodies (866-362-2769, www.groveparkinn.com).

NIGHTLIFE
This is the land of banjo music. To catch some of the finest, the Celtic pub and microbrewery JACK OF THE WOOD showcases live bluegrass and old-time mountain music. There's the New Orleans vibe and the dim lights of Tressa's; it's ideal for those of you who prefer smaller venues and blues and jazz.

EVENTS TO FLY IN FOR

The last weekend in July, Bele Chere, the Southeast's largest free outdoor festival with arts and crafts, food vendors, and live music, takes over downtown. Those in search of mountain crafts should attend the Craft Fair of the Southern Highlands, where more than 200 artists display their wares at the Asheville Civic Center in mid-July and again in mid-October.

WHERE TO STAY

Groups settle in nicely at the charming, all-suite Haywood Park Hotel in downtown Asheville. Some of their spacious suites adjoin, so all of you can stay within a pillow's throw of each other. 1 Battery Park Avenue (from $189; 828-251-1529, www.haywoodpark.com).

The Inn on Biltmore Estate gives you the chance to stay in poshly decorated rooms on the lovely grounds of the Vanderbilt manor (starting at $229; 800-624-1575, www.biltmore.com).

ONE CLICK AND YOU'RE OFF: Request a free visitors guide from Explore Ashville and inquire about their girls' getaway packages (888-247-9811, www.exploreasheville.com).

Sedona

ARIZONA

There's no better destination to catch up with friends and revive yourself than the glorious red rocks and mystical atmosphere of Sedona, Arizona. Tribal shamans came here for thousands of years to pray and seek guidance for their people. And these days Sedona is still considered sacred. The area's Cathedral Rock, Bell Rock, and Boynton Canyon are believed by some to be vortex centers, emanating electromagnetic energy. In fact, there are 15 vortex sites within a ten-mile radius of Sedona. But no matter what you believe, there is something unavoidably magical about the place. The towering rust-colored, sculpted sandstone dating back hundreds of millions of years has not only attracted talented artists, southwestern-style jewelers, and trained chefs, it has lured some extraordinary body workers for the best massages you've ever had. The older population also keeps this community very mellow—there's only one late-night dance club to be found. Therefore, it's the perfect place to spend hours entertaining yourselves with stories, laughter, backcountry

TIPS FOR REMAINING FRIENDS
WITH A ROOMMATE

- SNORING
  Be honest with each other. If your roommate lives alone, she may not know if she snores. What to do if your roommate snores: use silicone ear plugs.

- BEDTIME
  Prior to your trip ask your future roommate how late she watches TV or reads before turning off the light.

- TEMPERATURE
  Discuss with each other if you like to sleep in a cold or warm room so you understand what you both expect.

- WAKE-UP TIME
  Talk about how much time you each need to shower, dry your hair, and get ready to leave the room.

- SMOKING
  Even if your roommate does not smoke in the hotel room, her smoke-scented clothing can leave an odor.

- STAMINA
  If your physical abilities and stamina are different from your companion, you many not travel well together. Do you both have similar physical fitness levels for walking, stair climbing, carrying luggage, and dealing with jet lag?

- BUDGET
  Discuss your spending patterns and travel budget before the trip. How often do you like to splurge and for how much? Do you prefer to take taxis instead of public transportation or walking a few blocks?

hikes, scenic drives, and delicious meals. March through April and then September through October are the most pleasant times to visit.

SCENIC DRIVES

Two driving routes acquaint you with the area and help you plan where you'd like to spend the most time exploring on foot. Take Highway 179 south from the "Y" in town until you see the Chapel of the Holy Cross on your left, an architectural gem perched 200 feet above the road, with stunning views of the valley. Continue and you will see Bell Rock and Courthouse Butte next to each other on your left, and Cathedral Rock on your right.

Another drive starts from the "Y" on Highway 89A north and continue 16 miles to Oak Creek Vista (the overlook on top of the canyon), and then it's about a 20-mile drive back toward Upper Red Rock Loop Road. This Scenic Loop takes you into the nucleus of red-rock country. The route traces the foot of the multihued cliffs and deposits you at Red Rock Crossing, a spot where you might see the most spectacular sunset show ever. If you look at a map, these routes will make sense.

HIKE

Whether or not you "feel" the energy of the sacred rock formations in Sedona, their outstanding beauty will certainly make you feel something. Many of the area's stunning landmarks can be viewed from the road, but are best enjoyed up close on foot. Lace up your hiking boots and bring a pair of binoculars to see the hummingbirds, warblers, and flycatchers. Trailheads shoot out from everywhere—2.5-mile Boynton Canyon Trail and 4.2-mile Courthouse Butte Loop Trail are musts. Get maps and ideas at the visitors centers in Uptown, in Oak Creek Canyon, in West Sedona near the Cultural Park, or in Tequa Marketplace in the village of Oak Creek. You can buy a $5 Red Rock Pass here and you'll need it to park in some of the best hiking areas. Volunteers at the chamber of commerce will help you plan your hikes or day trips.

Sedona is not a city where we shake hands. We give hugs. This is a hugging city.

—Mary Ellen Hadley, 60s, Ten-year Breast Cancer Survivor,
Sedona, Arizona

BIKE

The Sedona area has achieved a world-class reputation for its mountain biking trails for all levels of riders. For rentals, maps, and information, go to Mountain Bike Heaven (928-282-1312) or Bike and Bean (928-284-0210, www.bike-bean.com).

GO NEW AGEY

All of you should have your auras read; you know, most of the men in your lives would never put up with it. Some of you may subscribe to things like psychic readings; others of you may think it's baloney. But you can't help be curious and get a few giggles out of it. The bright-purple Center for the New Age is like a supernatural department store. Browse the books, music, crystals, and jewelry in the gift shop. And you don't need an appointment for aura photography, aura cleansing, or shakra realignments; you can even channel a pet. If you want to be healed or rejuvenated, this is the place to go, with dozens of reiki healers, energy balancers, tarot readers, psychic readers, and full moon ceremonies and labyrinth walks. A free publication, *Four Corners*, lists many of the meditation and spiritual-growth workshops. It can be found in many of the health food stores, new age stores, or coffee shops. Many personal guides or shamans offer one- or multiday retreats with ceremonies, meditations, and trips to sacred or spirit-lifting places. Use a Web search engine and type in the words: Shaman, Sedona, and Retreat.

EXPERIENCE A VORTEX

There are four well-known ones in the Sedona area. You will find information at bookstores and the visitors centers, or search the Web using the keywords: Sedona, Vortex.

COOL OFF

No resort's pool could capture the beauty and fun of swimming at Slide Rock State Park. Upon entry, you walk through an old apple farm to Oak Creek, where the rock chutes make this nature's finest water park. This

There was one year, when it seemed as if all 23 of us were going through menopause. In retrospect, it was memorable and humorous due to the number of emotional outbursts.

—Priscilla English, 60s, Screenwriter, Los Angeles, California

is an ideal oasis for an afternoon of lounging about in the shallow pools, basking on the warm rocks, and riding down the rock slides, shrieking like youngsters. Note to self: A pair of old shorts over your bathing suit will save your tush from wear and tear on the rocks.

DINING IDEAS

CUCINA RUSTICA features rustic Italian and Mediterranean cuisine in an old-world setting, with beautiful fountains and antique doors from around the world, patio fireplaces, and al fresco dining. CUCINA RUSTICA has won awards for Best Fine Dining in Sedona and Best Ambience and Cuisines by Sedona Home and Garden. Located in Tequa Plaza in the picturesque village of Oak Creek, 7000 Highway 179 ($12–30; 928-284-3010, www.cucinarustica.com).

For the best views of sunset on the red rocks of Sedona and a truly memorable evening, dine at the exclusive AAA Four Diamond rated YAVAPAI RESTAURANT. Whether you dine indoors or outdoors on the terrace you will be surrounded by a 180 degree panorama of the flaming red-rock formations in Boynton Canyon. If you dine outdoors in the summer, each table has its own climate control to assure your comfort. Enjoy American and Southwestern cuisine for breakfast, lunch, dinner or Sunday Brunch. 525 Boynton Canyon Road ($25-50; 928-282-2900, www.enchantmentresort.com).

HEALTHFOOD IN THE GARDEN

For delicious, healthy food in a cozy garden setting with affordable prices and a friendly staff, try the HEARTLINE CAFÉ. Their roasted pear and butternut soup with spiced pecans is a must, and the grilled portabello mushroom over garlic mashed potatoes is excellent, too. Be sure to try breakfast at their less formal fireside café right across the parking lot. The breakfast burrito is memorable. 1610 W. Hwy. 89A ($7-27; 928- 282-0785, www.heartlinecafe.com).

ENJOY THE NIGHT SKY

Sedona has a "dark sky" ordinance so a new world of constellations awaits you in the clear Arizona desert night. Buy a book on constellations or join a stargazing tour so you can look at the sky through a telescope (www.sedonastarlight.com).

SHOPPING

Home to hundreds of artists, Sedona is catching up to Santa Fe in art commerce. Around the "Y" in town, one can find extremely high-end art (meaning good) that's worth viewing if not purchasing. Over at the cobble stoned Tlaquepaque Arts & Crafts Village, modeled after a traditional Mexican village, open plazas with fountains are bordered by 40 art galleries and clothing stores. There are many commercial galleries in town that feature turquoise and other Native American jewelry. Or search for authentic Native American jewelry at the open markets near the Dairy Queen in Oak Creek Canyon or up at the viewpoint at the very top of the Canyon Road. These displays are open from April to October.

BEST THRIFT/VINTAGE SHOP

Twice Nice is a thrift shop that looks and smells like a small designer boutique with equally high end clothing, you'll find treasures including vintage evening dresses from Bonwit Teller, Diane Freis, Ralph Lauren, Liz Clayborne, and Perry Ellis. The donations to this unusual shop, benefiting a worthy cause, can only be described as amazing: Native American and glamorous costume jewelry, paintings, sculpture, and art deco crystal. This little gem is also staffed by cheerful volunteers. All profits support a local community shelter for battered women and their children. They also donate clothing to the Navajo and Hopi Native American People and send children's heavy winter clothing to a village in Mongolia. 2070 Route 89-A in West Sedona (928-282-2563).

EVENTS TO FLY IN FOR

For over 25 years, jazz greats have converged in Sedona for Jazz on the Rocks, now held outdoors at the Radisson Poco Diablo Resort each September (928-282-1985, www.sedonajazz.com). During the holiday season, locals adorn the entire area with Christmas lights—on homes and trees—for an annual tradition referred to as Red Rock Fantasy. It's truly lovely to walk among the lights in the evenings.

NIGHTLIFE

You may be relieved to learn that Sedona is not known for being a party town. But most nights it's possible to find live music and soak it up with your girlfriends. The Highway Café offers live music, karaoke, singers, and bands. 1405 W. Highway 89A (928-282-2300). Check out *Red Rock Review* or *Red Rock News* for ideas and the latest schedules on who's performing where.

PAMPER YOURSELF

The Mii Amo Spa at the Enchantment Resort has won "World's Best Awards" for its Anasazi-inspired architecture, location beneath the red rocks, and outstanding menu of services, including an out-of-this-world Sedona Clay Wrap and Aromatherapy Massage. Expensive but unforgettable, and unfortunately, open only to Enchantment guests. Day packages start at $385 (888-749-2137, www.miiamo.com).

L'Auberge de Sedona Resort has a new spa which touts top-notch essential oils and natural ingredients as their signature selling points. They offer outdoor spa treatments next to a rushing river under the towering red-rock formations, and in-room treatments for those who prefer them. Hour-long massages start at $130 (800-891-0105, www.lauberge.com/spa.php).

Sedona's New Day Spa offers massages, body treatments, facials, waxing, and nail care. Massages start at $55 (928-282-7502, www.sedonanew dayspa.com).

WHERE TO STAY

Wherever you stay you must have a balcony or patio to savor the views. My favorite accommodations are in the adobe-style casitas of Enchantment Resort set in 70-acres of pristine red-rock country and surrounded by Boynton Canyon. They are a study in luxury (starting at $295; 800-826-4180, www.enchantmentresort.com).

There's also the Inn of Sedona, a Best Western hotel that is independently owned and operated. Taking advantage of the inn's location on a hilltop overlooking Sedona, each room has access to a large, terraced promenade deck for spectacular views of the red-rock formations. Enjoy the heated outdoor pool, spa, and free continental breakfast. Accommodations vary greatly according to season and occupancy rate. Ask for a AAA discount ($169-299; 928-282-3072, www.InnofSedona .com). The more basic Orchards Inn of Sedona is located on a hillside in the very heart of uptown Sedona, within walking distance from

My girlfriend and I have instituted "Run Away Days"— when we take a vacation day from work and run away from all our responsibilities. We do it a couple times a year. They typically last from 8:00 a.m. until we can't stay up any later. What we do may vary but the one consistent activity is lunch. We always order several small items and split them with a bottle of wine. The best discussions are over that bottle of wine and the dueling spoons for the last bite of dessert.

—Yvonne Decker, 50's, IT Professional, San Diego, California

restaurants, shops, and art galleries. Every room has red-rock views ($140-240; 800-474-7719, www.orchardsinn.com)

Many, but not all the B&Bs are listed at www.bbsedona.net. During peak season or busy weekends, call the Sedona Central Reservations, at 928-282-1518. They list about 90 percent of Sedona's properties and they can tell you where there are vacancies.

ONE CLICK AND YOU'RE OFF: The Sedona Chamber of Commerce will help you plan your reunion (800-288-7336, www.vis itsedona.com).

Banff

⤳ ALBERTA ⤶

Banff National Park serves as the ideal setting for girlfriends in search of adventure and spectacular scenery for a reunion. If you saw the film *Brokeback Mountain* you are already acquainted with Alberta's magnificent Canadian Rockies. With 2,464 square miles of wilderness, Banff presents the most stunning mountain views in the world: glaciers, ice fields, snow-capped peaks, crystal clear lakes, and raging rivers. A mere 90 minutes from the busy international airport of Calgary, Banff National Park is likely the most convenient wilderness locale for your get-together. The wondrous surroundings are inspirational and energizing for a group of gals looking to reconnect, relax, and recharge. Summer is cool (in the 70s) and winter ushers in the cold, but this is what makes their snow so powdery. No matter if you are hikers, bikers, skiers, or expert shoppers (or a mix of all of these), Banff National Park supplies year-round adventure. At 4,539 feet above sea level, the lovely mountain town of Banff on banks of the Bow River is unlike any national park village you've visited before. Both rustic and sophisticated, its alpine architecture, diverse restaurants, and bars serve as the perfect compliment to gallivanting around the wilds of the park.

BEST STRATEGY

Despite the wildness and enormity of Banff National Park, going sans tour group is the way to go. No guide and no hour-by-hour group activity lets you and your friends set your own pace and not worry about others. Staying in the town of Banff with a rental car, you can access many of the sights and day hikes on your own and enjoy the historic village. And if delving deeper into the backcountry by trail, raft, or helicopter tempts you, there are qualified local outfitters to take you there for a day or overnight.

SCENIC DRIVE

Pile into the car for a day, or several days of eye-popping roadside attractions between Lake Louise and Jasper on the 142-mile Icefields Parkway, which spans the length of Banff National Park. Undoubtedly one of the world's most scenic highways, the parkway leads you past more lakes than you can count and over a hundred glaciers—and straddles the Continental Divide. At 6,785 feet, Bow Summit is the highest point on the route and offers a spectacular mountain panorama via a short (but very fulfilling) hike to the Peyto Lake viewpoint. And for the finale, there's the 150-square mile Columbia Icefield, the snow of which feeds eight glaciers, among them the Athabasca, Dome, and Stutfield Glaciers, which are all visible from the road.

HIKING

Tucked into the backcountry of Lake Louise, two teahouses await hikers. (This is a great way to bribe those self-proclaimed non-hikers in your group to hit the trails.) Known as one of the most popular trails in the Canadian Rockies, the two-mile Lake Agnes Trail bring you to a 1910 cabin via a forested route that passes mountain lakes and waterfalls. You can then dig into your own packed lunch or choose from the teas and soups sold there. For more experienced hikers, follow the 3.3-mile trail leading to the Plain of Six Glaciers Tea House, not before encountering a series of switchbacks. You'll be rewarded at the historic teahouse with hot chocolate, teas, soups, and breads. A 40-minute walk farther, to the Glacier Viewpoint, and you'll get an unobstructed view of six enormous glaciers and witness minor avalanches—and Lake Louise as an electric-blue dot in the distance.

WINTER WONDERLAND

Until the 1970s, the Banff area would just about shut down for winter. Today it's still considered the off-season; however, the Icefields Parkway is open year-round. Nevertheless, November through May could be the best time for you to visit if you're in search of epic snow and discounted rates. A winter activity that you all must try is dogsledding. You'll adore the cute Alaskan huskies that pull you beneath the snow-covered Rockies in the crisp winter air. Nothing makes for a better photo op. For Nordic skiers, Alberta is bliss: Banff National Park maintains 75 miles of cross-country ski trails alone; Jasper National Park to the north and the Canmore Nordic Centre to the south offers world-class trails as well (Canmore was built for the 1988 Winter Olympics). And the "champagne" powder and long winter season of Alberta's downhill ski resorts is the envy of the ski industry. With a Tri-Area ski pass, you can schuss down the slopes of Ski Banff, Sunshine Village, and Lake Louise, the latter of which is considered to be the most scenic ski resort in North America (www.skibig3.com).

SHOPPING

Whether it's to buy your kids presents or just to window shop, there's an impressive assortment of interesting and rather upscale stores in the town of Banff. Didn't bring any hiking boots? Well, the excellent outdoor-gear stores can outfit you in the best ones made. There are also crafts by Canada's Native people, high-end art galleries, clothing boutiques, and plenty of chances to stockpile maple syrup. Meanwhile over at The Fairmont Banff Springs, shoppers can find all sorts of treasures in their 15 shops.

NIGHTLIFE

The town of Banff is a lively place after dark—it behaves more like a ski town than an outpost in a national park—with restaurants and bars lining the streets. Most notably, the Rose & Crown serves pub fare that's mouth-watering and you'll usually find a fire blazing on the hearth of this upstairs pub. Settle down for some live music. The St. James Gate is a traditional Irish Pub that was disassembled in Ireland and reassembled in Banff for those who enjoy toe-tapping live music and Irish fare. It doesn't cater to a specific age group, you'll be singing along with an energetic group of locals and tourists from 18 to 88. Live bands play as well at Wild Bill's Legendary Saloon, which has line dancing. Even if you're not a guest at The Fairmont Banff Springs, dining there is one of Alberta's finest experiences. The stateliness of its main rooms and views are inimitable. Sip Canada's famous ice wines and bask in the mountains outside the windows of the Grapes Wine Bar. Cheese fondue and a pint of beer at the cozy Waldhaus Pub are essential after a day hiking or skiing.

BEST DINING

LE BEAUJOLAIS RESTAURANT'S "BISTRO", considered by locals and critics alike as the finest in town, offers a sophisticated French menu combining the classics with an innovative twist. I remember the fabulous wild game dishes such as braised elk with wild boar bacon. Or try a Canadian specialty: Atlantic lobster, Quebec foie-gras, Alberta beef, or maple Grand Marnier soufflé. 212 Buffalo Street ($26 and up; 403-762-2712, www.lebeaujolaisbanff.com).

THE "X" TEAM

The "X" Team started fifteen years ago with five women in the same business, who decided to take a ski trip together. "X" stands for "extreme skiing" and not all of us qualify but we all can keep up and have a blast doing it. Word got out, and each year more women begged to join our "team," but we decided we had to cap it at 12 or lose the cohesiveness of the group.

We are a diverse group, ranging in age from 36 to 63 and living from London to Portland, some single, some married with children, but all in the same business; financial services—from presidents to saleswomen; entrepreneurs to members of large corporations. In addition to the fun of skiing together, we found we learned from one another, not only as career boosters, but also what music to listen to and how to dress. One woman is our fashionista and she has improved our appearances immeasurably!

We do probably discuss business 50-60 percent of the time we're together; however, our closeness is much deeper than as business colleagues. Now we'll find any excuse for a party. We celebrate birthdays and have welcomed three new babies, five new brides, and numerous new boyfriends, some keepers, some not.

No topic is off limits, but we have learned that it's best to avoid some subjects since our politics range from neo-conservative to flaming liberal.

But, there is one subject we never talk about—getting old! Why should we focus on menopause and physical ailments? After all, two in our group just welcomed their first children, both at age 45! We have a lot of great living ahead of us, and we fully intend to enjoy it.

Everyone knows the "old boys network"; this is the "new babes" time. It is a real support system. I love these women and they have made my life richer in very many ways.

—Lenore E. Thornton, 60s, Investment Management
Professional, New York City

COYOTE'S DELI AND GRILL is a Santa Fe–style intimate restaurant serving southwestern cuisine with flavorful and unique sauces. It is a favorite among locals who sit near the open kitchen. Healthy dishes range from soups and salads, to pasta and steak. 206 Caribou Street ($14-28; 403-762-3963, www.dininginbanff.com).

MAPLE LEAF GRILLE AND LOUNGE is a phenomenal restaurant with Canadian cuisine (Alberta beef, backcountry bison, local duck, wild game platter, Canadian cheeses) in a relaxed lodge atmosphere. 137 Banff Avenue, entrance on Caribou Street ($16-60; 403-760-7680, www.banffmapleleaf.com).

EVENTS TO FLY IN FOR

The Banff Centre each summer hosts four months worth of ballet, opera, orchestral and chamber music, jazz, fiction and non-fiction readings, and visual arts during the Banff Arts Festival. In late October, the Centre also screens nearly 50 of the world's best new mountain films—harrowing tales of adventure and cultural explorations that take you around the world—at the internationally recognized Banff Mountain Film Festival (www.banff mountainfestivals.ca).

PAMPER YOURSELF

Book appointments with the Fairmont Banff Springs for a Wildflower Body Polish or Mountain Stone massage at the award-winning, luxury Willow Stream Spa. You can reconvene after your treatments and idle together in the mineral pool, women's lounge, or on the terrace with panoramas of peaks (403-762-1772).

WHERE TO STAY

Styled after a Scottish baronial castle, the Fairmont Banff Springs and its 27-hole championship golf course stands on the bank of the Bow River cradled in a valley. It's breathtaking—with a price tag to match at $350 a night, unless you go off season and find deals online, then from $200. Be aware that nothing in Banff is cheap (800-257-7544, or 403-762-2211, www.fairmont.com/banffsprings).

Banff Caribou Lodge and Banff Ptarmigan Inn present moderately priced alternatives. The Banff Caribou Lodge is located at the far end of the commercial part of Banff Avenue, a ten minute walk to the shops and restaurants. Or you may opt for the free shuttle. At the lodge's Red Earth Spa massages start at $59. Underground parking, a large hot tub, and feather mattresses on the beds are a bonus at this affordable lodge (from $129 off-season to $229 in peak season; 800-661-8310, www .bestofbanff.com).

Centrally located, the Western-style Banff Ptarmigan Inn, managed by the same company as the Banff Caribou, is within walking distance of many Banff attractions (from $209 off-season to $250 in peak season; 800-661-8310, www.banffptarmiganinn.com).

ONE CLICK AND YOU'RE OFF: Ask Banff-Lake Louise Tourism about girlfriend getaway packages (403-762-8421, www.bannfflakelouise.com).

Savannah
❧ GEORGIA ☙

If you're a sucker for Southern charm, superlative antiquing, coastal beauty, and downhome cooking, then Savannah, Georgia, is the should-be site for your reunion. The 250-year-old history of Savannah takes you back in time to various eras of American history. It's an urban gallery that you'll love exploring in the midst of 100-year old oaks and blossoming magnolia trees. Considered the country's best walking city, Savannah was designed in 1733 around 24 squares—postage-stamp parks laid out in neat grids that most houses, churches, and stores face. The city abounds with well-preserved 18th- and 19th-century Federal, Italianate, and Regency-style houses and antique shops. You'll love wandering the streets, simply seeing where you'll end up, and peaking into curious shops full of handmade furniture from far-off places, hardware from old local homes, and some of the eyebrow-raising price tags of precious antiques. Revived in 1999 by the best-selling *Midnight in the Garden of Good and Evil,* a portrayal by John Berendt of Savannah's most

---

TRAVEL TIP .

With a subtropical climate, Savannah is a warm-weather vacation spot any time of year; perhaps avoid July and August if you can't bear hot, humid days.

I just can't get enough of Savannah. I've gone many times with a group of wild girlfriends. It is so enchanting and slow and sweet. I think of myself as a city girl, and there's nothing like going to Savannah to calm down. I find something new in every single square I walk through, every visit. The night ghost tours are so much fun, too. I've done them at least four or five times and I haven't seen a ghost yet. If you're a history nerd like me, you can get absorbed in the history. The fresh seafood can't be beat. I get she-crab stew every trip. It is like a lobster bisque in low country style—unpretentious but decadent. Wear your "buffet pants" because you'll gain five pounds, but it's worth it. You can diet when you get back home.

—Anne Rach, 20s, Television Producer, Orlando, Florida

intriguing eccentrics, the city's haunting grace and rich history quickly became a fixation of visitors. Those of you who have read the book, or seen the movie, will really enjoy seeking out the landmarks and legends mentioned by Berendt.

SHOPPING

Walking through the squares of Savannah is to window shop. And the buildings housing the varied stores are just as splendid as the shopping; they range from a former 1921 department store to an 1853 town house to an unrestored pre-Civil War mansion. On the Savannah River, the nine-block brick concourse of River Street is ideal for people watching, dining on seafood, buying knick-knacks, drinking a bloody mary, and viewing the giant ships go by. A former cotton warehouse, it's filled with more than 75 boutiques, galleries, artist studios, restaurants, and pubs.

BEST TOURS

There are nearly 40 tour operators in Savannah with their own spin on the city's highlights. On the Haunted Ghost Tour with Oglethorpe Haunted Tours you'll view a creepier side to the Historic District via trolley; carriages transport you over cobblestone streets as the coachman waxes poetic about the city on a Carriage Tour with Plantation Carriage Company ($20; 912-201-0001, plantationcarriage.com). You'll get a primer on the area's contemporary and colonial buildings with Architectural Tours of Savannah ($20; 912-604-6354, www.architec turalsavannah.com).

BEST LOW-COUNTRY FOOD

Savannah treats your taste buds to good ol' downhome cooking: creamy she-crab soup, crispy fried chicken and collard greens, grits and biscuits. And it is all cheap. CLARY'S CAFE has been serving breakfast since 1903. Join the crowds fueling up on omelets, grits, and steaming biscuits and pecan strawberry malted waffles. Be sure to view the stained glass rendering of the Midnight cover in the back. Try the crab cake benedict or the corned beef hash. 404 Abercorn Street at Jones. Daily 8-4 p.m. ($6-10; 912-233-0402).

At one of the three tables at WALLS BAR-B-QUE, dig into the devil crab, ribs, and sweet potato pie. Closed Sunday-Wednesday. 515 E. York Lane ($5-12; 912-232-9754).

BEST FINE DINING

Where do Savannah's elite dine when they want an excellent meal? At the OLDE PINK HOUSE. Inside this Georgian mansion built in 1771, you'll sample dressed-up low-country favorites such as blue crab with Vidalia onion sauce and she-crab soup. 23 Abercorn Street (starting at $15; 912-232-4286).

BEST MUSEUMS

The oldest art museum in the South, the Telfair Museum of Art, which includes the new Jepson Center for the Arts, was built in 1818 and served as the royal Governor's residence. It holds an impressive collection of American and European paintings and sculpture (www.telfair.org). The Juliette Gordon Low Birthplace, constructed between 1818 and 1820, is the birthplace of the founder of the Girl Scouts, and was named Savannah's first national historic landmark in 1965. It is operated by the Girl Scouts as a memorial to their founder.

RETREAT

All that walking will earn you a latte at the Sentient Bean, a café at the south end of the 20-acre, live oak-shaded Forsyth Park. Then stroll or laze about in Savannah's largest and arguably most lovely park. The Sentient Bean is located at 13 East Park Avenue (912-232-4447).

EVENTS TO FLY IN FOR

Extravagantly decorated houses in the city's four historic districts open to the public each March for the Savannah Tour of Homes and Gardens. For 15 days beginning at the end of March, zydeco, gospel, and Southern rock flood the city during the Savannah Music Festival, which stages internationally acclaimed acts in churches, old movie houses, and along the riverfront.

BEST DAY TRIPS

Bicycling through the streets of Savannah is another alternative to pounding the pavement and seeing its sights. Bicycle Link in downtown rents single-speed cruisers (912-233-9401, www.bicycle-link.com).

WHERE TO STAY

The historic district consists of distinguished inns and B&B's, vacation rentals ranging from garden apartments to carriage houses, and luxury

GIRL'S CAMP

～

There were nine of us. All women. All strangers. We had one friend who knew each of us and had decided we'd make a good team.

We threw our duffels into a pair of vans, then piled in and headed off for a weekend in a five-bedroom, rented cabin in the mountains. By the time we were smelling pine on that crisp fall Friday afternoon, remarkable friendships had begun to form.

That was 15 years ago.

Today, eight of us from that original group continue to meet annually for long "girls' camp" weekends. Our getaways have become cherished sanctuaries in each of our lives.

But eventually there was a problem. More friends wanted in. And we wanted to include them. So three of us decided to launch a second group, each inviting two friends to complete a new circle.

Over the years, our destinations have included rented homes on the gold coast of Baja, in Palm Springs, Carmel, and the Napa Valley

No matter where we go, the getaways are gifts to ourselves and one another. Our purpose is to unwind, catch up, refocus, renew, and nurture ourselves and each another.

—Alison DaRosa, 50s, Writer, San Diego, California

For me, it doesn't matter where you go with gal pals, it's always fun. It's not really about an exotic location. It's the stories and camaraderie.

—Susan Blouch, 50's, Consultant, Cleveland, Ohio

hotels. On the high-end of the spectrum, the Kehoe House is listed on the National Registry of Historic Places and regarded as one of the Savannah's most gorgeous B&Bs. 123 Habersham St. ($199-429; 800-820-0100, or 912-232-1020, www.kehoehouse.com).

Located in the historic district, the Mulberry Inn, owned by Holiday Inn, has a lovely outdoor garden for breakfast. You'll enjoy afternoon tea with cakes and cookies in the lobby accompanied by a live pianist (starting at $180; 877-863-4780, www.holidayinn.com).

For bigger savings, look into accommodations in Midtown, the Southside, and West Chatham, which are close to downtown.

ONE CLICK AND YOU'RE OFF: To plan your visit, contact the Savannah Convention and Visitors Bureau (877-728-2662, or 912-644-6401, www.savannahvisit.com).

San Diego

ఈ CALIFORNIA ☜

The best of both worlds—gorgeous beaches and a lively city—can be had in San Diego: a destination that promises great weather, food, shopping, and scenery for your mini-reunion. What you'll need to pack should give you an idea of what kind of trip this will be: a bathing suit, your best walking shoes, and a little sun dress. You'll spend more time outdoors here than in any other U.S. city, feeling that Southern California sunshine and ocean breezes on your skin.

San Diego is blessed with sunshine, 70 miles of sandy beaches, and days averaging 70 degrees. Add to that taco stands, farmers markets, upscale restaurants, diverse neighborhoods, great theater, and adventure. Wildlife here means more than pigeons: seals, migrating whales (from December through February), seal lions, and brown pelicans. You could get lost in the lush, 1,200-acre Balboa Park for a week, which is a good thing because it's also rich with museums, a world-famous zoo, and performing arts venues. A group picnic or power-walk in Mission Bay Park may be your thing; it's the largest man-made aquatic park in the country with coves, grassy areas, beaches, and athletes frolicking about. You may prefer watching surfers catch waves while you bask in the sun on the sand. Or there's always shopping for Mexican-inspired art.

BEST NEIGHBORHOODS FOR STROLLING

The Gaslamp Quarter with its restored 19th-century Victorian buildings with wide brick walkways and imitation gas street lamps has the character of any other city's "historic" district. First hit the art galleries and specialty shops, then find a sidewalk café for dinner and a club playing live jazz. Home to the House of Blues and Petco Park, the home of the Padres, it's a hopping neighborhood after sundown.

Beverly Hills meets the Mediterranean only 20 minutes from downtown San Diego, in the village in La Jolla. This posh community is popular for sandy beaches, palatial homes, and palm-lined streets filled with dining and shopping (or window shopping, as it's known for its little, independently owned, ritzy boutiques). Pomegranate has great antique and stylish jewelry, but is a definite splurge. 1152 Prospect Street (858-459-0629).

FOR GARDEN LOVERS

Balboa Park is like a town in itself. This 1,200-acre property is home to 15 museums, performing arts venues, and the zoo. But the eight gardens found here are not to be missed; highlights include a prize-winning rose garden, the Alcazar Garden, fashioned after the grounds of a castle in Seville, Spain, and the perfectly manicured Japanese Friendship Garden.

FOR BEACH LOVERS

Beaches fringe the city and finding a patch of sand couldn't be easier. If you're in want of a classic beach experience, the tiny island town of Coronado on San Diego Bay offers upscale shops, cafés, and stately homes plus a public white-sand beach (with a lifeguard) facing the Pacific. Locals who go to the

---

If you are a politically mixed group, as we are — try to schedule your reunions for non-election years to reduce friction.

—Priscilla English, 60's, Screenwriter, Los Angeles, California

beach choose La Jolla Shores, because it is less windy, the water is clean and a bit warmer, and there are lots of lifeguards and people.

IF YOU PREFER A WILDERNESS BEACH

Torrey Pines State Beach, at the north end of San Diego, is backed by 300-foot cliffs and hiking trails of the Torrey Pines State Reserve. The beach stretches 4.5 miles north to the city of Del Mar. Often uncrowded, it's a great escape and chance to spot sea lions, dolphins, and migrating whales. The La Jolla area is also a beautiful setting for snorkeling and kayaking with Hike Bike Kayak San Diego (866-425-2925, www.hikebike kayak.com) and learning how to surf with Surf Diva, which for a decade has been teaching women of all ages how to hang ten (858-454 8273, www.surfdiva.com).

MUST-SEE MUSEUMS

The San Diego Zoo dates back to 1916 and is one of the preeminent zoos in the world (619-231-1515, www.sandiegozoo.org). Wear comfy clothing and shoes, pack water, and expect to walk a few miles. There are 100 acres of natural habitats for more than 4,000 animals from Africa, Asia, Australia, and North and South Americas. You'll giggle watching the polar bears paddling in their water tank; and your hearts will pound as you peek in on the jaguars in Cat Canyon. The Monkey Trails and Forest Tales is an amazing installation and the zoo is one of only four in the U.S. with giant pandas. If you all are looking for fine art, there's plenty to choose from in the park. But the Mingei International Museum stands out as a favorite among ladies: It's a collection of folk art from numerous world cultures. Note: Admission to a handful of Balboa Park's museums is waived on Tuesdays, on a rotating basis (619-239-0512, www.balboapark.org).

PAMPER YOURSELVES

La Jolla's Spa at Torrey Pines indulges guests with marine- and botanical-infused treatments in their 9,500-square foot Arts & Crafts–inspired center at the Lodge at Torrey Pines resort. Around you are the greens of a golf course, the ocean, and Torrey Pines State Reserve. Plan to book treatments a month ahead of time (50-minute massage from $140; 858-453-4420, www.spatorreypines.com).

BEST SHOPPING

There are nearly 200 shops in Horton Plaza, an outdoor mall with some unique (very Southern Californian) architecture in the midst of downtown.

HOW TO NAVIGATE A NEW CITY

Here's how to get around a new city easily:

- Preparation is critical. Read guidebooks and research online before you start planning your trip. Use the terms "Convention and Visitor's Bureau" and "Tourist Board" when you do your online city search.

- Before you leave, buy a good map of your destination city and familiarize yourself with areas of interest. Some city websites offer free maps.

- Hotel location is paramount for easy navigation and safety. Locate your hotel on a map to ensure its proximity to restaurants, theaters, museums, shopping, and entertainment. Give serious consideration to how you'd like to move around the city. Do you want to use public transportation? If so, is your hotel located near a major subway station or bus stops?

- Think about whether you really need to rent a car. Hotel parking in the center of the city can be exorbitantly expensive. In most cases car rental is necessary only if you wish to spend a few days in the countryside.

- Once you've arrived in the new city and settled in at your hotel, take a bus tour to get an overview of neighborhoods and tourist attractions. You can return later on your own to spend more time in areas that interest you.

- Ask for help. Your best source for on-the-spot information will be local residents. They maneuver around the city every day and know the commuter patterns and pitfalls of each mode of transportation.

You can all find what you're looking for (just about every store is here) in this colorful complex. Looking for something quainter? Seaport Village resembles a New England town by the sea. Inside, small one-of-a-kind shops, galleries, and restaurants come with views of the photogenic Coronado Island. Add to that free concerts on weekends and street musicians entertaining shoppers.

BEST DAY TRIPS

Drive north on Historic Highway 101/Pacific Coast Highway, a route through the seaside towns of Del Mar and Solana Beach. You may want to rent a convertible for this one. Or head east to the quaint mountain community of Julian, known for its fall apple festival—and occasional snowfall in winter. And to the south, there's always shopping in Tijuana over the border in Baja California, Mexico, a hectic but colorful city that demands alertness and stamina from you.

BEST DINING

It could be argued that **THE PRADO AT BALBOA PARK** resides in the most beautiful building in San Diego. The Spanish Colonial-style House of Hospitality, built in Balboa Park for the 1915 Exposition, now is a dining landmark serving Latin and Italian cuisine accompanied by a popular sangria. The enormous interior is ideal for any group. 1549 El Prado ($23-42; 619-557-9441, www.cohnrestaurants.com).

For the freshest seafood in San Diego, eat where the locals go; **POINT LOMA SEAFOODS** where the owners buy seasonal fish directly from local fishermen daily. You can count on clean, fresh shellfish and mollusks, as well as locally caught California Spiny Lobster during the season, October through March. This local lobster, with no claws, is renown all over the world for its firm, sweet tail meat. Try the Pacific Swordfish, another locally caught delicacy. Fish foodies who live in the area swear that the "fish tacos" are the best in Southern California. On the Waterfront, 2805 Emerson Street at Scott Street, two blocks off Rosecrans Street ($6-16; 619-223-1109, www.plsf.com).

Reserve a table at the **OCEAN TERRACE BISTRO**, part of the well-reviewed George's at the Cove in La Jolla. The sunset view of the Pacific is spectacular. Don't be lured into the fine dining restaurant—head directly upstairs to the outdoor Ocean Terrace Bistro where the view is twice as good and prices are half what you'd pay in the dining room. With views of the Pacific beneath you, you'll all dig into affordable masterpieces such as Thai Inspired Fish Stew and Grilled Mahi Mahi. 1250 Prospect Street, La Jolla ($16-28; 858-454-4244, www.georgesatthecove.com).

If you want Mexican food and seek something more upscale than a taco shack, head to one of the MIGUEL'S COCINA restaurants. They're among the best sit-down Mexican joints to order authentic fish tacos, enchiladas, and carnitas. 1351 Orange Avenue, Coronado (619-437-4237) and 2912 Shelter Island Drive, Point Loma (619-224-2401, www.brigantine.com/miguels).

EVENTS TO FLY IN FOR
The Summer Shakespeare Festival in Balboa Park stages three plays between June and October at the impressive Old Globe Theater, which throughout the year puts on plays and musicals, many Broadway bound (619-234-5623, www.theoldglobe.org). You can all place your bets and cheer for your horse at the Del Mar racetrack. The Del Mar racing season begins in mid-July and closes in early September. This historic racetrack was the stage for the famous Seabiscuit race in 1938.

BEST THRIFT SHOP
Encore of La Jolla is where many of San Diego's best-dressed women shop for their European and American designer clothing. The shop offers high-end recycled clothing it buys from clients around the country. It sells nothing on consignment; everything is in pristine condition, many items still with original price tags. You'll find women's sizes from 2 to 14, and pay from $2 for a T-shirt to $2,500 for a floor-length mink coat. Prices are generally about 25 percent of what you'd pay retail. You'll find bargains like a $295 Fendi jacket, or pay $250 for an Escada pantsuit, $450 for an Armani coat. There's a whole department of St. John knits, racks of Chanel suits. Upstairs, everything is $99 or less. 7655 Girard Ave. (858-454-7540, www.encorelajolla.com).

PLACE TO STAY
If you and your girlfriends are looking for a one-of-a-kind lodging experience, book a Cape Cod-style cottage on a historic pier above the Pacific, where you'll fall asleep to the soothing sound of the rhythmic waves beneath you. The 23 cottages at Crystal Pier Hotel have private patios, fully equipped kitchenettes and floor to ceiling glass walls. You can jog the beach at dawn and watch the sunset from your lounge chairs on the patio. The living area, bedrooms, and kitchens are decorated with a nautical theme. If you want a resort with lots to do, bellhops, room service, and amenities, then this is not the place for you. If you're game for a cozy bungalow perched over the ocean with views, serenity, and peace, then check out the cottages at the Crystal Pier Hotel, located on Ocean Blvd.

The largest units (A to F) are located further out on the pier and offer more privacy on the patio decks, which are angled with the best views of the ocean. At the hotel on land, there are six additional rooms facing the ocean for the same price as the bungalows. There is usually a two- or three-night minimum. Their website doesn't do them justice (winter rates start at $225; 800-748-5894, www.crystalpier.com).

The Pacific Terrace Hotel is located in Pacific Beach just north of Crystal Pier in the heart of the San Diego surfer community. The hotel sits atop a 50-foot cliff with nothing between it and the ocean but a boardwalk, a few palm trees, and about a hundred feet of sand.

Book a spacious ocean-view room to take advantage of the great people-watching from your balcony, which overlooks the pool and the beach which is sprinkled with dozens of sun worshipers and surfers. Amenities and décor rival the high quality of most boutique hotels; continental breakfast, a heated pool, hot tub, fresh cookies daily, wine hour by the pool, a wet bar with a microwave and a refrigerator in every room, turn-down service with chocolates at night, a 42-inch plasma TV, and massage in your guest room, in a private massage room, or at a poolside, ocean-view cabana. The service is top notch. The beach front location is terrific, however street parking is difficult in the area so expect to pay $15 a night for hotel parking. For those with no car there is a bus stop at the end of the road that takes you directly to the Gaslamp district. Starting at $380, call the hotel for various discounts. 610 Diamond Street (800-344-3370, 858-581-3500, www.pacificterrace.com).

If you prefer a very polished, sophisticated, big hotel, check out the the Omni, located in downtown San Diego, just steps from the historic Gaslamp Quarter. Ask about the Select Guest Program, which offers a number of choices, including high floor corner rooms with amazing views of the bay, Coronado Island, and Gaslamp Quarter. You may bag a very low rate online. Valet parking is expensive, $26 per day with unlimited in and out service. However, there is a multistory parking garage across the street where parking is $8-13. Rates start at $149 low season; $239 is the high season weekend rate. Special offers online. 675 L Street (800-843-6664, or 619-231-6664, www.omni hotels.com).

ONE CLICK AND YOU'RE OFF: San Diego Convention & Visitors Bureau (619-236-1212, www.sandiego.org).

CHAPTER SEVEN

Best Places to Heal

❧ DONNA'S STORY ❧

Donna, a stay-at-home mom from Ridgefield, Connecticut, thought she was doing everything right. She volunteered for the PTA and drove her son to games and practice for two sports and her daughter to a private school for the handicapped. She raised three kids, mostly by herself, because her husband traveled 240-plus days a year. She had even packed up the kids, the house, and her life to move seven times for her husband's job.

"I stuck by my man and gave everything to him," says Donna. "Through sickness and health....I took my vows very seriously."

After the kids left home, Donna hoped to travel with her husband, but he told her he was too tired and hated to travel. She was tired of waiting, so six years ago she booked a hiking trip in Montana's Glacier National Park with an all-women's travel company.

"It was fabulous," she says of the trip. "I got hooked and started taking two all-women trips a year, one domestic and one overseas. I learned to kayak and surf in Kauai, to climb mountains in the Rockies, to sail in the British Virgin Islands, and to raft the raging rivers of Montana. The women on these trips were from all walks of life, all colors and backgrounds. Ninety-five percent of the women were married or had been married. I listened to their stories and loved the female companionship. I made all kinds of friends: gay, single, married, career women, grandmas."

Donna thought her marriage of 28 years was perfect. "But you never know what tomorrow will bring," she explains. "I woke up one morning married and happy, and boom, the next day my husband tells me he's no longer romantically in love with me and wants a divorce." It was a total surprise and Donna was devastated. She learned later, with the help of a private detective, that her husband lived two totally different lives, one as a church-going, respectable husband and father, and another with a younger woman in a different state. He had been cheating on her for 18 years.

"He asked for a divorce four days before I was scheduled to depart on a hiking trip in Switzerland," she says. "I was a mess, I couldn't sleep or eat, but I went. If I was home, I would have stayed in bed and cried. On the trip, I kept busy and bonded with all the women in the group. It was a huge sisterhood. Everyone had stories and even if they hadn't gone through a divorce, they gave me strength. Everyone was so compassionate and supportive. They enabled me to be strong."

She soon discovered that some of their stories were even worse than her own. One woman had recently become a widow. Another woman had a huge celebration for her 30th wedding anniversary, which all their friends attended, and their grown kids flew in from around the country. Her husband even gave her a diamond ring. But the morning after, at breakfast with the kids, he announced he was moving out. It was also for a younger woman. She'd been duped just like Donna, who learned from her travel companions that you can be devastated, but you get over it and still have a very full, exciting life.

Donna also prefers joining an all-women's trip so she doesn't have to round up girlfriends to join her or do all the planning. "I go on 'cruise control' the moment I leave the house," she explains. "All the details are planned and when the trip is over I feel like I've been away three weeks instead of only one. We accomplish so much every day. We might hike in the morning, raft in the afternoon, or shop. I met two wild friends on the Kauai trip and we got rub-on tattoos on our butts. My tattoo showed a skeleton surfing. Another time I came back with a fake belly-button piercing. It gave my kids a little rush when I showed them the tattoo and piercing. We had a lot of laughs."

Donna attributes her healing to her strong faith and a supportive group of travel buddies. "Now I'm very excited about life," she says. "Traveling has helped me realize how much I can do and how much beauty there is in the world."

❧ JOAN'S STORY ❧

"We all have a secret fantasy that we'll get through life without pain, grief, heartbreak, or loss. It's wishful thinking that you and you alone were born under a lucky star and will have no major setbacks. So we're always a little shocked when the bad times arrive," explains Joan. In the mid-1980s when her 56-year-old mother was dying of breast cancer, she remembers, "At times I couldn't breathe, think, or take in what was occurring." When her mother's health began a rapid decline, Joan decided to move home to take care of her. She had been married for a mere four months. At the end of her mother's life, everyone in the family pitched in—dad, brothers, and sisters—but Joan nursed her day and night, week after week, for three months.

"During that difficult time, I found my solace in nature. When my brother or sister would sit with Mom, I would take a break and go hiking. I drew new strength from the energy that emanates from the trails and trees. One day I came to a grove of aspens and each leaf was shimmering gold." says Joan. "It seemed they were cheering for me."

After her mother's death, Joan returned to her husband in Colorado where her healing began on the trails of the Rocky Mountains. As she hiked through her grief, she reminisced about her mother. "She was a fabulous role model," says Joan. "She always hung out with women. Dad was 'way into it,' not like some husbands who are threatened, resentful, or jealous. During a short period when the cancer was in remission, Mom went to Cambridge, England, with six girlfriends for a study abroad experience. She loved it! She was an English major in college and this was a chance to rekindle her passion for literature. We all supported her and encouraged her to go." Just last month Joan heard from her mom's best friends in Salt Lake City. They have held a birthday party for her, in her absence, every year for the past 20 years.

Joan has followed her mother's example. She travels with girlfriends and often joins a core group of women from the North Central Rockies for all-day hikes to stay centered and deepen her friendships. They range in age from

28 to 65 years old. They hit the trails every Friday. On their most recent outing they celebrated a member's 55th birthday with a picnic and trek up to Columbine Lake, above Winter Park ski resort. "The wildflowers were in bloom and the hike was perfect for different ages and ability levels. I walked with every single woman during the trip. You get beyond contrived conversations—like where you ate, or what movie you saw, and into more meaningful thoughts. During this hike I casually mentioned nursing my mother during her illness and another hiker quietly piped in, 'me, too.' Then we shared our stories," says Joan. She admits it was cathartic to describe her fear and pain during this devastating time in her life to someone who had had a similar experience. Amid the wildflowers of the Rockies they talked about the lessons they had learned and the gifts they had received through the loss of their mothers. The experience made them more compassionate and showed each of them how to help other people who go through the process.

It makes one wonder about her husband. Can a new relationship survive separation and grief? "My husband thought he was marrying a joyful, fun, spunky woman. When I moved home to nurse Mom he was very concerned. And for the first year of married life, I was a grieving person," explains Joan. "That was 21 years ago and our marriage is strong and has weathered other less traumatic events," replies Joan. Her most restorative energy comes from the mountains. "After all," Joan says, "Prada and feeling sorry for myself are two luxuries I can't afford."

Glacier National Park

☙ MONTANA ☙

Perhaps nothing puts life into perspective and rebuilds your self-esteem more than hiking among glaciers. Situated in a remote corner of northwestern Montana, which is a state that redefines "remote" as we know it, lies a region of incomparable splendor: Glacier National Park. These protected lands hold a special place on the list of the world's natural wonders. With its glaciers now receding, the park has become even more precious. The beauty of glacier-coated mountains manages to push life's obstacles to the side, and to be humbled by these fields of snow and ice is to be uplifted by them, too. There are 700 miles of maintained trails that in summer (June through September) lead you up into a stunning high-alpine setting, past dramatic waterfalls and icy blue lakes to the foot of these glaciers, where you can place your hand on one or dip your toe

A driving trip with a girlfriend is the best way to heal. Take good music, crank up the tunes, sing and talk it out as you put miles behind you and let it all roll by.

—Jan Butchofsky-Houser, 50s, Professional Photographer,
Nogal, New Mexico

in the lake created by its runoff. You'll find yourself using your strength and determination to make it to the next overlook and then the next. The pounding of your heart in your ears as you climb to 7,000 feet will restore your self-confidence. There's also the excitement of crossing paths with the park's prolific wildlife such as eagles, moose, bighorn sheep, or even grizzly bears. All the park has to offer will fortify you. Even though this is the country's most rugged territory, the National Park Service has made it rather user friendly. It accommodates visitors with historic lodges, a new bus system, and well-marked trails, plus there's an airport with car rentals in the nearby town of Kalispell, close to the park's western gate.

BEST GUIDED TRIP
AdventureWomen, the oldest adventure travel company for active women over 30, has lead trips to this area of the world for 15 years. Their seven-day guided tour of the park in August includes hiking with expert female guides, driving the breathtaking Going-to-the-Sun Road, and whitewater rafting the Middle Fork of the Flathead River. Nights are spent in the park's lodges and the tour also dips into Canada's Waterton Lakes National Park. If you're looking to connect with other women and thrive off of their encouragement, this is the trip for you (starting at $2,695; 800-804-8686, www.adventurewomen.com).

DO-IT-YOURSELF TRIP
It's very doable to take this journey without joining a group. You can stay at the park lodges or campsites, or in the motels or B&Bs in the towns outside the park entrances, and map out your own itinerary of hikes and sites. In 2007, the park expanded its bus system to serve the entire length of the Going-to-the-Sun Road with 12 stops along the way. And if you're feeling hesitant about taking longer hikes alone, you can always join one of the group hikes with Glacier Guides, which is the only backcountry guide service permitted to operate in the park. AdventureWomen uses their experienced and enthusiastic guides ($86 a day; 800-521-7238, www.glacierguides.com).

It's a healing experience to travel with the same women year after year, from hiking the Montana Mountains to trekking in Timbuktu. We listen to each other's life stories and share a passion for adventure. Time is marching on and we want to see it all before our legs give out.

—Susan Eckert, 50s, Founder, AdventureWomen, Bozeman, Montana

SCENIC DRIVE
The 50-mile Going-to-the-Sun Road bisects the wilds of this million-acre park. From the lowest elevation in Glacier to the Continental Divide at the 6,646-foot Logan Pass, the highway twists and turns around mountainsides affording staggering views everywhere you look. It's best to hit the road early in the day to avoid the rubberneckers. The road is open in its entirety from early June to mid-October (with some scheduled closures over the next few years due to road construction).

BEST DAY HIKES
The mellow half-day hike to the high-alpine Iceberg Lake is the perfect warm-up. Via a ten-mile, round-trip trail from Swiftcurrent Motor Inn in Many Glacier, hikers get an eye-opener when they arrive at a lake surrounded by 3,000-foot cliffs on three sides. In the spring avalanches crash down this cirque, and well into July it's possible to still see a fleet of icebergs in the lake. The Highline Trail is one of the premiere hiking trails in the park. From Logan Pass on the Going-to-the-Sun Road, this trail runs north, tracing the Continental Divide, eventually ending at the Canadian border. But a shorter version of this long trail can be done in a day: At the Granite Park Chalet, nearly eight miles from the trailhead, it meets up with a trail that loops back to the road, making this hike 11.6 miles long in total. It's a spectacular, mostly flat (but long) trip on which you'll likely encounter bighorn sheep and mountain goats.

HIKE TO A GLACIER
From Many Glacier Hotel or the Swiftcurrent Lake picnic area, the Grinnell Glacier Trail begins a five-mile journey to one of the largest remaining glaciers in the park. Past waterfalls, forests, slopes covered in wildflowers, and sparkling lakes, you arrive at Upper Grinnell Lake filled with chunks of floating ice at the hem of the 300-acre glacier. Although it's not a good idea to explore the glacier on your own (it's riddled with crevasses), you can get right up to it and dip your toes in the freezing cold lake.

BEST DINING

AdventureWomen's favorite spots to eat include **SERRANO'S** in East Glacier Park, **PARK CAFÉ** in St. Mary, and **TWO SISTERS CAFÉ** near Babb, all on the east side of the park. Serrano's serves what's been called the best Mexican food in Montana ($9-18; 406-226-9392, www.serranosmexican.com). "Welcome Aliens!" beckons to hungry hikers from the roof of Two Sisters Café, a funky joint that serves homemade meals made with love; they also make a mean pie and lime margarita ($7-24; 406-732-5535, www.twosistersofmontana.com). And the salads, bison steaks, and 17 different kinds of pie are always fresh at the Park Café ($8-12; 406-732-4482, www.parkcafe.us). While all the park lodges have dining rooms, the food tends to be overpriced (and not that great). But the gorgeous views can make up for that.

BEST PLACES TO STAY

Located by the eastern entrance to the park in East Glacier, the rustic Glacier Park Lodge was constructed using 40-foot Douglas fir beams, which you can admire from their grand lobby (starting at $129; 406-892-2525, www.glacierparkinc.com). Built in 1915 by the Great Northern Railroad, Many Glacier Hotel on the shores of Swiftcurrent Lake in the northeast corner of the park is the most popular lodge. The Swiss influence comes through not just in the décor but the surrounding peaks that resemble the Swiss Alps (starting at $142; 406-892-2525, www.glacierparkinc.com). Nearby, the modest Swiftcurrent Motor Inn serves as the starting line to some of the park's best hikes, Iceberg Lake among them (starting at $55; 406-892-2525, www.glacierparkinc.com). Lastly, the Lake McDonald Lodge on the western edge of the park was constructed as a hunting lodge in 1913 and today that intimate-cabin atmosphere still comes through (starting at $120; 406-892-2525, www.glacierparkinc.com).

ONE CLICK AND YOU'RE OFF: Glacier National Park (406-888-7800, www.nps.gov/glac).

San Miguel de Allende

⌒ MEXICO ⌒

There's something about San Miguel de Allende that encourages you to take risks, to learn something new, and to reinvent yourself. The generosity, joy, and good-naturedness of the local people is contagious. Four

HOW TO PLAN A GETAWAY
WITH A GROUP OF WOMEN

- Ask someone to be the organizer: One person needs to be the organizer to find a date that works for everyone, to spearhead communications, and to start looking for accommodations.

- Pick a date: Select the date as far in advance as possible and commit to how much time everyone can spend on the trip. Do you want to travel for a long weekend or a week? This can be the most difficult part of your planning. Ask everyone to commit the dates in ink to their work and home calendars. Include the trip dates in the subject line of every e-mail communication about your girlfriend getaway.

- Agree on a budget: Assess how much everyone plans to spend. Do you want to go far or stay close to home, travel by car or plane? These decisions will impact your budget. *TIP:* You can save a lot of money if you travel weekdays, off-season, and to less touristy destinations. Best days to travel for cheaper plane tickets are Monday, Tuesday, and Saturday.

hours north of Mexico City in the cool hills of the Mexican Interior, San Miguel de Allende is bathed in the sound of ringing church bells and the warmth of the sun. Its narrow cobblestone streets, old pink and terra-cotta-colored buildings, blooming gardens, and an enormous gothic-inspired church are right out of a postcard from Spain—a couple of hundred years ago. The nucleus of this 17th- and 18th-century Spanish colonial town, which played a major role in the country's War of Independence, is the Jardin (the town square). It is rimmed with cantinas, boutiques, and galleries, musicians performing, and vendors selling just about anything (baskets, rugs, saddles, avocados, and pomegranates).

- Discuss activities: Canvass the group to find out what everyone wants to do; sit and talk, go to shows, spas, resorts, evening entertainment, cultural events, biking, hiking, and kayaking? Peruse this book for unique ideas.

- Search for accommodations: Ask everyone if they have friends or family members with a condo, beach house, mountain home, or apartment that your group can use or rent. Condos or homes are practical because they have kitchens and living rooms where you can all hang out. If your budgets permit, maybe you'd all prefer a spa vacation or a weekend at a fabulous resort.

- Research Special Events: In many descriptions in this book I've included the special heading "Event to fly in for" for many of the destinations. For example: a free Jazz Festival in Golden Gate Park in San Francisco or the South Beach Wine and Food Festival in Miami may be activities you'd enjoy.

- Commit with a deposit: Everyone contributes a non-refundable deposit of $100. This money goes into a "kitty," which the organizer can use for reservation deposits. When everyone has agreed on a date and committed money, there are fewer cancellations. Remember, the deposit is non-refundable.

Everything is within walking distance. Locals are friendly and follow an old-fashioned way of life that's worlds away from yours. The weather is typical of any paradise: sunny and 80 degrees. And the food is outstanding (and varied). It's no wonder that American, European, and Japanese expats call this home. You'll find the resident gringos here very social, welcoming you into their active and artistic community. On any given day there are photography, painting, and Mexican folk art exhibits. It's hard to avoid attending one of the many workshops and schools in town when everyone around you is writing a novel and learning digital photography. Perhaps what you need is a complete immersion: Spanish lessons to draw you into another world all together. San Miguel de Allende also possess a strong spiritual side; there's a collection of old churches, yoga and meditation studios, spas, hot springs, and a roster of religious fiestas to take your mind off life back home. And at 6,400 feet, the vistas of the surrounding semidesert mountains are a dose of medicine in themselves. Busy season here runs from mid-December to April and again from June to November, when the days are clear and sunny and the nights are cool. Fall and the month of May are considered the slower season, when it's easier to get a rental home or hotel room and workshops don't sell out as quickly.

TAKE A COOKING, LANGUAGE, OR ART CLASS

From a tiled kitchen inside a colonial hacienda estate in the countryside near town, join Mexican food scholar and chef Kristen West for cooking classes such as Salsa 101, Culinary History, Elegant Entertaining, and Holiday Entertaining. Learn how to create flavorful Mexican specialties with ingredients from the organic garden. Classes are demonstration as well as hands-on and include recipes and tasting of the foods prepared. (210-200-8758, www.casaluna.com). Take your bathing suit with you to swim in the pool or soak in the Jacuzzi after class. The Instituto Allende, the famous art center with Bachelors and Masters in Fine Arts programs, holds a series of workshops that include jewelry making, stained-glass window building, and painting (011-52-415-152-0190, www.instituto-allende.edu.mx). The school also teaches Spanish, but the Warren Hardy School is the preferred program in the expats' circle (011-52-415-152-4728, www.warrenhardy.com).

Ever since Visiting San Miguel the first time in the early 1970s I knew in my bones that this was a place where I wanted to live. Maybe it's something about the wonderful light which makes each vista a magical site to behold, or maybe it's the kindness and love of life exhibited by the local people who say good morning, good afternoon and good evening without fail to friends and visitors alike, or maybe it's the mysterious energy that seems to spark creativity and spontaneity more times than not. All I know is that my life has been enhanced by San Miguel and I'm forever grateful!

—Dianne Kushner, 50s, B&B Proprietor, San Miguel, Mexico

There's this country western song with the cowboy's lament of betrayed love. "He's got you, I've got Mexico." I know what he means: Years ago I went south to ruminate over a thorny romance, and ended up loving Mexico better than I loved the man. And I've still got Mexico.

—Lynn Ferrin, 60s, Writer, San Francisco, California

PAMPER YOURSELF

For only $55 you're indulged with a hot-stone massage, a foot reflexology massage, and an herbal footbath at the spa at Hospicio 46 Centro. An hour body massage is only $27 (www.smaspa.com). If you prefer something more active, Yogi Lydia Wong will help get the kinks out in a unique yoga dance class (305-735-3519, www.sanmiguelyoga.com). Hey, she's done it for Angelica Huston and Jack Nicholson. On the road to the nearby town of Dolores Hidalgo, today a town more famous for its scrumptious ice cream than its prominent role in the first Mexican Revolution, La Gruta awaits tired bodies with three serene thermal pools, one of which leads to a steamy stone grotto where the mineral spring bubbles forth (011-52-415-185-2099).

BEST TOURS

The two-hour walking tour led by English-speaking docents of the historic Centro of San Miguel departs at 10 a.m. Monday, Wednesday, and Friday from in front of La Parroquia, the imposing church in the heart of town that is one of Mexico's most famous. The two-hour Sunday House and Garden Tour visits three different San Miguel properties each week, departing at noon from the Biblioteca ($15; 011-52-415-152-4987).

BEST SHOPPING

For the colorful pottery that has made this region famous, visit Arcilla at Recreo 5A or Terra on Calle Cuadrante. La Fabrica de Aurora Arts & Design Center, an old converted textile factory at the northern edge of town, has become a showcase for local painters, sculptors, jewelers, and furniture makers. At San Miguel Shoes on Calle Reloj you can pick up a pair of "San Miguel Combat Boots," a rugged (but cool-looking) sandal designed especially for walking on the town's slippery cobblestones and stone-slab sidewalks. The bold colors of cotton Mexican apparel from Girasol Boutique Willa Mina on Calle San Francisco will liven up your wardrobe. At Productos Herco (aka Casa Cohen) you can buy all sorts of brass, bronze, and iron items, including door knockers, fireplace accessories, fanciful animal drawer pulls, and incredible sink fixtures. And Definitely Darla, at the corner of Recreo and Correo, sells jewelry you'll find you simply need to have: colorful beaded necklaces and silver bracelets with inlaid stones.

BEST DAY TRIPS
Less than two hours by bus or car will get you to more equally fascinating and historic towns with new streets to explore. Guanajuato is a particular favorites of mine. But if you're a hiker, you must make time for the trails of El Charco del Ingenio Botanical Garden, 225 acres of Mexican flora, a reservoir with migratory birds, and panoramas of the surrounding canyon. There's also horseback riding with Coyote Canyon Adventures into a surprisingly deep arroyo with a river at the bottom. Included are a campfire meal, hiking, and swimming ($75-125; 011-52-415-154-4193, www.coyotecanyonadventures.com).

BEST DINING
San Miguel is recognized as one of the best food destinations in Mexico, with many cuisines to choose from. For traditional Mexican food, premium steaks, lobster, jumbo shrimp, and frog legs, dine at EL CAMPANARIO, a half block from the square. El Campanario has live music every weekend, plus the archetypal restaurant waiters will give you an exuberant welcome at 34 Canal Street ($30-50 for two; 011-45-152-0775). Inside the Hotel Casa Linda, NIRVANA fuses Asian and Mexican cuisine and serves its modern dishes in a lovely old courtyard. 101 Mesones

---

San Miguel has all the history, culture, and art to make it worth a visit—but the truly amazing thing about getting into the life here is becoming part of the multilayered and eccentric expat community of artists, writers, bon vivants, and sophisticated world travelers. Among them are many wonderful, eccentric women from all over the world. They have come here to undertake a new adventure, to reinvent and revitalize their lives, and it's both invigorating and inspiring to meet them and witness their energy for each new day.

—Annie Reutinger, 50s, Businesswomen, San Miguel, Mexico

($50-75 for two; 011-52-415-150-0067, www.restaurantenirvana.com). With drop-dead views of La Parroquia, dine on light and fresh internationally inspired dishes on the rooftop of **LA CAPILLA**, considered to be town's most elegant restaurant and most expensive. 10 Cuna de Allende ($75-100 for two; 011-52-415-152-0698, www.lacapilla.com).

EVENTS TO FLY IN FOR

San Miguel de Allende doesn't need an excuse to have a fiesta; they have them all the time. The most famous is New Year's in the Jardin with fireworks; La Candelaria (dedicated to fertility) celebrates the arrival of spring in early February with a garden show and plant sale in the Parque Juarez; and in April Semana Santa (Holy Week) brings the most elaborate religious processions in Mexico to the streets of town. Then Dia de los Locos, a wild and crazy parade held the third Sunday in June, takes place. Independence Day kicks off at 11 p.m. on September 15 with an enormous gathering in the Jardin with fireworks all night long and into the actual day of the celebration. And an arts-and-crafts festival precedes Day of the Dead and All Saints Day on November 1 and 2. Despite their morbid undertones, these are joyful celebrations considered to be the most traditional of the Mexican fiestas dating back to the pre-Hispanics times.

PLACES TO STAY

The rooms and suites in Casa Luna's Pila Seca and Guebrada locations look like the setting of a romance novel: wrought-iron beds, stone hearths, exposed-beam ceilings, intimate lighting, vibrant colors, and views of lush gardens with fountains. Several rooms have private patios. Both the colonial-style Casa Luna Inns are so dramatic they have been featured in numerous books about Mexican style and architecture (starting at $160 including a five-star breakfast; 210-200-8758, www.casaluna.com). Villa Marisol, located farther from the square offers very reasonable rates for their simply decorated quiet rooms. 35 Pila Seca (starting at $115 including breakfast; 011-52-415-152-6685, www.villamirasolhotel.com). Or choose between 70 homes, from studios to seven-bedroom villas, managed by San Miguel House Rentals (starting at $650 for a week; 512-351-4304, www.san-miguel-house-rentals.com).

ONE CLICK AND YOU'RE OFF: Mexico Tourism Board (800-446-3942, www.visitmexico.com). For dependable online sources, visit Internet San Miguel (www.internetsanmiguel.com) or Portal San Miguel (www.portalsanmiguel.com).

Yoga Retreat

WILLIAM SEWALL HOUSE, MAINE

Numerous yoga retreats nationwide and in Canada nurse their guests back to physical and psychological health with a loving atmosphere, healthful food, and the simplicity of country living. Although only one option is described here, other excellent programs in North America offered in Chapter 9, Pampering Retreats.

The William Sewall House in Maine is a place of solace. The intention of its owners, husband-and-wife duo Donna Sewall Davidge and Kent Bonham, is to integrate yoga with nature: Close to the north end of Baxter State Park, 90 miles from Bangor (which many guests fly into), the property is surrounded by wilderness prime for biking, hiking, swimming, canoeing, or simply reflecting on your life. They also intend to continue the house's legacy as a place of healing. The Sewall House was built in 1865 by Donna's great-grandfather, an established nature guide in the late 19th century who had a lifelong friendship with Theodore Roosevelt, who came to Sewall House as a college student to recuperate from asthma. Today the building is on the National Registry of Historic Places. In 1997, the couple bought it and soon after opened it as yoga retreat from June 15 to Columbus Day (mid-October).

Donna, a certified Kundalini yoga teacher (her yoga video, "The Challenge," was a top-ten pick by *Yoga Journal* in 2000), brings to Sewall House 20 years of yoga and meditation experience and a masters in nutrition. She is adored for her patience, encouraging nature, willingness to learn, and friendliness. No matter if you're a veteran yogi or a beginner, there's a silencing of the mind and loosening of the body to be gained in Donna's daily yoga and meditation classes. Kent adds his passion for vegetarian cooking, yoga, and music. The twosome work very hard—and it shows—to maintain this house of five private, sun-flooded bedrooms, each with full-size antique beds and dainty wallpaper, and cozy communal areas (including a living room with a fireplace and a reading nook, and a large wraparound porch with chairs). On your journey back to spiritual or emotional health, you'll be joined by no more than ten fellow guests in search of the same curative effects. To fully reap the benefits of the retreat, five days are needed. In this time you'll feel yourself unwinding, the yoga renovating your body, the food cleansing you, and the meditation clearing your mind.

PEACE AND HEALING

When my five-year relationship dissolved and he moved back to Connecticut after living together for a year, I was shaken with sadness but felt some hidden hope emerging. I had to learn how to be single in New York again. To start the process of healing and renewal, I needed to get away to a quiet retreat, where other women could nurture me by listening. That's when I discovered Kripalu Center in Lenox, Massachusetts (see p. 177). It was perfect for me at that time of my life—within my meager budget, unpretentious, and the antithesis of the high-end, glitzy spas that double as adult day camps. Every morning for five days I awoke at 6 a.m. to the soothing sound of monks chanting in the chapel. I welcomed each new day with sunrise yoga, and went to all the classes. The sharing sessions, in particular, were very healing. Everyone talks about their problems and you get lots of support. By the end of my stay, I was so happy to take my own problems back, because everyone else's problems seemed very heavy duty. I didn't want to leave because I felt so secure. It wasn't just the yoga, it was the peaceful and healing environment.

—Valarie D'Elia, 50s, Broadcast Travel Journalist,
New York City, New York

A TYPICAL DAY

Guests rise (by choice) for an 8 a.m. meditation session, a silent sitting for never-evers to experts with Donna leading the way, held in the converted "shed," which they transformed into a lovely studio. Then at 8:30 a.m., for an hour and a half, she guides students through a Hatha/Ashtanga-based class. Incorporating the Vinyasa, poses that flow from one to another, it's an energizing practice. Over breakfast, options for the day's activities are discussed. There may be canoeing on Mattawamkeag Lake, hiking in Baxter State Park, biking around the country roads (with the bikes provided by the house or your own), or swimming among waterfalls ($20 per person

Two bouts of near-fatal oral cancer cost me more that half of my tongue and lower jaw and a host of body parts that were harvested for unsuccessful reconstruction attempts. Just as my official treatment ended, I began to exhibit symptoms reminiscent of the cancer, so I went to California to say goodbye to my sons. At the end of that visit, most of which I spent staring at the glistening San Francisco, my husband said "You've done more healing in ten days of looking at that water than you have in six months of treatment." He was right and I have been gazing at the water ever since. It's been thirteen years since the cancer from which I had a two per cent chance of survival and I know that the water has been a huge factor in my healing.

—Terri Tate, 60s, Registered Nurse, Sausalito, California

for arranged hikes or lake tours). It's all up to the guests, and if you want to stay at the house and read on the porch, you're free to do that as well. There's a "Midday Munch" around 1 p.m. And at 5 p.m. Donna leads a Kundalini class; this discipline focuses on energy work and breathing. Then some guests enjoy a sauna or a massage before sitting down with everyone for a family-style dinner.

SING YOUR HEART OUT
Mantra work is a big part of Donna's Kundalini practice. The afternoon class typically ends with 5 to 11 minutes of chanting, soothing and catchy songs composed by Kent and accompanied by him on the guitar. The harmony of the other voices in the class meld into an inspirational hymn, much like Gospel music. You'll find yourself abandoning your inhibitions as you begin to raise your voice after each verse. Kent plays again for shavasana, soothing you during this final, relaxing pose.

MEALS
Kent and Donna buy much of their produce from a local Amish community. Kent then whips up these fresh ingredients into absolutely delicious vegetarian meals that won't make you miss meat one bit. Breakfast may consist of homemade yogurt and granola and fruit. Then the Midday Munch may be leftovers or a salad. And dinner, served with salad and homemade whole-grain bread, is where Kent's ingeniousness

in the kitchen really shines: His coconut Thai curry, lentil stew, and an imaginative peanut stir-fry in a philo pastry are among guests' favorites. (You can now understand why some guests get excited about eating the leftovers at lunch.)

BEST HIKE
If you're looking for a confidence booster, take on one of the East's most infamous peaks. The highest in the state, Mount Katahdin in Baxter State Park has challenged day hikers, backpackers making their way along the Appalachian Trail, and teenage campers being dragged up by their counselors for ages. It's a majestic (and challenging) peak that just about stands alone, offering endless views to New Hampshire, the coast, and Canada. There are many ways to get to the top, but no matter which way you decide to go up, bank on needing the entire day with a very early morning start. And for those of you who can stomach it, the Knife Edge traverse along the peak truly lives up to its name.

BEST BIKE RIDE
There's very little traffic on the roads around Sewall House, making them prime for bikers wanting some peace and scenery. In particular, Belvedere Road is a seven-mile loop with jaw-dropping views of Mount Katahdin.

PAMPER YOURSELF
Exceptionally talented local masseuses apply a blend of Swedish massage and trigger-point techniques in a quiet room off the yoga studio ($80 for an hour massage). Off the studio you'll also find the sauna, which guests can use any time.

ONE CLICK AND YOU'RE OFF
The Sewall House (starting at $200 a night for single occupancy, including meals and two daily sessions of yoga and meditation; 888-235-2395, www.sewallhouse.com).

KRIPALU CENTER FOR YOGA AND HEALTH
Located in the Berkshires of western Massachusetts, this center offers year-round Healing Retreat packages beginning on Sunday, Monday, or Tuesday for three, four, or five nights. It is not available on weekends or during holidays. The Healing Retreat Package includes all meals, daily healing arts sessions, daily yoga, sauna, whirlpool, workout room, hiking trails and meditative labyrinth, aromatherapy, footwork reflexology, and other treatments. The three-night package starts at $610 for a dormitory

room with shared bath or $900 for a private room with private bath (866-200-5203, www.kripalu.org).

Key West

If a beach vacation (read: turquoise water, umbrella drinks, palm trees, and walking around in flip-flops) is your kind of therapy, look to the southernmost point in the United States: Key West, Florida. The 113-mile, 42-bridge highway just above the ocean that leads you to this edge of the world symbolically removes you from everything you need to leave behind at home. While Key West may no longer be the outpost Ernest Hemingway fell in love with—it has grown into a cruise ship destination—it's still possible to immerse yourself, in its nooks and crannies, in the far-flung, paradisiacal setting that put a spell on him. Forever gorgeous are the placid waters of the Gulf and Atlantic, tropical flora, and rich sunsets. The beach-bum, laid-back vibe that inspired Jimmy Buffett's "Margaritaville" even now pervades Key West here and there. A small and flat island town, Key West is ideal for women looking to escape on their own or in a small group. It's safe and easy to get around (bikes are the preferred mode). And ladies appreciate its flamboyant side: both the gay and Cuban and Caribbean populations here make it a festive, artistic, and welcoming community. High and lowbrow coexist contentedly in Key West. You can join the tourists at the bar of Sloppy Joe's (where Hemingway used to tie one on) to hear live music through the night on the bustling (and sometimes rowdy), mile-long Duval Street. Or attend a concert by the Key West Symphony Orchestra or a play at the Tennessee Williams Theater. And then on side streets you can discover unique galleries, restored Victorian homes, tin-roofed bungalows, local hangouts, and cute B&Bs. If solitude is what you seek, May and September are months that see fewer crowds and a summer-like climate. And if the energy and bustle of peak season allures you, Christmas through Easter may be when you'll want to make your therapy appointment with the beach.

BEST BEACH
Solitude seekers should head to Fort Zachary Taylor State Park. Its gorgeous big beach and waters that are home to live coral and multicolored fish give

you a better sense of privacy than elsewhere on the island. Glass-bottomed kayaks, snorkel gear, chairs, and umbrellas can be rented.

GO FOR A SPIN

Biking is the best way to get around Key West—and the most fun. Tour the streets of the historic Old Town district and its 19th-century clapboard homes and gardens with flowers wafting perfume. Paradise Scooter Rentals loans bikes and scooters for the day or week out of two locations in town. 430 Duval Street (305-293-1112) and 112 Fitzpatrick Street (305-292-6441, www.paradisescooterrentals.com). Get your hands on a copy of Sharon Wells's *Walking and Biking Guide to Historic Key West* to learn more about the area's architecture and legends.

PAMPER YOURSELF

The Indonesian-inspired SpaTerre opened at the Ocean Key Resort in 2005. Their signature Tropical Essence Massage incorporates a rare blend of oils from the Pacific islands (50 minutes for $110). At the very least, treat yourself to a manicure ($40). Or practice your downward dog with Yoga by the Sea on Higgs Beach next to the White Street Pier early in the morning or just before sunset ($10; 305-295-7017).

BEST SUNSET

About an hour before sundown, the 80-foot Schooner Liberty, a replica of the tall ships from the 1800s, sails out of the harbor and into the open sea. With a glass of wine in hand, you'll take in the sound of the wind in the sails as you watch the sun's descent. Even if you're solo, go! ($45 for an afternoon sail or $65 for the sunset sail; 305-292-0332, www .libertyfleet.com).

PACKING TIP

Remember that the luggage compartments on airplanes are not pressurized. Bottles with spray pumps often leak. To prevent messy leaks, fill bottles only three-quarters full and put each one in a plastic bag.

Root down to reconnect with your divine self. Take a moment to thank yourself for all your efforts and all that you do. Thank your body and acknowledge your body for all it does for you. Welcome the self back to the self with great respect and great love.

—Megan Scott, 50s, Ph.D. Exercise Physiologist,
Anasara Yoga Teacher

BEST DAY TRIP

You'll be whisked away to Dry Tortugas National Park, 70 miles west of Key West, in a seaplane gliding just 500 feet above the blue-green ocean. Below you coral atolls, marine life, and shipwrecks appear. When you arrive at arguably the country's most remote National Park, you can explore on your own this incredible refuge with migratory birds, fantastic snorkeling to wrecks and reefs in shallow water, and the behemoth Fort Jefferson (starting at $229 for a half day; 800-950-2359, www.seaplanesofkeywest. com). A 2.5-hour ride on the *Yankee Freedom II* ferry will also get you to Dry Tortugas ($149; 800-332-0013, www.yankeefreedom.com).

BEST DINING

In the open-air courtyard looking out onto Duval Street, dine on conch spring rolls and yellowtail snapper garnished with mango prepared by the distinguished chef at MANGOES. 700 Duval Street ($24-38; 305-292-4606, www.mangoeskeywest.com). Seafood lovers look to the waterfront CONCH REPUBLIC SEAFOOD COMPANY for freshly plucked-from-the-sea grouper, oysters, shrimp, and tuna. 631 Greene Street ($17-35; 305-294-4403, www. conchrepublicseafood.com). For flavorful Cuban cuisine, sit down for a meal of traditional dishes and homemade sangria at the family-run EL MESON DE PEPPE. Remember to order a side of platanos maduros (fried plantains). 410 Wall Street ($8-17; 305-295-2620, www.elmesondepepe.com).

EVENTS TO FLY IN FOR

You could find yourself rubbing elbows with writers such as Amy Tan, Calvin Trillin, and Tobias Wolf at the Key West Literary Seminar in January. Four days of seminars and panels are interpersed with intimate parties attended by literary greats. The Key West Craft Show in January and the Old Island Days Arts Festival in February bring artists and craftspeople to town. Think of it as Mardi Gras by the sea. Fantasy Fest runs for ten days at the end of October with outrageous masking and costuming, parties, pageants, drag queens galore, and a parade filled with enormous floats.

PLACES TO STAY

Two of the three buildings that make-up the Island City House Hotel in Old Town were built in the late 1800s. You'll appreciate their airy, sun-lit rooms and taking breakfast in the courtyard under the palms. 411 William Street (starting at $170 in low season to $399 in high season; 800-634-8230, www.islandcityhouse.com).

Set amid tropical landscaping in a former private estate, the Gardens Hotel offers the service and amenities of a boutique hotel at an affordable rate (starting at $200 in low season to $645 in high season; 800-526-2664, www.gardenshotel.com).

Overlooking the Gulf, the rooms at the Ocean Key Resort & Spa will lift your spirits with their Caribbean colors, Jacuzzi tubs, and large balconies. Across from lively Mallory Square, the hotel offers convenience and on-site pampering. Zero Duval Street (starting at $399 in low season, but pricey at $595 in high season; check out Web specials; 800-328-9815, www.oceankey.com).

ONE CLICK AND YOU'RE OFF: Florida Keys Tourist Development Council (800-527-8539, www.fla-keys.com).

Monterey Peninsula

⟶ CALIFORNIA ⟵

A road trip along the Monterey Peninsula is a prescription for a broken heart: It's a therapeutic and liberating journey on one of the most scenic roads in the world. Between Monterey and San Simeon on California's Coast Highway (Highway 1), you'll drive along a dramatic section of the West Coast, skirting the Santa Lucia Mountains, traveling through canyons, over towering bridges, and next to cliffs above the brilliantly blue Pacific. It's a thrilling joyride of picture-perfect sights that will make you want to roll down the windows and sing along with the car radio. In particular, the 90-mile stretch of the mostly undeveloped, rugged Big Sur coast is sure to snap you out of your woes. Escaping into the wilds of Big Sur via hundreds of miles of hiking trails, viewing whales, sea lions, and harbor seals in their natural habitat, and unwinding in the solitude are known to have a curative effect. It's what has lured artists, poets, and craftspeople since the early 1900s. This was John Steinbeck's back-yard; Henry Miller called it home; and countless other writers have lauded the beauty of Big Sur. They, as you will, found their inspiration here. Simply digging your toes into the sand of its beaches, listening to the pounding surf, spotting migrating whales, poking around tide pools, and cruising the coast in your car will do wonders for your state of mind. There's a delicate balance of all this natural wonder with civilization at its best. You'll love the bohemian flair of Big Sur, where you can find meditation workshops, yoga studios, spas, and quirky museums. Equally as charming are Monterey with its wharf and world-class aquarium, Pacific Grove and its Victorian homes, Carmel-by-

BREAKFAST ATTIRE

When we stayed at Ventana Inn & Spa along the Big Sur coast, we weren't sure what the dress code was for an 8 a.m. breakfast so we made sure we were presentable. We wore freshly pressed clothes that matched. Ha Ha! When we arrived at the breakfast room in the lodge, 99 percent of the guests were in PJs and bathrobes. Now we have stayed in resorts all around the world and this was a first for us. But then it was California, and we are quick to adapt. So the next morning we walked to breakfast in our robes and spa slippers. It was very liberating, if slightly cold when the wind blew.

Our next stop was the Boulders Resort in Arizona. It was 104 degrees by noon. So we got up early and went to breakfast in our robes, of course. What a mistake. The resort doubles as a golf/tennis country club and the local residents turned out in their "Sunday best," literally, and we were in our robes.

—Kathleen Casey, 50s, Teacher in the South Bronx,
South Salem, New York
—Vicki Mendelson, 50s, Advertising Executive,
South Salem, New York

the-Sea's galleries and shopping, and Pebble Beach with its renowned golf resorts. You can dine alfresco in adorable cafés, peruse art and shops, and stay in hotels that range from rustic lodges to posh resorts—and never stray too far from the beauty and ruggedness of the Monterey Peninsula. While late April through September is the busiest season, October coincides with Indian summer, making it just the right time for a quiet getaway.

BEST HIKING

The trails at Point Lobos State Reserve (just south of Carmel) take you to white-sand beaches, rocky headlands, coves, and tide pools. Since the park sticks out into the Pacific, the views are frequent and staggering. Inspired by the poet's quote about Big Sur, the Robinson Jeffers Walk led by Stephen Copeland of Big Sur Guides & Hiking brings you to secret spots with verdant canyons, waterfalls, and coastline. Or his three-hour meditation walk may be the cure for what ails you: It starts off with yoga and then takes you on a hike in silence (starting at $75, lunch included; 831-658-0199, www .bigsurguides.com). Farther south from Carmel on Highway 1, Julia Pfeiffer Burns State Park maintains short trails to spectacular scenes, among them an 80-foot waterfall tumbling from granite cliffs and a perch over the sea for spotting migrating gray whales (January, March, April, December).

GIDDY-UP

With Molera Horseback Tours you can treat yourself to a dreamy trot on the white-sand beach with the sounds of the ocean and the sea air washing over you. They also offer rides at dusk (starting at $50; 831-625-5486, www.molerahorsebacktours.com).

MUST-SEE MUSEUMS

Get up close to sharks, sea otters, and sea turtles in the magnificent Monterey Bay Aquarium (831-648-4888; www.mbayaq.com). The Henry Miller Memorial Library in a redwood grove in Big Sur displays the work of the author, who lived in Big Sur for 18 years, and is home to a sculpture garden and an outdoor stage for performances (831-667-2374; www.henry miller.org). Insert yourself into the world of beloved, Nobel Prize-winning writer John Steinbeck at the National Steinbeck Center in his hometown of Salinas (www.steinbeck.org). And near San Simeon, 98 miles south of Monterey, the palatial estate of newspaper mogul William Randolph Hearst welcomes visitors to view the 65,000-square foot Mediterranean-style mansion with a 5,000-volume library and lush botanical gardens. Five different tours are offered, including an evening tour that is truly special. Reservations are required (800-444-4445, www.hearstcastle.com).

MOST SCENIC DRIVE

The private 17-Mile Drive through Pacific Grove and Pebble Beach winds along the Pacific, through the 8,000-acre Del Monte Forest and famous golf courses, among them the prestigious Pebble Beach Golf Links. Pull into turnouts to take in sights such as Bird Rock (which attracts lots of shorebirds, sea lions, and harbor seals) and a sandy beach, and for picnic areas on the ocean. Lunch fixings can be picked up at the gourmet Pebble Beach Markets across from the whitewashed Lodge at Pebble Beach or the Pacific Grove entry gate.

PAMPER YOURSELF

At Ventana Inn's Allegria Spa, splurge on their signature aromatherapy massage in the Zen Garden ($120 for 50 minutes). The property is perched 1,200 feet in the clouds above the Pacific and is considered to have the premier accommodations on the Big Sur coast (starting at $485; 831-667-2331, www.ventanainn.com).

BEST DINING ALONG THE COAST

With a glass of pinot noir and a precipitous view of the ocean 800 feet below, you'll sit down to filet mignon, swordfish, or the popular Ambrosia burger at NEPENTHE, a redwood and glass building suspended over the coast on the property that Orson Welles bought for Rita Hayworth in 1944. (Later, Henry Miller lived here.) Highway 1, Big Sur ($13-35; 831-667-2345, www.nepenthebigsur.com).

BEST TOWN FOR STROLLING

On the shady streets of Carmel, you'll swear you ended up on the pages of *Hansel and Gretel*. Adorable courtyards and cottages draped in vines house shops with wondrous finery: Fine local wines, rare collectibles, jewelry, fine art, monogrammed linens, and European lingerie. Seek out the Carmel Art Association: It's a mini-museum of local artists' work and is Carmel's oldest gallery. The turquoise waters and sugar-white sands of Carmel City Beach are never more than a few blocks away. See Chapter 10 for more about Carmel as a getaway for retail therapy.

EVENTS TO FLY IN FOR

Highway 1 lends itself to the Big Sur International Marathon in April. Nearly 3,000 runners participate in this scenic 26-miler (a half marathon is held in October), and hordes of spectators line the course to cheer them on. In May the Big Sur Experimental Music Festival welcomes more than 70 musicians redefining the parameters of modern music.

When you've been dumped you should to go to a place where you can talk your heart out. You need to have instant access to other people who will listen to you, but not couples, just human beings. For example, go on a walking trip where you schmooze your head off. During an organized walk you have your choice of lots of ears. On a bike trip you are alone, but when walking or even doing volunteer work you tend to talk to other people a lot. So you can take your dump and dump it on some else. You hope you'll meet someone whose dump is worse than your own.

—Phyllis Stoller, 60s, Founder Women's Travel Club, New York City

---

June's Big Sur Hidden Gardens Tour gives you access to a half dozen home gardens. Then the Carmel International Arts Festival takes over Main Street during a weekend in September. And in the same month, the world's longest running jazz festival, the Monterey Jazz Festival, brings hundreds of musicians to seven stages for three nights and two days.

PLACES TO STAY
Beneath skyscraping redwoods 25 miles south of Carmel, the historic Big Sur River Inn keeps 20 unfussy rooms with balconies looking onto the Big Sur River (starting at $115 in low season; 800-548-3610, www.bigsur riverinn.com). Sixteen snug, Mongolian-style yurts make up the ten-acre Treebones Resort, a rustic hideaway 65 miles south of Monterey. The cozy and furnished yurts overlook the ocean or the mountains and fill you with a sense of serenity. Rates include a tasty waffle bar each morning (starting at $185; 877-424-4787, www.treebonesresort.com).

FOR A SPLURGE AND A VIEW
Ventura Inn & Spa, Highway 1, Big Sur, offers 62 rooms with fabulous ocean or forest views. It is perched 1,200 feet above the Pacific in a quiet wooded area with panoramic views of a 50-mile expanse of the Pacific Ocean. The atmosphere and service are low-key. Ask for a room that has been recently renovated. Look for special winter rates (starting at $350; 831-667-2331, www.ventana inn.com).

ONE CLICK AND YOU'RE OFF: Monterey County Convention and Visitors Bureau (888-221-1010, www.montereyinfo.org).

CHAPTER EIGHT

Home & Garden Tours

~ LAVERNE'S STORY ~

"Everyone should experience the hospitality and history of the South at least once," says 80-year-old Laverne, who has lived in California her entire life. During World War II Laverne was part of a theatrical troupe that entertained GIs at military bases throughout the South. For decades she regaled her daughter, Renee, with her memories: antebellum mansions, pastel-colored row houses, live oaks draped with Spanish moss, palm-tree-lined promenades, swirling fans, and jasmine-scented air. Laverne often talked about revisiting the South with Renee to see the old piazzas, gaslit alleys, and cobblestone streets.

But her husband's health declined. Just when Laverne's duties as caretaker seemed overwhelming, Renee found a way to give her mom a break. She booked a trip to Charleston and Savannah during the annual spring Festival of Houses and Gardens. Before anyone could protest,

Renee organized helpers to take care of dad and she packed her sunscreen, sandals, and sketchbook.

To make it easy for both mother and daughter, they joined a lively group of ladies on a women-only tour. "We soaked up the gentile ambience, strolled the narrow streets admiring the 18th-, 19th- and 20th-century American architecture, and viewed the private gardens and interiors of Charleston's finest homes," says Laverne. Charleston, Beaufort, and Savannah are places where you won't find a Starbucks or McDonald's in the center of town. Instead they dined on low country cuisine: crab cakes, hush puppies, and fresh collard greens. "We really loved the seafood and many Southern dishes," adds Renee, "as well as the smiling waiters who served with a 'Yes, ma'am.'"

For many years Renee had participated in the annual Garden & Architecture Tour in her community in Marin County, California. "It is always interesting to visit homes and gardens in other parts of the country. The southern gardens are a bit more formal than the Californian gardens, and the antique-filled homes are decorated much more elaborately than our casual Californian homes," says Renee. "Traveling in the South also gave us a deeper sense of American history and the very important roles women played during the Civil War and in plantation life."

"Although I love my husband very much," Laverne points out, "it was great to have an escape from being a 24-hour caregiver, and our trip was especially memorable because I shared it with my daughter." Renee agrees, "I always love an adventure with my mother. We have traveled in many areas of the world and have wonderful memories to share."

Charleston

⮞ SOUTH CAROLINA ⮜

The country's best-kept colonial city, Charleston makes for an excellent destination to have your female tribal gathering because it's such an easy city: easygoing, easy to get around, easy to plan a visit to, and easy to please everyone in your group. Founded in 1670 on the coast of South Carolina, Charleston is a "living museum." It has an astounding assortment of colonial, federal, Gothic Revival, and art deco architecture, the oldest museum in the country, and the earliest churches in the South. (For this reason as well as its early religious diversity and tolerance, it also carries the designation of the Holy City.) Charleston brims with old piazzas, secrets alleys, cobblestone streets, historic B&Bs, and antebellum mansions and plantations. Gardens in the

To sit in the shade on a fine day and look upon verdure is the most perfect refreshment.

—Jane Austen

---

historic district continually burst with blossoming flowers no matter the season. Waterfront Park, a palm-tree-lined promenade with benches and fountains and views of the boat-filled harbor, makes for prime people-watching and time for unwinding. And what the local restaurants can do with a few simple ingredients (shrimp, oysters, rice, okra, and green tomatoes) will excite every palette among you: Here southern cooking means a mingling of French, Spanish, African, and Caribbean cuisines. The warmish climate year-round makes Charleston a great place to gather anytime (if humidity and 90-degree days are a killer for any of you, you better avoid summer). Whereas with a big city you have to concern yourself with a strategy and getting your money's worth, in Charleston you'd be hard-pressed to find a hotel, activity, historical site, or restaurant that won't knock everyone's socks off—even your finicky sister's.

BEST HOME AND GARDEN TOURS (OPEN ALL YEAR)
Drayton Hall is the oldest (ca.1738) U.S. preserved plantation house open for public viewings. The main house is an amazing example of Georgian-Palladian architecture and the grounds—125 acres of earth and old oak trees—will take make you feel as if you're Scarlet O'Hara. 3380 Ashley River Road (843-769-2600, www.draytonhall.org). The Aiken-Rhett House is the jewel in the crown of Charleston. Built in 1818, this urban villa still contains some of its original artifacts; go into the rooms and take a peek. You'll be both amazed and impressed by our foremothers. 48 Elizabeth Street (843-723-1159, www.historiccharleston.org). If you're interested in seeing a well-preserved, "still working" plantation, visit Boone Hall. The grounds envelope you with space and beauty; the architecture, gardens, horses, and world's longest oak-lined avenue are truly impressive. There also well-preserved slave cabins. You're transported back to the Old South. 1235 Long Point Road, Mt. Pleasant (843-884-4371, www.boonehallplantation.com).

BEST PRIVATE HOME AND GARDEN TOURS (ONCE A YEAR)
One of the most celebrated annual tours of the area is the Fall Tour of Homes and Gardens that allows you to visit remarkable 18th-, 19th-, and 20th-century American architecture. This tour is open for five weeks, normally from the end of September through October. 147 King Street

FAVORITE PUBLIC GARDENS
IN THE WEST

To find public gardens across the United States, contact the American Public Gardens Association at www.aabga.org.

- HUNTINGTON BOTANICAL GARDENS
  Best time to visit: Winter and spring.
  Approximately 150 acres.
  Don't miss the Japanese Garden January to May.
  1151 Oxford Rd., San Marino, California
  www.huntington.org

- SAN FRANCISCO BOTANICAL GARDEN
  AT STRYBING ARBORETUM
  Best time to visit: Spring through summer. 55 acres.
  Ninth Avenue at Lincoln Way, San Francisco, California
  www.sfbotanicalgarden.org

- THE LIVING DESERT
  Best time to visit: November through April.
  1200 acres.
  47-900 Portola Avenue., Palm Desert, California
  www.livingdesert.org

- VANDUSEN BOTANICAL GARDEN
  Don't miss the Rhododendron Walk.
  5251 Oak Street., Vancouver, B.C.
  www.vandusengarden.org

- UNIVERSITY OF WASHINGTON
  BOTANICAL GARDENS
  Best time to visit: Spring through summer. 230 acres.
  2300 Arboretum Dr. E., Seattle, Washington
  www.uwbotanicalgargens.org

(843-722-4630, www.preservationsociety.org). The Festival of Houses and Gardens ushers in spring (mid-March to mid-April) with extensive tours of the interiors and gardens of some of Charleston's finest homes. This festival has been running for more than 60 years. 40 East Bay Street (843-723-1623, www.historiccharleston.org).

BEST NEIGHBORHOOD FOR STROLLING

On the streets of the old French Quarter you go back to a different era: The gaslit alleys and cobblestone streets are reminiscent of when the French Huguenots occupied Charleston in the 17th century. Today, dozens of galleries, with over a hundred artists' work, have taken over the district. The first Friday in March, May, October, and December, Art Walk keeps 30 of the galleries open in the evening with artists in attendance and wine and cheese.

MUST-SEE MUSEUMS

America's oldest museum, the Charleston Museum, reconstructs the history of the city and the South. The museum also maintains two lovely 19th-century homes that can be visited with a combination ticket. And the special exhibitions at the Gibbes Museum of Art are clever assemblages of American art with a low-country influence.

TAKE A CLASS

An informal class is an excellent way to spend time together: Learn something new (about each other, too) and have a few laughs. In their modern, well-stocked kitchen, Charleston Cooks has an extensive lineup of small culinary classes taught by the finest chefs in the South. Check their schedule to see who's cooking up what when you're in town. The store is worth a visit too if you're forever in search of new kitchen gadgets (from $25; 843-722-1212, www.charlestoncooks.com).

BEST SHOPPING

Seven days a week, local vendors set up their wares at the City Market, a covered (but open-air) bazaar of jewelry, candies, tapestries, and sweetgrass basket weavers fashioning items for sale. There are also permanent shops to browse, among them ice cream parlors scooping delicious flavors.

FOR GARDEN LOVERS

At the Magnolia Plantation meander over seven bridges, through a topiary garden, a quarter-mile maze (a replica of Henry VIII's), and through the

> **To me a lush** carpet of pine needles or spongy grass is more welcome than the most luxurious Persian rug.
>
> —Helen Keller

rooms of the main house abundant with Early American antiques. This quintessential southern plantation is considered to be the oldest major public garden in America. It's a great place to lose yourself for awhile (from $7; 800-367-3517, www.magnoliaplantation.com).

BEST NIGHTLIFE

Charleston has a thing for rooftop bars. And the Market Pavilion Hotel has the best one. It's the newest hotel in the city, and its harbor and skyline views from the poolside Pavilion Bar are spectacular. Its list of fancy drinks (among them the Paviliontini) is surprising affordable for a luxury hotel (877-440-2250, www.marketpavilion.com).

BEST DINING

There's nothing terribly extravagant about the much talked-about HOMINY GRILL. (Most dishes are under ten bucks.) But the creativity that goes into their shrimp Creole, pork ribs, chicken 'n a biscuit, and fried green tomato BLT make up for its lack of sophistication. 207 Rutledge Avenue (843-937-0930, www.hominygrill.com).

For a classier atmosphere, try SLIGHTLY NORTH OF BROAD, affiliated with Charleston Cooks. It has elegantly updated low-country standards and an impressive dining room with an open kitchen. In season, try the soft shell crab sandwich. 192 East Bay Street ($15-40; 843-723-3424, www.mavericksouthernkitchens.com).

BEST DAY TRIP

A 30-minute drive to Kiawah Island delivers you to ten miles of dune-fringed Atlantic coastline and five award-winning golf courses. Turn your visit to Charleston into a beach vacation and stay at one of the island's resorts or rent an oceanfront home for the group.

EVENTS TO FLY IN FOR

The special events at the Charleston Food & Wine Festival in March are loads of fun. Aside from demonstrations, seminars, and book signings by chefs, there's the entertaining gospel Sunday brunch and Blues, Brew and BBQ. Also in March, the Historic Charleston Foundation holds its annual fund-raiser, the monthlong Festival of Houses & Gardens. Over a hundred owners of historic properties all over the city open their doors and gardens to visitors. Beginning Memorial Day weekend and running for 17 days, Spoleto Festival USA, the satellite of the acclaimed Italian arts festival, stages opera, jazz, theater, and orchestral, chamber, and contemporary music performances in old churches, theaters, and parks all around downtown—a tradition that started in 1977.

WHERE TO STAY

In the center of the historic district, the three-story, antebellum Kings Courtyard Inn has elegantly appointed rooms with canopied beds, Persian rugs, and original architectural features. 98 King Street (starting at $130; 866-720-2949, www.kingscourtyardinn.com).

For more B&Bs in the historic district like this one, visit the Charming Inns of Charleston website (www.charminginns.com). Check their "Hot Deals" section for affordable room rates.

The Charleston Convention and Visitors Bureau has put together girls getaway packages with the Wild Dunes Resort, 20 minutes from downtown on the Isle of Palms. Perks such as massages, champagne, and rounds of golf are combined in reasonably priced packages. The beachfront property consists of two 18-hole golf courses, a tennis center, spa, restaurants, and pools. It's a quiet oasis close to the city that gives you time together in private.

ONE CLICK AND YOU'RE OFF: Charleston Area Convention and Visitor Bureau (800-774-0006, www.charlestoncvb.com).

Newport

⤳ RHODE ISLAND ⤳

Newport has it all: Stunning coastal scenery, amazing architecture, and an exciting downtown waterfront. Founded in 1639, Newport is full of historical sites as well as hundreds of preserved colonial houses and buildings. During the 19th century Newport was the place for wealthy Americans to vacation, a fact marked by the mansions they built along Bellevue Avenue. Today this beautiful tree-lined street is peppered with Gothic Revival cottages, shingled houses, and luxurious French- and Italian-style palaces.

Newport is also famous for sailing; it's been host to the America's Cup, and its harbor is a regular resting point for boats from around the world. It's a great place from which to take a chartered sunset cruise: The views are postcard perfect. This is also a place of festivals—food, music, beer, and more food—all year-round. You're never short of things to do, and the people are so warm in spirit that you won't want to leave. Somehow this city feels like a home away from home.

BEST HOME & GARDEN TOURS (OPEN ALL YEAR)

Rough Point Mansion, the late estate of heiress and avid art collector Doris Duke, is the place to view her famous international art collection and fine furnishings. The mansion is impressive in its own right as are the grounds, both of which overlook the ocean. 680 Bellevue Avenue (401-849-7300, www.newportrestoration.org). Belcourt Castle, completed in 1894, was designed in the style of King Louis XIII of France. This gilded age architectural masterpiece has been lovingly preserved—its Gothic ballroom, French oak staircase, and Russian chandelier with 13,000 prisms are a few of the many treats you'll encounter on your visit here. 657 Bellevue Avenue (401-846-0669, www.belcourtcastle.com). The Breakers is an amazing Italian Renaissance–style palazzo based on the 16th-century palaces of Genoa and Turin. The 70 rooms in this mansion boast beautiful Parisian furnishings, and there's a 45-foot-high central great hall. 44 Ochre Point Avenue (401-847-1000, www.newportmansions.org). Marble House, completed in 1892 and modeled after the Petit Trianon at Versailles, contains 500,000 cubic feet of marble. It has an unusual Chinese teahouse that sits on a surrounding seaside cliff. 596 Bellevue Avenue (401-847-1000; www.newportmansions.org).

BEST PRIVATE HOME & GARDEN TOURS (ONCE A YEAR)

One of the best-kept secrets is the Secret Garden Tour, which takes place over two days in both the fall and spring (dates change annually so check the website for specific dates). During these tours the gardens of some of Newport's most exclusive and private houses on Bellevue Avenue are opened to the public. 33 Washington Street (401-847-0514, www .secretgardentours.org). In December the city hosts a candlelight tour of 18th- and 19th-century private homes. The tours run from 4 to 7 p.m. (401-293-0965, www.christmasinnewport.org).

BEST WALK

Cliff Walk is a 3.5-mile path that travels between the well-maintained grounds of Newport's mansions and the awe-inspiring Atlantic. The path begins at the western end of Easton's Beach at Memorial Boulevard and carries on southward. The level of the trail is easy to moderate. (401-849-8048, www.cliffwalk.com).

BEST SHOPPING

Newport has lots of quaint specialty stores; Bellevue Avenue and Thames Street are full of them. Try Grenon's of Newport for fine watches. 210 Bellevue Avenue (401-846-0598). Stardust excels at antiques, especially Harmony Kingdom figurines, which are made from crushed marble. 359 Thames Street (877-782-7378, www.stardustri.com). Frazzleberries is fantastic for country home furnishings and gifts. 475 Thames Street (401-841-9899, www.frazzleberries.com). Bowen's Wharf, which has been around since the 18th century is today home to more than 20 high-end clothing, galleries, jewelry, and gift shops, such as Terra Zapato, Geoclassics, and Terrida. Bowen's Wharf (401-849-2120, www.bowenswharf.com).

BEST TOUR

Enjoy a glass of champagne and appetizers as you watch the sunset from the serenity of a boat in Newport's beautiful harbor. Here you'll experience a different view of the city and horizon's edge. Gansett Cruises, Bowen's Wharf Ferry Landing (401-787-4438, www.gansettcruises.com).

BEST MUSEUM

The award-winning Museum of Newport History is a good way to get to know the city. Its collection is a fascinating array of artifacts from the 17th century up through the 20th. There's also a museum store. 127 Thames Street (401-841-8770, www.newporthistorical.org).

BEST DAY TRIP

Tiverton Four Corners is a colonial-style village made up of 18th- and 19th-century buildings. Some of the houses and shops have gambrel roofs and cedar-shingle siding. There's an old stone wall and plenty of working farms surrounding the village. The 21.5-mile (37-minute) drive from Newport in itself is a treat.

BEST RESTAURANTS

TUCKER'S BISTRO is the best place to eat in Newport. It feels like a Parisian bistro from the 1930s. The atmosphere, décor, and food all complement each other. Try the skillet roasted littleneck clams, seared Long Island duck breast, and for dessert the Tahitian vanilla crème brûlée. 150 Broadway ($21-30; 401-846-3449, www.tuckersbistro.com). **SPARK** is a bright, fun place with live Latin music and inventive food. The grilled scallop and asparagus salad is tasty, as is the grilled Atlantic salmon with quinoa. You can bring your own wine here, which adds to the festive feel of the place. 12 Broadway ($18-28; 401-842-0023, www .sparkrestaurantandcatering.com). **EVERYDAY GOURMET** is a great place for a low-key breakfast or lunch. The food is superb, healthy, and hearty. The omelets are incredible, and the corn chowder will fill you up and keep you warm throughout the day. 677 Thames Street ($5-16; 401-619-1580, www.everydaygourmetnewport.com).

WHERE TO STAY

Castle Hill Inn and Resort sits on a stunning 40-acre peninsula. The rooms are spacious and tastefully decorated. The views are incredible. You'll feel relaxed before you even step into your harbor/beach house or Swiss-style chalet. 590 Ocean Drive (starting at $259; 888-466-1355, www.castlehillinn.com). Vanderbilt Hall is a modern mansion with a great private roof deck and secluded garden terrace. There's a fantastic spa and the hotel's welcoming reading areas are perfect for a little afternoon rest and relaxation. The rooms are enormous. There's also an indoor pool and attractive bar. 41 Mary Street (starting at $159; 401-846-4255, www.vanderbiltrc.com).

Those who dwell among the beauties and mysteries of the earth are never alone or weary of life.

—Rachel Carson

EVENTS TO FLY IN FOR

The Newport Mansions Wine and Food Festival is a delicious event with wine auctions, a Sunday jazz brunch, galas, and great food. Held the last weekend in September, this is a festival your palate won't want to miss. Rosecliff and Marble House (401-847-1000, www.newportmansions.org). If you enjoy beer and/or German culture then the Columbus Day weekend International Oktoberfest is just up your street. Oh to rejoice to all things hop-like! Newport Yachting Center, 4 Commercial Wharf (401-273-7310, www.newportfestivals.com). The Newport Music Festival (July) brings in classical musicians for concerts set within the city's famous mansions (401-849-0700, www.newportmusic.org).

ONE CLICK AND YOU'RE OFF: www.gonewport.com or www.destination newport.com.

Pasadena

⤳ PASADENA, CALIFORNIA ⤳

Pasadena's motto is "simply more"; a description that couldn't be more true. This city has everything and then some—gorgeous houses and gardens, world-renowned art centers and museums, tremendous restaurants, extensive shopping, and endless outdoor activities. Aesthetically it is a striking place with the San Gabriel Mountains looking down on it, constant blue skies, a Mediterranean-style climate, and arching architecture. When you're immersed in one of Pasadena's historically designated districts (there are 16!), you'll find it hard to believe that downtown Los Angeles is only nine miles away. But it is and you will know it when you walk through Pasadena—a place that prides itself on being pedestrian-friendly, a place that embraces its artistic roots and limits skyward development. Pasadena feels European but with an American essence. It is a good balance of Old World meets New.

BEST HOME AND GARDEN TOURS (OPEN ALL YEAR)

Descanso Gardens is a real treat. With an iris garden, bird observatory, lilac garden, enchanted railroad, Japanese garden and teahouse, as well as a heritage house and exhibit to name but a few of the garden's unique destinations, this place has a little something for everyone. It's also a great place for kids. 1418 Descanso Drive, La Canada (818-949-4200, www .descansogardens.org). The Tournament House and Wrigley Gardens is the headquarters of the Pasadena Tournament of Roses Association. Formerly owned by chewing-gum giant William Wrigley, Jr., the Italian Renaissance-style mansion retains much of its original splendor with a marble staircase and fine wood paneling. Wrigley Gardens' 4.5 acres of floral displays include 1,500 different kinds of roses. Free public tours of the house are given on Thursdays, February to August, from 2 to 4 p.m. The gardens are open to the public 24 hours a day, year-round. 391 S. Orange Grove Boulevard (626-449-4100, www.tournamentofroses.com). The Gamble House is an affectionate salute to arts and crafts architecture. The house will inspire and intrigue. Tours available Thursday through Sunday, 12 to 3 p.m. 4 Westmoreland Place (626-793-3334, www.gamblehouse.org).

BEST PRIVATE HOME AND GARDEN TOURS (ONCE A YEAR)

The Spring Home Tour (last Sunday of March), allows you to visit some of Pasadena's most impressive early 20th-century houses. Tours themes change every year (626-441-6333, www.pasadenaheritage.org). During the last weekend in April many residents of the 1900- to 1930s-style homes in Bungalow Heaven, Pasadena's first landmark district, open their doors for the annual Bungalow Heaven Home Tour (626-585-2172, www.bungalowheaven. org). The Garfield Home Tour takes place in the second oldest historic neighborhood in Pasadena—Garfield Heights. This self-guided tour allows visitors to view up to seven gorgeous historic houses that range architecturally from Victorian to Spanish Revival (626-388-2174, www.garfieldheights. org). During the first weekend in December the must-see Holiday Look-In Home Tour—now in its 41st year—gives visitors the opportunity to view four area homes artfully decorated by professional florists with a holiday season theme (626-793-7172, www.pasadenasymphony.org).

BEST SPAS

The spa at the Langham, Huntington Hotel & Spa is renowned for pampering its guests. You will find everything here to make you feel a million miles away. Perfection! 1401 S. Oak Knoll Ave. (626-568-3900, www.pasadena.langhamhotels.com). The Cote D'Azur Spa is pure relaxation. Try the 15-minute, $30 Tea Break—shoulders, neck, hands, and feet—treatment. This is a great place to unwind. 74 N. Fair Oaks Avenue (626-396-3030, www.cotedazurspa.com).

MUST-SEE MUSEUMS

The Huntington Library, Art Collections, and Botanical Gardens beckon visitors from far and wide to its feast of art and culture. There are three art galleries and a library that is home to an amazing collection of rare books and old manuscripts. The gardens are a pleasure to get lost in—207 acres of awe-inspiring beauty. This world-class collection will make any jaw drop. 1151 Oxford Road, San Marino (626-405-2100, www.huntington. org). The Norton Simon Museum shows a wide range of art from the Renaissance to van Gogh, Picasso, and Rembrandt. Sculptures are on exhibit here too. Wednesday to Monday 12-6 p.m; Fridays 12-9 p.m. 411 Colorado Boulevard (626-449-6840, www.nortonsimon.org).

EVENTS TO FLY IN FOR
The Pasadena Art Weekend (second weekend in October and March) is a free extravaganza of eye-opening art and culture (626-795-9311, www .pasadenaartweekend.com). The Tournament of Roses (New Year's Day) is nearly three hours of floats, fun, and festivities. This televised annual event reaches over 40 million Americans; it's how many bring in the New Year, in person or via their TV (626-449-4100, www.tournament ofroses.com).

BEST DINING
A favorite for celebrations is **BISTRO 45** with its French/Californian menu and its numerous awards. It has cozy dining alcoves and maplewood floors. Its menu includes pomegranate martinis, grilled sea scallops, and an organic white peach melba with ginger ice cream that will bring you to tears (good ones). This is the place for a special night out. 45 S. Mentor Avenue ($19-34, 626-792-2676, www.bistro45.com). For a cozy, low-key Mexican restaurant with super food, atmosphere, and prices, go

TRAVEL TIPS

The climate is perfect year-round in Pasadena, so any time of the year is a good time; although it does get very crowded for the Tournament of Roses on New Year's Day. Pasadena is 28 miles from Los Angeles International Airport, 15 miles from Bob Hope/Burbank Airport, and 37 miles from LA/ Ontario International Airport. Allow a good three days to visit Pasadena.

where the locals go: YAHAIRA'S CAFÉ. Located in the Playhouse District of Pasadena, it serves delicious snapper burritos and tortas (Mexican sandwiches)—try the *de lomo con aquacate* (pork, tomato, and avocado). This is a great destination for breakfast or lunch; both are served seven days a week. Dinner is served Thursday through Saturday. 698 E. Colorado Boulevard ($8-11; 626-844-3254, www.yahairascafe.com). For superb Indian cuisine and atmosphere, book a table at RADHIKA'S, where all of your senses will be catered for. The tandoori paneer tikka, lamb shank kashmiri, and lemon saffron biryani are almost too good to be true. On weekend nights the restaurant has traditional Indian folk music and belly dancers. 140 Shoppers Lane ($12-18; 626-744-0994, www.radhikas.com).

BEST PLACES TO STAY

They really know how to look after their guests at the Westin and have one of the best bars I've ever scene in a hotel, with a library and scrumptious margaritas. This is a very special place. The rooms are modern and comfortable, and many have views. Be careful though: You're charged for using the bottled water in your room, and you must pay extra for Internet use and car parking. 191 North Los Robles (starting at $169; 626-792-2727, www.starwoodhotels.com). If you're looking for something more decadent, try the Langham, Huntington Hotel & Spa where you'll have more than 380 guest rooms and suites, as well as cottages, to choose from. This is the place for tennis, swimming, spa treatments, and five-star dining. Just try not to think about how much it's going to cost you. 1401 S. Oak Knoll Avenue (starting at $269; 626-568-3900, www.pasadena.langhamhotels.com).

ONE CLICK AND YOU'RE OFF: www.visitpasadena.com.

Alexandria

ঙ VIRGINIA ঙ

Alexandria is well known for its charm. Founded in 1749, 50 years before Georgetown (now an area of Washington, D.C.), the city is steeped in history. It is in fact on the National Register of Historic Places due to its abundance of 18th- and 19th-century homes, town houses, and historic attractions. Be sure to walk its tree-lined streets where oaks and magnolias gracefully stand and squirrels leap from branch to branch; admire the federal and Georgian architecture where red, blue, and green doors, polished door knockers, boot scrapes, and cobblestone streets create a feeling that this modern place still has one foot stuck in the past. And then there are the locals; you know Alexandria is special when you see how crazy the residents are over their dogs and how they indulge in their love of sweets. Dog-friendly watering bowls sit in front of hotels, restaurants, and shops; and the dogs are (weather permitting) dressed in fashionable coats, sweaters, and collars. The sweet shops are heavenly and there are plenty of them to admire along with ice cream parlors, bakeries, and cupcake stores. Alexandria is a very walkable city with neighborhoods like Old Town, filled with historic houses; so put on your walking shoes, ladies, and bring your cameras because this is a city to remember.

BEST HOME AND GARDEN TOURS (OPEN ALL YEAR)
Completed in 1753, the Carlyle House went from being a political and social nest to a major military headquarters during the French-Indian War. The house is unique because it is the only 18th-century Palladian-style house in all of Alexandria made of stone. Adult tickets are $4; closed Mondays. 121 N. Fairfax Street (703-549-2997; www.nvrpa.org/parks/carlylehouse). George Washington's Mount Vernon Estate and Gardens was home to George and Martha Washington and is the most visited historic estate in America. The 500-acre property has more than 20 18th-century structures and 50 acres of 18th-century gardens. You'll also find the tombs of George and Martha Washington, Washington's greenhouse, a memorial to the accomplishments of 18th-century slaves, and a museum. Adult tickets are $13. 3200 Mount Vernon Memorial Highway (703-780-2000, www.mountvernon.org).

BEST PRIVATE HOME AND GARDEN TOURS (ONCE A YEAR)
The Annual Tour of Historic Alexandria Homes takes place at the end of September. You'll visit seven houses located in the heart of Old Town; they are some of the city's most beautifully restored and decorated. Tickets are $30 in advance; $35 on tour day. 221 King Street (703-683-5544, www.thetwig.org). During the last weekend in November/first weekend of December, Alexandria hosts the Holiday Scottish Walk with a fabulous holiday designer tour that allows you to visit the seasonally decorated homes of local residences. Advance purchase adult tickets are $30. 101 Callahan Drive (703-549-0111; www.scottishchristmaswalk.com). Virginia's historic Garden Week has been going strong for 76 years. Around the third week of April the gates of more than 250 gardens, houses, and historic landmarks open to the public for tours. It's

considered "America's largest open house" and is truly a spectacular event. Ticket prices range from $10 to $35. 221 King Street (703-838-4200, www.vagardenweek.org).

BEST PUBLIC TRANSPORTATION
There's a free trolley that meets you at the King Street Metro Station; jump on and off with the audio tour and map. It runs from 10 a.m. to 10 p.m. daily.

BEST SHOPPING
The Old Town boutique district has a collection of 19 unique fashion, beauty, jewelry, children's gifts, and home specialty stores; here you'll find merchandise that you cannot find at the mall (www.oldtownboutiquedis trict.com). Imagine Artwear will open your eyes, and it's worth the splurge for one-of-a-kind imported silk jackets, scarves, dresses, and jewelry. 1124 King Street (703-548-1461; www.imagineartwear.com). At Hysteria you need to make an appointment for the boutique's private salon where, in addition to its elegant, designer clothing selection, you'll relax with a cocktail and hors d'oeuvres. 125 Fairfax Street (703-548-1615, www.shophysteria. com). Diva Designer Consignments is a great place to find secondhand designer clothing, shoes, and accessories. Don't be surprised if you find that Chanel suit or Prada handbag you always wanted. 116 S. Pitt Street (703-683-1022, www.divaboutique.com).

TRAVEL TIP

Water taxis cross the Potomac River to the National Harbor and Gaylord National Resort. You can also take a water taxi to Georgetown and Mount Vernon (your taxi fare will include entrance to Mount Vernon). Travel time from Dulles International Airport to downtown Alexandria is 23.3 miles, a 37-minute drive. From Washington National Airport to downtown Alexandria, it's 7.3 miles, an 11-minute drive. And from Baltimore-Washington International Airport to downtown Alexandria, it's 40.1 miles, a 53-minute drive.

BEST TOUR

The Ghost and Graveyard Tour takes you back to 18th-century Alexandria when your guide tells you stories about the good old haunted days. It's a one-hour tour that spans six spooky Old Town blocks. Adult tickets $10. 221 King Street (703-519-1749, www.alexcolonialtours.com/graveyard .html).

BEST MARKET

The nation's oldest continuously operating farmers market takes place every Saturday, year-round, from 5:30 a.m. to 10:30 a.m. on Market Square. Among other things, you'll find handmade jams, floral wreaths, hand-knitted scarves, and baby clothes. 301 King Street (www.alexandriava.gov/market).

BEST MUSEUM

The Stabler-Leadbeater Apothecary Museum was in nonstop operation from the time of George Washington until the 1930s. It is one of the oldest pharmacies in the nation, and there are more than 8,000 objects on display, from pill rollers to hand-blown medicine bottles. There's even an archive of journals, letters, prescriptions, and formula books. 105-107 S. Fairfax Street (703-838-3852, www.apothecarymuseum.org).

BEST RESTAURANTS

The MAJESTIC CAFÉ has the best table-side prepared Caesar salad that I've ever tasted. It's made with white anchovies packed in vinegar so there's no salty flavor. The scallops with avocado mousse and the chestnut soup are pure bliss. The décor is American classic and the family-style Sunday dinner is something special. 911 King Street ($20-27; 703-837-9117, www.majesticcafe.com). VERMILLION offers contemporary American and has a wine list that would impress the most conservative sommelier. It has great signature dishes, like Virginia rockfish with black couscous and Pennsylvania duck with pommery mustard. The pecan pie with cherry ice cream and chocolate sauce will make you cry, it's so good! 1120 King Street ($20-36; 703-684-9669, www.vermilionrestaurant.com).

WHERE TO STAY

Located in the middle of all the action is my favorite hotel, the Monaco. This small boutique hotel (with 241 rooms) evokes southern Virginian hospitality; the lobby is a dramatic Adriatic blue and the rooms follow the color scheme of the Union soldiers: brown, black, cream, red, and orange. All rooms have flat-screen TVs and the hotel is pet-friendly. During weekdays you have access to complimentary bikes and wine tasting. 480 King

Street (starting at $189; 703-549-6080, www.monaco-alexandria.com). The Morrison House is a classic redbrick building with 45 stylish rooms in Old Town. In-room spa treatments include massages and facials, and you can even choose from a variety of pillow sizes. (Pet friendly.) 116 S. Alfred Street (starting at $199; 703-838-8000, www.morrisonhouse.com).

EVENTS TO FLY IN FOR

The Scottish Heritage Festival and Harbor Parade of Lights rings in the holiday season with more than a hundred clans marching and playing bagpipes, dressed in their kilts and clan tartans. During the evening more than 60 decorated boats float past the waterfront in a festival of lights. There's also a Christmas marketplace and Celtic concert. 101 Callahan Drive (703-548-0111, www.scottishchristmaswalk.com).

ONE CLICK AND YOU'RE OFF: www.visitalexandriava.com.

Litchfield

⟡ CONNECTICUT ⟡

You feel as if you're stepping back in time in Litchfield, one of the best preserved 18th-century villages in all of the United States. Litchfield is a sleepy little town without billboards, burger chains, or bright lights. It's the type of place to stroll through, the type of place that makes you wonder if our modern way of living is truly better than that of the past. Litchfield is and remains a community that exists within its original colonial-style buildings; even the town's businesses work out of these architectural masterpieces. The town's centerpiece is a pretty lawn called the Green. Litchfield is nestled in the hills of Northwestern Connecticut, about two hours from Manhattan.

HOME AND GARDEN TOURS

The best time of year to visit Litchfield's gardens is in the spring or summer, when the flowers are in full bloom. All of the gardens are a 20-minute drive apart, so depending on your enthusiasm you can easily visit two or three in a day. The Glebe House dates back to 1750. This former minister's house, or glebe, is now a museum with fine period paneling and furnishings from the era. The first American bishop of the Episcopal Church was elected here in 1783. The house's garden is the only one in the U.S. designed by Gertrude Jekyll, the greatest modern gardener of the 20th century. 49 Hollow Road, Woodbury (203-263-2855, www.theglebehouse.org). The Kellogg Estate in Derby has 120 different hybrid tea rosebushes. In December local garden clubs decorate rooms within the estate, which the public can view free of charge (203-734-2513, www.ct.gov). Bellamy-Ferriday House and Garden in Bethlehem has a parterre garden shaped as a serpentine with a circular pool and statue. There's an 18th-century apple orchard on the premises and apparently one of the country's largest collections of rose literature. 9 Main Street, Bethlehem (203-266-7596, www.ctlandmarks .org/bellamy.php). Topsmead is an English Tudor-style house set on 511 acres of open land. The grounds are open year-round. Guided tours run June through October. Two miles east on Route 118, east on E. Litchfield Rd., then south on Buell Rd. (860-567-5694, www.friendsctstateparks .org/parks/topsmead).

MUST-SEE GARDEN CENTER
White Flower Farm is five acres of gardens and greenhouses; it is Eden at your fingertips. Route 63, Litchfield (800-503-9624, www.whiteflowerfarm.com).

ANTIQUE LOVERS
Jeffrey Tillou on the Green specializes in American furniture and 18th- and 19th-century American folk art. 33 West Street (860-567-9693, www .tillouantiques.com).

GREAT PHOTO OP
The First Congregational Church is beautiful; its charming white steeple sits proudly on Litchfield's Green. You may visit most days until 5:30 p.m. (860-567-8705, www.fcclitchfield.org).

EVENTS TO FLY IN FOR

The Annual Litchfield Open House Tour prides itself as being "the oldest continuously running house tour on the East Coast." Tours allow you to visit country estates and the town's North and South Streets (860-567-9423, www.litchfieldct.com/cjr/tour). In fall, the autumn colors in the Litchfield Hills are breathtaking. Go for a scenic walk, drive, or bike ride through the falling leaves.

TAKE A WALK

The 4,000-acre White Memorial Foundation and Conservation Center is Connecticut's largest nature preserve. There are 35 miles of hiking trails. Visitors also like to cross-country ski and camp here. This is a great place for bird- and butterfly-watching. You never know what kinds of animals you'll cross paths with. One of the preserve's best trails goes along the Bantam River to a mile-long elevated boardwalk that circles around Little Pond. This path takes you through a forest and wetland environment. It's a gentle three-mile hike and you may even see a turtle or two along the way (860-567-0857, www.whitememorialcc.org).

BEST DINING

One of Litchfield's hot spots, the **WEST STREET GRILL** certainly lives up to its reputation as THE place for fine food, ambience, service, and celebrity sightings. This stylish but relaxed American bistro cooks up local and organic produce, fish, poultry and game. There are no daily specials because co-owner James O'Shea believes every dish is special. And it's true; this place makes the best Maryland-style crab cakes I've ever tasted. And the deserts—the bread and butter pudding will transport you to O'Shea's native Ireland. It really is that good. Reservations strongly recommended. 43 West Street ($22-37; 860-567-3885, www.weststreetgrill.com). Another downtown local favorite is the **VILLAGE RESTAURANT**. Its unpretentious, casual atmosphere, and great homemade soups, sandwiches, and pizzas are a winning combination. There are heartier meals to choose from as well; you can't go wrong with the roasted lean pork with sautéed onions and a garlic aioli. 25 West Street ($16-35; 860-567-8307).

EAT AL FRESCO

When the weather is nice **THE HOPKINS INN RESTAURANT** is the place to be. The food here is Austrian-inspired, the waitresses wear dirndls, and next door there's a vineyard. The flagstone terrace sits in the shade of a giant chestnut tree, and you have a spectacular view of Lake Waramaug. Entrées include such classics as wiener schnitzel, rahmschnitzel, and backhendl with lingonberries. For desert try the Toblerone sundae or strawberries Romanof. 22 Hopkins Road ($21-27; 860-868-7295, www.thehopkinsinn.com).

PLACES TO STAY

The Old Riverton Inn is quaint, friendly, and heavy in atmosphere. It was built in 1796 as an old stagecoach stop and is now a listed historic building. Surrounded by rivers and forests, this inn is a great place to chill out. Locals love the inn's restaurant which serves great duck and fish entrées. Rates range from $100 to $160. 436 East River Road, Riverton (starting at $99; 860-379-8678, www.rivertoninn.com). If it's indulgence you're after, book a room at the popular Mayflower Inn and Spa, a 25-minute drive from downtown Litchfield. This inn is nestled within 58 acres of rhododendrons, cypresses, and blue atlas cedar trees. Here you can wander through winding gardens or take in a game of tennis on the private courts. There are four spa treatment rooms and two good restaurants on the property too. 118 Woodbury Road, Route 47, Washington (starting at $520; 860-868-9466, www.mayflowerinn.com).

ONE CLICK AND YOU'RE OFF: www.litchfieldhills.com.

CHAPTER NINE

Pampering Retreats

Traveling doesn't always mean relaxing. In fact, traveling can be the oppo-site of any word meaning to unwind. Planning, packing, camping, cooking, mapping routes, it's all rather exhausting, isn't it? There are times when "going somewhere" means relaxing and pampering ourselves, taking care of our bodies and minds. And at a destination spa these are your only responsibilities. It's worth the splurge!

You may ask yourself, why go away when you can go to a day spa in a mall for a massage or a facial? Destination spas, like those featured in this chapter, are actually health retreats designed for a "tune up" over three or more days. Unlike day spas, they combine pampering treatments with moder-ate to hard exercise, healthy eating, and a comfy bed at the end of the day, all in a gorgeous setting. Experts also educate you about new ways to improve your diet, nutrition, skin care, and mental and physical health. I've selected retreats where the long-term benefits are more than skin deep. So invite a girlfriend and make an investment in a destination spa and yourself.

I go away every year with two close girlfriends, whom I met in the newspaper business when we were all in our 20s. We've helped each other through love affairs, divorces, kids' dramas, sick mothers, and job disasters. One year when we got together we were all going through different crises so we decided to pamper ourselves. We met in the Napa Wine region in the small town of Calistoga, known for its spas. We soaked in warm water, challenged each other to sit in the mud baths, got massages and pedicures, and took turns assuring each other we would survive the child or the man who was dragging us down. We came away confident that even if other people disappointed us in our lives, we still have each other.

—Susan Swartz, 50s, Journalist, Author, *The Juicy Tomatoes Guide to Ripe Living Over 50*, Sebastopol, California

MARY'S STORY

Some women, like Mary, become spa enthusiasts reluctantly. There was a time when the very word "pampering" put her off. In her 50s, she was the executive director of a large foundation, happily married, mother of three boys, three step-children, and busy with 11 grandchildren. Three years ago her husband, Steve, overheard one of her close friends rave about her annual trips to Rancho La Puerta in Mexico, so he gave Mary a week at the spa for her birthday (with the friend's group). Mary was not pleased and she fought the idea for six months.

"I felt it was all too self-indulgent. I didn't want to do this for myself," Mary explains. "But he kept saying, 'go, you'll have fun,' and he was so persistent." Steve enlisted her three sons to chip in and encourage her too. The pressure was on, and how can you say "no" to the four most important men in your life? "So I thought I might as well go," she says.

Mary was surprised by what she discovered about herself during a week at the spa. "It was the first time in my life that I had no responsibility for anyone else," Mary recalls. "I only had to decide what walk to take, what class to attend, and what part of the buffet to eat from. My experience was very holistic. It touched every part of my soul, body, and mind."

Who would have guessed that Mary, who loves lazy weekend mornings, would get up every day at 5:45 a.m. for a hike? The group dynamics and enthusiasm carried her through and took her to levels she never imagined. After her morning hikes, she chose between a stretch class, yoga, Pilates, or weight training. Afternoons were at a slower pace, with nurturing activities: meditation, a gentle stroll through the organic garden, a walk through the labyrinth, cooking classes, or creating an herbal wreath. She had a massage or beauty treatment every day, but those were only a small part of the whole experience. In the evenings resident artists talked about their work. After one lecture on photography, she was hooked, so she continued the class all week. "Photography stirred a new passion within me and since I've returned home, I use my camera all the time to capture the beauty in my world," says Mary. "I have a new hobby."

She only knew one woman in the group when she arrived, but remarkable friendships began to form over the first organic lunch. In the relaxed atmosphere of the ranch, they wore sweat pants and no make-up. All superficial formalities dropped away. "I deepened the bonds with NEW friends, as well as with myself," she says. "At meals we talked about everything from the very deeply spiritual to problems with our families to mundane topics like our make-up and hair. Often, in our bathrobes and slippers, we continued talking late into the night."

Rancho La Puerta changed Mary's life the way a normal vacation doesn't. She returned stronger physically and has incorporated new healthy habits into her life. She altered her diet—less protein, more fresh fruit and vegetables. At the ranch, Mary was attuned to nature—observing the world around her. By continuing yoga, stress control, and a more active lifestyle, Mary brought that peace back home with her. "My experience was not about pampering in the sense of massages and facials," says Mary, "but in what I feel is the true sense of pampering—nurturing your soul."

New Age Health Spa

⤳ NEW YORK ⤶

Two hours north of New York City and about a thousand miles away from reality, New Age Health Spa caters to guests seeking a holistic overhaul. Although it's best known for its dedication to detoxification and spiritual well being, hippie-dippy the New Age Health Spa is not. On 280 acres in the Catskills, this comfy camp for adults accommodates 72 guests at a time in five recently remodeled, whitewashed cottages. (Fortunately, there are no TVs or phone in the rooms.) Its spectacular Cayuga Yoga and Meditation Center, constructed of gorgeous Western Redwood, houses a grand stone fireplace, heated floors, and a large golden statue of Buddha. The calming effects of this structure will turn anyone into a yoga and meditation convert. Your time here is supplemented with the spa's detoxifying mud wraps, multidisciplinary massages, and gentle facials. Many of their fruits and veggies come from an on-site greenhouse and orchard—their juice-fasting program is popular with those looking to jump-start a diet. But the food is anything but Spartan. Its impressive "eco-adventure" program includes an outdoor climbing and ropes tower, hiking the surrounding 3,000-foot peaks, cross-country skiing, or snow-shoeing. And there's a lengthy menu of fitness classes that includes the latest exercise trends and a calendar filled with make-you-smarter evening lectures on all sorts of topics.

LAY OF THE LAND

Cayuga Yoga and Meditation Center, spa, fitness complex, indoor and outdoor swimming pools, whirlpool tubs, hiking trails, Alpine Tower, tennis courts, a sweat lodge, a labyrinth, and a bird sanctuary.

THE FOOD

The menu here is mostly vegetarian with vegan options as well as fish and chicken entrées available at dinner. Their almond-crusted trout, the strawberry and spinach salad, and the homemade Spa Pizza (loaded with veggies) are worth mentioning. The salad bar is a marvel, replete with mounds of salad greens, veggies, and sprouts from the property's three greenhouses and garden. The chefs also use this bounty (including the fruit from the orchard) in New Age recipes. Those interested in their cleansing, detoxifying, juice-fasting program take three meals consisting of fresh raw juice, which may be supplemented throughout the day with spring water and lemon, potassium broth, or herbal tea.

Make an appointment with your hairstylist right before you leave on vacation and tell her/him that you'll be traveling. A good travel haircut makes a big difference—you don't want to spend lots of time in the bathroom blow-drying your hair every day. Remember your hair is something you wear with every outfit and every pair of shoes. To feel good about yourself, your hair needs to look great. It's about pampering yourself.

—Jane Hope Gordon, 60s, Owner, Salon des Artistes,
Sausalito, California

GET SMART

Experts are invited to speak on topics such as "Getting Out Of Your Head: How To Relax & Stop the Chatter" and "Relax Your Back." Lectures on how to eat better are held every day at 2 p.m. And cooking classes are held every Tuesday.

Also, don't miss out on visiting the greenhouse. Stop in on your own or take the tour on Thursdays.

GET YOUR HEART RATE UP

If you need motivation and creativity out of a fitness class to take your mind off the pain (and boredom) of working out, there are classes such as toning with the body ball, Pilates, interval training, belly-dancing, step aerobics, an abs workout, and cardio boxing.

GET OUTDOORS

Start the day with a brisk, two- to three-mile group walk at 7 a.m. Then head out to Minnewaska State Park and other more challenging terrain in the Catskill Mountains for a few hours of hiking with a provided backpack and lunch. The spa's own Alpine Tower, a 50-foot climbing wall with three sides of rope ladders, swinging logs, a seesaw, and a wall of handholds to get you to the top, redefines your definition of adventure (and gives you an amazing workout). It's a safe and controlled environment that let's you push your fears and test your problem-solving skills. May through October, you can sign up for weekly climbs. If there's snow on the ground, take out a pair of snowshoes or cross-country skis for a winter workout.

ZEN OUT

Those in search of a fit mind should commit to their "spiritual program": a head-to-toe, inside-and-out course of therapy that includes cardio, yoga, meditation, and lectures, much of it held in the sun-drenched Cayuga Yoga and Meditation Center. (You can just attend the individual classes.) And in the tradition of the Native Americans, the spa has built its own sweat lodge out of willows for guests to use from May through September. When water is thrown on fire-heated stones, the round hut fills with steam, purifying towel-wrapped guests through sweat.

BEST SPA TREATMENTS

In the Healing Stone Massage, smooth hot stones are applied to the back and used to knead away tension, aromatherapy is worked into it, and there's a focus on balancing your body's energy centers or chakras, which can get clogged when we are stressed or fearful ($200 for 100 minutes). And

TUNED TO HEALTH

When I was in my 20s my mom introduced me to her favorite spa in Utah, a special place that she had visited five times with her girlfriends. She wanted me to understand the importance of taking time off and focusing on my health. At the time, she didn't realize she was giving me a precious gift: a safe place to go and recoup in future tough times. I needed that refuge several years later after a traumatic car accident in which my oldest friend and I were hit as pedestrians. Her severe injuries in the near-death accident left her in the hospital recovering for months, where I supported her—the best I could. My world spiraled down and turned negative, and all my healthy habits vanished. So I decided to set aside five days to return to Red Mountain Spa to rest, eat right, exercise, and gain strength. I ate at the communal "Captain's Table" every night with different guests who were very low key and approachable. I talked to everyone. Slowly I let myself feel the pain and sadness of the past year, which helped me get over the trauma. The other guests were not focused on superficial beauty, they were at the spa to push themselves a little physically and refocus their lives on their health, and I did the same. The whole experience was extremely nurturing. It jump-started a more balanced life: I got motivated to exercise more, and I eventually lost 30 pounds. It's not hard to set aside several days to fine-tune your physical and mental health, and it's worth every second.

—Sally Garbarini, 30s, Film and Theater Producer,
San Francisco, California

the Paradise Mountain Rain treatment is an indulgent recipe for fatigued skin: deep-sea salt scrub, mud wrap, Vichy shower, and Pomegranate and Cranberry Body Butter (110 minutes $200).

CALLING ALL BIRDERS
The Bald Eagle Watch, which is held every Sunday and Thursday during the months of April through October, brings guests to see as many as 20 baldies that stop in the area for a visit.

ALONE TIME
If you're in need of silence and time to yourself, strike out on the property's five miles of maintained trails over streams, through deep woods, and past a pond and gazebos.

SPECIAL PACKAGES
Every month, a weekend is devoted to a special practice of yoga (Vinyasa, Power, or Hatha) with a visiting, well-known yogi. Four seasonal juice fasts are held a year as is a yoga and juice fast weekend once a year. Every November and May, a Birding Weekend is centered on watching the bald eagles with local experts from The Audubon Society. There's also a cooking workshop in early December that prepares you for healthy holiday entertaining. And various spa packages are always offered.

WHAT'S INCLUDED
Accommodations, three meals a day, and unlimited classes and lectures. Weekly rates start at $1,634; mini-weeks (Sunday to Friday) start at $1,229 with two qualifying treatments for free; and nightly packages start at $209. Prices fluctuate by season (peak rates are in effect Fridays, Saturdays, and holidays as well as every day from July through September).

ONE CLICK AND YOU'RE OFF: New Age Health Spa (800-682-4348, www.newagehealthspa.com).

Deerfield Spa

ᘒ PENNSYLVANIA ᘓ

The supportive atmosphere and simplicity of country living are what draw women to the Deerfield Spa in East Stroudsburg, Pennsylvania, an hour-and-a-half drive from New York City. Guests tend to be laid-back, comfortable in sweats and very friendly. It's a nurturing place for learning how to do yoga or Pilates, or getting the support and encouragement you need to kick-start a diet. (The Deerfield Spa is so good at monitoring your caloric intake it tricks your body into feeling amazing on 1,500 calories a day.) Plus, it's very affordable. In the middle of the forested Pocono Mountains, the property consists of 12 acres with a sprawling green lawn, flowerbeds, and grazing deer. It's open from April to October and at maximum capacity with only 33 guests, who share a big old Victorian house and an annex cottage, both with cheerful wallpaper and wicker furniture. Although sitting on their wraparound porch reading a book could be all the pampering you need, there are incredible facials and massage to splurge on. The founder's hospitality has been passed on to her daughter, who continues the legacy of the 25-year-old business of treating guests like family. The waiters call you by your name, and the therapists have been there for so long that return guests get to know them. Think of it like staying at a friend's weekend home (assuming your friend is a chef and a masseuse).

LAY OF THE LAND

Fitness equipment room, studio, a heated outdoor pool, a gazebo-enclosed hot tub, sauna, spa treatment rooms, and a sports court for basketball, volleyball, and tennis.

THE FOOD

Meals here are calorie counted and served restaurant-style. You select your three meals the day before. Dishes include chicken, fish, and veggies and there's always lots of fresh salad with homemade dressings. In particular, the creamy lentil soup, turkey Reuben, and spinach quiche are outstanding. All you get is 500 calories, but you'll be amazed how far that will get you. On Sundays, there's a buffet—and "Watch the Calories" signs on tables to keep you in check.

GET YOUR HEART RATE UP

The most fun you'll have in a pool since you were a kid is a water fitness class. There's a "noodle" class that uses a buoyant prop with exercises—it's a blast. There is also instruction in the pool with weights. In the heat of the day, getting into the water is bliss. Also, if you've never tried Pilates (been too intimidated?), they give you the chance to learn on mats as well as on the reformer (a rack that is utilized in the exercises).

THE BEST TREATMENTS

The facials here, for whatever reason, are amazing. Perhaps it's because their aesthetician, who has magnificent skin herself, customizes the treatment to your skin type. Try the micro-dermabrasion ($95 for 25 minutes). Or she may recommend the LumiLift procedure for you, which sounds more invasive than it really is: It's like getting a face-lift and chemical peel in one from a couple of flashlights ($175 for 50 minutes). It's been called "lazy person's yoga," but the effects of a Nuat Thai massage make limbs feel longer, muscles feel like dough, and joints loosen. Buddhist monks originated this practice 2,000 years ago. Using pressure and compression, the therapist gently folds your body into postures on the floor and stretches you never thought you could do ($75 for 50 minutes). And the warmed-stone massage is always a favorite ($85 for 50 minutes).

NIGHTLY ENTERTAINMENT

The spa goes out of its way to make sure you have a laugh here and there. In the evenings, line dancing, an astrology seminar, and bingo are offered once a week, in addition to seminars on health and yoga classes.

GET OUTDOORS

Join one (or all) of the eight hikes that are offered every week with a naturalist. They are divided into three different levels and there's typically a two-hour morning hike and a two-to-three-hour afternoon hike. Bring your hiking boots or sturdy sneakers to walk the famed Appalachian Trail, which runs through this region, and on the 13 miles of trails in the Pocono Environmental Education Center.

ALONE TIME

Take in the splendor of the lush Poconos and read a book on the wrap-around porch of the main house.

WHAT'S INCLUDED

Accommodations, three meals a day, and unlimited classes and workshops. Weekly rates start at $850; mini-weeks (Sunday to Friday) start at $800. Weekly guests are treated to a 50-minute Swedish massage; mini-week

My friends are my estate.

—Emily Dickinson

guests receive $150 toward personal services. Special discounts on opening and closing weeks are offered.

ONE CLICK AND YOU'RE OFF: Deerfield Spa (800-852-4494, www .deerfieldspa.com).

Lake Austin Spa Resort

ᔕ TEXAS ᔕ

Lake Austin Spa Resort is a Garden of Eden for those seeking the convenience of a resort with pampering and gourmet food but with a rustic twist. Thirty minutes from downtown Austin, the resort is situated in Hill Country, the central region of Texas with semi-arid rolling hills colored with oaks, junipers, and mesquites. This is the panorama one wakes up to each morning on Lake Austin, a reservoir on the Colorado River, threaded with mist on its mirror-like surface at dawn. Deer roam the property, waterfalls flow through terraced gardens, blooming vines drape over arbors, clay pots burst with flowers and fruit dangles from fig, peach, and pear trees for plucking. The architecture is best described as an uberdecadent ranch style. Every one of the 40 rooms and suites has a private patio and offers either lake views or looks out onto Japanese meditation gardens. (But the fluffy down comforters and the in-room lavender bath and body products could be what wins you over.) The multimillion dollar, 25,000-square foot Lake House Spa was completely renovated in 2004. The mostly wooden interior is inviting and includes some divine features such as outdoor treatment areas, spots with cushy seating for curling up and reading, and a lovely outdoor pool with cabanas. Their extensive offering of classes addresses the hottest workout trends (BOSU, anyone?), and incorporates the old favorites too, while the spa practices ancient remedies (Cupping?) on down to the good old American manicure. There are informative and practical lectures to round out your time here. After such full days you will be relaxed, believe it or not, and amply rewarded with exquisite meals that you won't believe aren't naughty. Read on to find out what BOSU is.

LAY OF THE LAND
The Lake House Spa, two outdoor pools, an open-air indoor Junior Olympic-length pool, whirlpool, the Treehouse fitness complex, a yoga dock, and walking trails.

THE FOOD

The breakfast, lunch, and dinner menus here read like the table of contents in a Julia Child cookbook. At first glance you may wonder what wild mushroom pizza with truffle oil, duck confit with pickled red onion and Roquefort crumbles, or bleu cheese stuffed beef tenderloin with blackberry demi-glace will do to your figure. Thankfully, Chef Terry Conlan's looking out for you: Each entrée is limited to only five grams of fat per serving. You also have the option of eating at the spa's Aster Café. And there's always room service.

GET SMART

As part of the resort's Discovery Programs, guest lecturers give evening talks on such subjects as Texas Hold 'Em, aromatherapy, knitting, and astronomy. Chef Conlon also shares his kitchen wisdom in a few classes a week. And the weeklong Culinary Experience invites different guest chefs to conduct wine classes, cheese tastings, and hands-on cooking classes. (There is no extra fee for this workshop.)

GET YOUR HEART RATE UP

Getting fit never was this fun. There is salsa aerobics, spinning, Pilates, and kickboxing among many other activities. You can also finally find out what BOSU is: a half-dome object you balance on while performing exercises. Can you say core strength?

GET OUTDOORS

Rise early for a refreshing paddle on Lake Austin before breakfast: You'll find it glassy, silent, and stained with the glow of the rising sun. Follow it up with a short hike through the neighborhood, or a nearby preserve, or sign up for the Mount Bonnell Expedition, which takes you up the 785-foot peak for views of Town Lake and downtown Austin.

PACKING TIP

I can't stress this enough—leave your expensive jewelry at home. Why take a chance? Fake pearls or inexpensive costume jewelry will do the trick.

ZEN OUT

Daily yoga, meditation, and tai chi classes are held. If the weather is nice, a wooden dock over Lake Austin serves as the sun-drenched studio for a variety of yoga classes.

BEST SPA TREATMENTS

Intrigued by Eastern medicine? There's an assortment of fascinating and ancient practices to relieve stress and achy muscles. Manaka Tapping Treatment involves a wooden peg placed on an acupuncture point that is gently tapped to relieve tightness or pain (50 minutes for $155); or Calming Cupping, which applies glass cups to draw fresh oxygen-rich circulation into muscles ($90 for 25 minutes). The resort's Healing Garden grows many of the herbs the spa uses, such as eucalyptus, lavender, and sage, which are then utilized in the Gifts of Our Garden's body scrub, massage, and body wrap in an outdoor tent ($315 for 100 minutes).

ALONE TIME

Relaxing under a cabana by the outdoor Palm Pool makes for a great rest. Pre- or post-treatment read a book, listen to your iPod, or just zone out as you sink into the chaise lounges with afghans in the spa's Blue Room. You may prefer its outdoor screened porch, with a row of rockers looking out to the lush gardens and pools.

SPECIAL PACKAGES

The Spa Refresher includes a $330 spa-and-fitness allowance (starting at $1,830 per person for three nights), whereas the Ultimate Spa Pampering package includes $645 of spa-and-fitness services (starting at $2,070 per person for three nights).

WHAT'S INCLUDED

Accommodations, three meals a day, and unlimited classes and lectures. Three-night packages start at $1,555 per person, and weekly rates begin at $3,070 per person. For last-minute specials, check the website.

You don't get to choose how you're going to die or when. You can only really decide how you're going to live.

—Joan Baez

ONE CLICK AND YOU'RE OFF: Lake Austin Spa Resort (800-847-5637, www.lakeaustin.com).

Red Mountain Spa

⤳ UTAH ⤲

No matter what initially brings you to Red Mountain Spa in Utah's Mojave Desert in the first place, having exhilarating adventures in its glorious landscape is inevitable. It is an adventure spa, after all. The unique geology of spires, domes, caves, and undulating canyons is painted in reds, pinks, and oranges. Trails fans out from the resort for biking and hiking; its backyard is Snow Canyon State Park, and two national parks are down the road. Beginner outdoorswomen are in good hands here: There's a staff of experienced guides, and Red Mountain Outfitters is a shop frequented by locals for the selection of outdoor gear. The resort can accommodate 174 guests at a time, making it the second largest destination spa in the country. Guests are housed in adobe-like buildings that blend into the canyon walls—every room and Villa Suite has a view. In 2006 the Sagestone spa and salon debuted in a renovated, three-story, geodesic-domed building, where its long list of luxurious services helps guests unwind from their hectic lives. And Red Mountain Spa pays respect to the land's first inhabitants through Native American cultural and spiritual practices. While many folks choose to take advantage of the myriad adventure options, some arrive focused on losing weight, and others simply come to relax. By custom-tailoring their services—through special packages as well as helping guests create their own program—the spa can be whatever you need it to be based on what's going in your life at that time.

LAY OF THE LAND
Sagestone spa and salon, fitness center, indoor pool, outdoor pool, two whirlpools, tennis court, the Red Mountain Outfitters clothing and gift store, and a labyrinth.

THE FOOD
You won't find rabbit food anywhere on the menu at the Canyon Breeze restaurant. Breakfast and lunch are served buffet-style, while dinner is a seated affair. (If you're traveling alone, the Captain's Table is a great way to get to know other folks traveling solo.) For dinner, there's an

I took my daughter to Red Mountain Spa as a "goodbye gift" before she went to college, 3,000 miles from home. Our separation, two weeks later, was softened by sweet memories of watching the most colorful sunsets imaginable over the red-rock cliffs, spires, and domes from our hammocks by the pool; trying to take photos of ourselves in fluffy spa robes—cucumber slices over our eyes—awaiting our massages, early morning hikes into the spectacular canyons; elegant dinners of duck, elk, beef, fresh fish, fruit soups and vegetable dishes; and guiltlessly snarfing up warm, homemade chocolate-chip and oatmeal-raison cookies.

—Marybeth

extensive menu with "Adventure Cuisine" selections marked and calories subtly indicated. If you're on a rigorous fitness regimen, the PowerFuel option provides needed extra calories (beef tenderloin with sweet potato pancake and sautéed spinach); Call of the Wild entrees focus on natural local ingredients, and 25 percent or less of their calories come from fat (char-grilled bison with spinach risotto); the Green Cuisine selection is free of animal products and the lowest in calories (butternut squash gnocchi with black bean Sauce); and the Detox choice includes ingredients free of toxins such as vegetables and free-range chicken.

BALANCE YOUR LIFE

Classes here focus mainly on making lifestyle adjustments. And giving you guidance in this transformation are the spa's chef, resort nutritionists, life coach and visiting experts. The monthly School of Adventure Cuisine program is a popular cooking course that helps guests bring healthy (and tasty) eating habits home with them. You can also educate yourself about your body with on-site bone density testing, blood cholesterol screening, postural assessment, and gait analysis.

GET YOUR HEART RATE UP

The creative and varied aqua workouts are almost always full in both the indoor and outdoor pools. It could be that the water is the place to be in the heat of the day or perhaps it's the natural resistance the water provides. Dancing is also a preferred exercise at Red Mountain: Get long and lean in the New York City Ballet Workout or burn some serious calories in the Cardio Salsa class.

GET OUTDOORS

You haven't experienced Red Mountain Spa until you get out into the surrounding red-rock country. The resort offers an extensive mountain biking program; it's a great place to learn how if you've ever wanted to. There are also daily morning hikes accessing 30 different local trails. You can join one of three levels of hikes to match your pace and the distance you'd like to do. These group hikes are an excellent way to get to know other women. And putting an educational spin on your hikes are Outdoors Skills classes such as archaeology walks, rock climbing, travel sketching (starting at $40). Their guided day trips include hiking Zion National Park, through stunning slot canyons, and Bryce Canyon National Park, where you'll hike around curious hoodoos (starting at $199).

ZEN OUT

The Awareness Walk is a meditative journey through an enchanted landscape of rust-colored canyons and buttes. After a silent walk, you sit for a meditation session, absorbing the sounds and smells of the desert. And behind the property, a Native American-inspired labyrinth has been built for guests. Instructors can lead you through the ways to achieve inner peace here.

BEST SPA TREATMENTS

The Desert Rain Massage is like taking a sleeping pill. You are bathed with a refreshing Coconilla bath gel and then relax as warm rain falls from above and you receive a full-body massage. This deeply relaxing, deeply restorative water massage is best before bed (50 minutes for $110). The Rocks Leg Massage is a must for anyone who is hiking every day. The massage of your lower body uses anti-inflammatory oils and analgesics to soothe tired and achy ankles, calves, quads, and hamstrings (50 minutes for $110).

ALONE TIME

Hammocks are scattered all over the property for private relaxation in the shade. Down in a hidden grotto, hammocks look out onto the red-rock canyons. And at night, when the galaxy lights the sky, rocking in a hammock is ecstasy.

SPECIAL PACKAGES

There are more than a dozen packages to choose from. Get three of your pals together for their Girlfriends' Spa Roadtrip for four days/three nights. St. George is located 90 minutes from Las Vegas. The Girlfriends Package for four includes a two-bedroom Villa Suite, a 50-minute Swedish massage per person, a $100 gas card for the group, three daily meals, complimentary bike rental, and more (starting at $365 a night or $1,185 per person for three nights). The five-night Eat Well Feel Well Culinary School gets you eight hours of private cooking classes ($2,765 per person for five nights). And the Detox Week helps get you started on a 30-day purification of your body—flushing out all that fast food, caffeine, and sodium—with special massages, body wraps, and nutritional support (starting at $429 a night or $3,003 for seven nights).

WHAT'S INCLUDED
Accommodations, three meals a day, and unlimited classes and workshops. Room rates start at $369 per person, per night. You can save a bit of money December through February and June through August. And often you can find last-minute deals on their website.

ONE CLICK AND YOU'RE OFF: Red Mountain Spa (800-407-3002, www.redmountainspa.com).

Rancho La Puerta

⮞ BAJA CALIFORNIA, MEXICO ⮜

If your idea of a restorative vacation is getting in shape, look just over the border from San Diego to Rancho La Puerta in Baja California, Mexico. A fitness resort first and foremost (and spa second), the ranch instills in its guests the principles of a fit and healthy lifestyle. When the ranch was founded in 1940, it was the first fitness resort in North America. In the beginning, guests paid $17.50 for a week, pitched a tent, ate off the organic farm, and exercised in the sage-scented foothills. Today the ranch is still relatively affordable, the guests' clothing is casual, the mood is laid-back and hiking remains one of its best workouts. But it has also matured over the past 65 years into an incredible holistic retreat with more than 300 gym classes a week that range from tennis clinics to Salsaerobic classes to Pilates, Pulitzer Prize-winning guest speakers, a stand-alone cooking school on the organic farm, and 87 deluxe, terra-cotta cottages each with a private garden and patio. So determined to send you back home fitter and wiser, they recommend you come for a week. But you'll hardly mind. You're treated to a cultural immersion with Mexican cooking and design, and Rancho La Puerta sits beneath a mountain thought to be sacred on 3,000 acres of preserved land that extends to the U.S. border. Set between the sea and desert at an altitude of 1,750 feet, the property includes 32 acres of blooming gardens and a six-acre organic farm, which yields all the vegetables, herbs, and fruit used by the chefs and spa aestheticians. Mediterranean-like in climate, Baja California can practically guarantee you agreeable (never humid) 80-degree days year-round.

LAY OF THE LAND
Three pools, three health center buildings (one male, two female), five hot tubs, three saunas, four lighted tennis courts, eleven gyms, a track, two volleyball courts (one sand), a basketball court, and a labyrinth.

THE FOOD
The heart of the ranch, the two-level dining room welcomes guests to eat in the glory of high ceilings with exposed wooden beams, spiral staircases, colorful Mexican rugs, and chandeliers, plus there's a veranda for outside dining. Breakfast and lunch are buffet style, while dinner is served. The ranch's low-fat diet is mostly vegetarian and the Mexican influence really livens up the menu. Favorites include their signature guacamole and chile rellenos, plus there's typically the choice of fish. (The seafood comes from a nearby open-air market where local fishermen sell their catch of the day.)

GET SMART
Every minute of the day there's something to be learned at the ranch. It may be in a watercolor class, the weekly cooking demonstration by the spa's chef, or a talk on such topics as safe weight loss. Occasionally notable celebrity speakers give talks: Roger Ebert, Bill Moyers, and Madeleine Albright are among those who have visited.

GET YOUR HEART RATE UP

You'll laugh and sweat while learning how to move to African, Caribbean, country, funk, and Latin music in various dance workouts. Or you may prefer to work on your tennis game. Four days a week, two classes are offered, a beginner and intermediate, each focused on improving different aspects of your game: serving, volleying, backhand, etc.

GET OUTDOORS

Each morning, all before 7 a.m., various levels and distances of hikes depart from the ranch. Walk across the property to a Mexican-style breakfast at the resort's organic vegetable farm two miles away. Or for something more rigorous, the Pilgrim Trail is a steep 3.5-mile hike. You can also sign up for a three-day hiking program with more challenging 5- and 13-mile hikes, offered between November and the end of March.

ZEN OUT

Finding your way through the labyrinth, a meditative path modeled after the one at Chartres Cathedral in France, is like a walking meditation. At night, it's lit by luminaries for strolls under the moon. The morning Woodlands Meditation Hike is a silent guided walk in the foothills of sacred Mount Kuchumaa. Seated meditation classes are also held daily. And sometimes Meditative Dinners are arranged: meals without conversation often accompanied by inspirational music.

BEST SPA TREATMENTS

The first treatment to be offered at the ranch was an herbal wrap meant to ease the muscles of guests worn out from exercise. Today the Aromatherapy Wrap, one of four wraps offered, rolls you up in a snug, fragrant bundle of hot linens with special oils and herbs (30 minutes for $45). The Hot Riverstone Massage is a top pick for those looking for heat and massage to dissolve knots ($85 for 50 minutes).

ALONE TIME

With 36 hammocks dotting the property, there are plenty of opportunities to spend time on your own.

SPECIAL PACKAGES

Dozens of Special Weeks are offered throughout the year. In August, the resort sets aside its facilities, staff, and rooms exclusively for the use of ladies over two Women's Weeks. There are also weeks in which experts are invited to teach various disciplines of yoga, dance, or Pilates, as well as writing and art. Check the ranch's calendar for these themed weeks. (Prices are the same as weekly rates.)

WHAT'S INCLUDED
Accommodations, three meals a day, unlimited classes and lectures, and transfers to and from San Diego on Saturdays. Weekly rates start at $2,795 per person. Prices drop slightly in the off-season (June through December 30).

ONE CLICK AND YOU'RE OFF: Rancho La Puerta (800-443-7565, www.rancholapuerta.com).

CHAPTER TEN

Retail Therapy

❧ MARGE'S STORY ↩

There is no doubt—Marge is a born shopper. For the past six years, she and five girlfriends from Calgary, Canada, have taken a weekend trip in November. They bill the weekend excursion as a Christmas shopping trip, dedicated selflessly to their families, friends, and loved ones. This fun-loving group simply talks, eats, and shops—no dues, no rules, no worries.

They head east or west, to New York, Chicago, Las Vegas, or San Francisco for a spiritual retreat of markdowns, closeouts, and rack-ravaging. They give each other advice on holiday presents and make the whole task a game of finding marvelous surprises. "Of course we love bargains," says Marge. "Filene's Basement, in Chicago and New York City, was one of our best finds."

After hours of shopping, they always have a Show and Tell, either with a drink before dinner or in their PJs before bed. "Last year in New York

'Tis the thrill of the hunt. Just a fun thing to do with the girls.

—Marybeth

one of us paraded into the hotel room with a wonderful prize: a tiny pink fur coat with matching boots and a hat for her granddaughter," explains Marge. "We oohed and aahed and passed it around to inspect."

Although Marge doesn't collect anything in particular, she has shopped all her life with a drive that implies she does. She has a list of more than 30 people for whom she buys holiday presents. "So beginning in the summer, I have my eyes wide open—observing, thinking of what would be suitable or a nice surprise for each person," she says. And, Marge admits, holiday shopping is so much fun because you end up buying a lot for yourself too.

Marge, who was a devoted wife, mother, and homemaker in her younger years, after her kids left home evolved into an adventure traveler and international shopper.

In the past few years, Marge has joined numerous women's hiking trips to places like New Zealand and Vermont and has expanded her circle of shopping companions. She's learned to pack an additional bag because she usually needs to ship home an extra suitcase filled with purchases. When asked if there is one place she loves to shop above all others, she confessed her passion for Santa Fe. "I love New Mexican food, architecture, art, crafts, and landscapes," she says. "Santa Fe is a great place to buy art work, silver or turquoise jewelry, one-of-a-kind clothing, and even eclectic items like a vintage Japanese silk kimono."

Marge asserts that shopping together with her girlfriends is a form of entertainment as well as team building. "I believe that women need time to spend with women, be they old friends or new gals with a common interest," says Marge. "Philosophies, values, and idea exchanges abound when my female pals travel with me, and shopping is a great vehicle for this."

⮞ BETSA'S STORY ⮜

True to its noble name, the Ladies Discoursive and Digestive Society can talk and eat with the best of 'em. "We aren't too shabby with a credit card, either," says Betsa, founding member as well as an author and photographer from Ohio.

This gaggle of friends in Greater Cincinnati has been together for 16 years, through births and deaths and bad hair choices. They travel a couple of times a year, fearless leaders and map-challenged followers bonded together. Sometimes it's to a cabin in the woods, sometimes a reclusive spa, and sometimes a big-city hotel. But never fail, there's always time made for shopping.

These women are power shoppers, multi-taskers long before anyone dreamed up the name. They can run a conference call, text message orders for the family dinner, and buff their manicure all at once. It's no wonder they can pop into a museum gift store or an outlet mall and knock out their Christmas list in 15 minutes.

"What's the most fun though, is the feeling of luxury on a Ladies trip," says Betsa. "Suddenly you have dedicated time to shop, free moments in which you're not supposed to be anyplace else or doing anything else for anyone else. Most women are rushed and distracted when they 'have' to shop: It's a rare gift to ourselves when we can relax, breathe, and 'get' to shop. And there's always a Lady nearby to give her yea or nay to the eternal shopping question, 'Whaddya think?'"

"Each evening, we have the Ritual Display of Purchased Products," she adds. "Over wine and cheese, everyone has to fess up to her hoard—whether it's from Victoria's Secret or Williams Sonoma. The Ladies need to see, touch, and smell every single item—in case they want to buy it themselves the next day." And for dedicated shoppers there will always be another day, another sale, and another opportunity for a bargain.

Santa Fe

⮞ NEW MEXICO ⮜

Women with a weak spot for silver jewelry, Southwestern art, and Mexican food adore Santa Fe, New Mexico. The strands of history intertwining here—from Native American to Mexican to Catholic missionary to famous modern-day artists, namely Georgia O'Keeffe—have left behind gorgeous collectibles and traditions. Today art galleries, its newest legacy, stand over 250 strong; in fact, Santa Fe competes with New York and Los Angeles in art commerce. Throughout the streets surrounding its 400-year-old plaza (yes, you read that correctly), you can wander into hundreds of shops and galleries in old adobe buildings and get the feeling you've gone back in time. You'll be in awe of the surrounding high-desert landscape viewable from street level, the savory green chili-infused cuisine, and the marvelous sunsets painting the capital city and the Sangre de Cristo Mountains purple. And at 7,200 feet, Santa Fe enjoys a uniquely dry climate and a big blue sky with sunshine 300 days of the year. It's a year-round destination with hot summers (but cool evenings), brief thunderstorms, and winters that can be chilly (and it does snow). There's really no bad time to visit for shopping, but you may want to time your trip to some of its famous markets and festivals to get in some serious southwestern shopping.

BEST FOR JEWELRY SHOPPING
In front of the Palace of the Governors on the northern side of the plaza, dozens of Native American craftspeople sell classic southwestern jewelry. On blankets side-by-side, handmade silver necklaces, earrings, rings, bracelets, pins, and bolo ties with unique patterns and stones are displayed. Because you're buying directly from the artist, you're getting a better deal than in the shops.

BEST WESTERN VINTAGE SHOPPING
Double Take at the Ranch stocks Western and vintage clothing such as embroidered cowboy shirts and silver-and-turquoise jewelry. You will get a kick out of rummaging through the racks and trying on the flouncy skirts and fringed suede jackets. 321 S. Guadalupe Street (505-820-7775).

BEST SHOPPING FOR BARGAIN HUNTERS
Jackalope is a bizarre bazaar. Inside there are bargain-priced rugs, patterned bed throws, ceramics, red-chili lights, and a good selection of world music. Outside is a labyrinth of booths chock full of cowboy hats, jewelry, and Mexican and Native American goods. Plan to spend at least an hour here and maybe get some Christmas shopping done. Also many of the rugs, jewelry, and clothing you've ogled in Santa Fe can be scored for much less at the Tesuque Flea Market held on most weekends north of town. Jackalope, 2820 Cerrillos Road (505-471-8539). Tesuque Flea Market, Highway 84/285 located next to the Santa Fe Opera. Closed Tuesday and Wednesday (505-670-2599, www.tesuquepueblofleamarket.com).

BEST FOR ART LOVERS
Canyon Road's 80 or so galleries, in adobe buildings standing one after another on this narrow road, require at least a full day. Eye (or invest in, if you can) Navajo blankets, the famous black-on-black pottery of Maria Martinez, wildlife photography, and Russian paintings. And tucked in between the galleries are upscale Western-wear shops, cafés, and restaurants.

Don't schedule too much physical activity on your first full day in Santa Fe. The elevation is 7,000 feet, and most people feel the need to take it easy.

—Marybeth

HAVE TEA

In The Teahouse on Canyon Road, you can choose from a 13-page list of teas and settle into their den-like café with art on the walls, couches you can get lost in, and a fireplace. In the colder months, use it as a warming hut after paying the galleries a visit.

MUST-SEE MUSEUM

The Georgia O'Keeffe Museum holds the largest collection of New Mexico's most famous artist's work in the world. Many recognizable paintings hang here that may decorate your own walls—albeit as posters. You can also visit O'Keeffe's residence of nearly 40 years in Abiquiu, north of Santa Fe. Here you can see the iconic landscape that inspired her masterpieces. Tours of her home and studio require reservations well in advance. 217 Johnson (505-946-1000, www.okeeffemuseum.org).

DAY TRIPS

Bandelier National Monument, Anasazi ruins an hour northwest of Santa Fe, offers a glimpse back to 900 years ago when the ancient civilization populated this high desert. High above in the canyon walls, ancient cliff dwellings remain for you to explore via trails and ladders. Another nearby wonder, Tent Rocks National Monument, between Albuquerque and Santa Fe, lets you hike among immense ghost-like volcanic tuffs. Simply driving on the secondary roads up to Taos or down to Albuquerque is also bound to yield striking landscapes, peculiar shops, and historical sites. You never know what you'll come across in these parts. Bandelier National Monument (505-672-3861, www.nps.gov/band). Tent Rocks National Monument (505-761-8700).

BEST DINING

MARIA'S NEW MEXICAN KITCHEN pours unquestionably the best margaritas in Santa Fe—period. Imagine fresh lemon juice, triple sec, and your choice of more than 100 tequilas, including 100-percent agave varieties, and piping-hot blue corn enchiladas and chili rellenos smothered in green chili sauce

Wherever my sister, mom, and I go, we look for thrift shops. We check in the phone book for thrift stores. My sister will give each of us $20 and we go in and shop for each other, and when we go home we wrap up our treasures and give them to each other. Then we hoot and laugh and exchange or trade them. We have found all sorts of goodies; brand new Stewart Wiseman black alligator shoes for $3.50 or a Coach bag for $4, a Dunny Burke purse for $19 and an Armani Jacket sample for $15. We find thrift shops wherever we go.

—Kathy Musser, 50s, Executive, Retirement Community, Akron, Ohio

---

for not too much dinero. Cuisine is Southwestern, barbecue, and Mexican. 555 W. Cordova Road ($10-30; 505-983-7929, www.marias-santafe.com).

For an equally affordable and yummy meal, sit at the bar at cozy **RIO CHAMA STEAKHOUSE** and order the Chama chili and a glass of their finest red. A real indulgence is dining at **COYOTE CAFÉ** or **SANTACAFÉ**, both elegant and highly acclaimed restaurants with a fancier spin on New Mexican cuisine. Rio Chama Steakhouse, 414 Old Santa Fe Trail ($15-38; (505- 955-0765). Coyote Café, 132 W. Water Street ($28-38; 505-983-1615, www.coyotecafe.com). SantaCafé, 231 Washington Avenue ($22-32; 505-984-1788, www.santacafe.com).

EVENTS TO FLY IN FOR
The open-air Santa Fe Opera, situated in the pinon- and sagebrush-cloaked hills outside of town, stages five operas in repertory from late June through August. Tickets to this famous tradition can be tough to procure, so book well ahead of time (www.santafeopera.org). In late August the best Native American artisans convene on the plaza for the prestigious Santa Fe Indian Market. A colorful tradition dating back to 1712, Santa Fe Fiesta every autumn marks the return of the Spanish to Santa Fe in 1692 after 12 years of exile with weeklong festivities. It's the country's oldest continuous celebration with arts-and-crafts fairs, Mariachi music, religious parades, and the burning of Zozobra (a 40-foot-tall paper effigy). Then in December the city becomes illuminated with farolitos (called luminarias in Albuquerque), which are candles in paper bags that line the rooftops of buildings and homes. There's a warmth about this time of year despite its cold (but dry) temperatures.

WHERE TO STAY
One of the oldest hotels in the country, La Fonda is situated on the plaza, merely steps from the shops, museums, galleries, and cafés of downtown.

Authentic southwestern décor and antiques fill the grand interior, and the Belltower Bar is the best place in town to watch sunset. 100 E. San Francisco Street (starting at $189; 505-982-5511, www.lafondasantafe.com).

The newly renovated AAA Four Diamond Eldorado Hotel and Spa is decorated in a Santa Fe style and many rooms have kiva fireplaces, terraces,or balconies. A remarkable Southwest art collection graces the interior spaces. It is within walking distance of the plaza and fine restaurants. 309 West San Francisco Street (online specials starting at $199; 505-988-4455, www.eldoradohotel.com).

ONE CLICK AND YOU'RE OFF: Santa Fe Convention and Visitors Bureau (800-777-2489, www.santafe.org).

The Berkshires

⌖ MASSACHUSETTS ⌖

If you fancy classic American antiques and window shopping on Main Street, U.S.A., then you've found your next vacation spot: the Berkshires. Blue bloods from Boston turned the mountains of western Massachusetts into a sprawling resort two centuries ago and, boy, did they like to shop. Thirty-two towns make up the Berkshires, each with stores aplenty. You'll love being able to shop as Americans once did: walking down historic streets to locally owned specialty stores with distinct character. The 70 cultural venues throughout the Berkshires make for excellent shopping, too. The Hancock Shaker Village, Edith Wharton's home, the Clark Art Institute—the list goes on and on—all sell wonderful books, posters, and trinkets in their well-stocked gift shops. And as luck would have it, there's no sales tax on clothing in Massachusetts, subsequently you may feel justified in revamping your entire wardrobe. In the Berkshires you're never too far from the beauty and solitude of forests, mountains, lakes, and rivers.

BEST ANTIQUING

The oldest town in the Berkshires, Sheffield has more antique shops on its streets than any other town in the region. The old carriage houses of historic homes were converted into antique stores with a wide array of wares. A close second and third for antiquing are Great Barrington and Egremont.

BEST MAIN STREET

Stockbridge is right out of a Norman Rockwell painting. Actually, it was his inspiration: He called the town home for the last 25 years of his life. Bakeries, galleries, and retail shops in late-19th-century buildings and the Red Lion Inn, which began as a stagecoach tavern in 1773, constitute Main Street, with the southern Berkshires mountains in the background.

BEST OUTLET SHOPPING

Nearly 70 discount clothing and housewares stores in Lee sell stylish labels for less. There's no sales tax on clothing, remember, so you may as well outfit the whole family in Polo, J. Crew, Coach, Izod, and Calvin Klein (413-243-8186, www.primeoutlets.com).

BEST VINTAGE SHOPPING

You'll find a wide selection of vintage clothing (in excellent condition), jewelry, and linens, as well as antiques at Nora Martin Antiques in Pittsfield. 446 Tyler Street (413-499-0927, www.norasantiques.com).

MUST-SEE MUSEUMS

At the Norman Rockwell Museum in Stockbridge, wander through the largest collection of the artist's original work. Believe it or not, the masterworks of Renoir, Degas, Sargent, and Homer are hanging in the Berkshires, too: The Clark Art Institute, best known for its French Impressionist paintings, is a highly respected museum in Williamstown. Dozens of former mills now make up MASS MoCA in North Adams. When it opened in 1999, it became the largest contemporary art museum in the United States, occupying one-third of the city's downtown business district and housing enormous installations in its airy rooms. The complex alone is a sight to behold. More can be found on museums in the Berkshires under "Tanglewood" in Chapter 2, Spirit Boosters.

PAMPER YOURSELF

The newest addition to the Berkshires softer side, Williamstown's Intouch Massage and Day Spa opened in a former gristmill hovering over the Green River. A 90-minute massage will set you back only about $90, and you can rent their riverfront hot tub for a private soak. In July and August, their yoga classes are held on the deck (413-458-3235, www.intouchdayspa.com). Canyon Ranch and Cranwell Spa and Golf Club, both in Lennox, and Kripalu Center for Yoga and Health, in nearby Stockbridge, offer enticing packages for girlfriends, mothers and daughters, bridal parties, and moms to be. Canyon Ranch (800-742-9000, www.canyonranch.com). Cranwell

Spa and Golf Club (800-272-6935, www.cranwell.com). Kripalu Center for Yoga and Health (800-741-7353, www.kripalu.org).

NEED A GOOD READ?

The Bookstore in Lenox, Massachusetts, is a favorite among locals as well as visitors. You will find best sellers, regional interest titles, and books by regional authors. The knowledgeable and well-read staff will offer personal recommendations of authors and favorite books. Call for a schedule of author appearances, book-signing parties, and poetry readings. 11 Housatonic Street (413-637-3390).

TAKE A BREAK

Give your credit card a rest with a hike up Mount Greylock, the highest peak in Massachusetts. From Lanesborough, you can set out on a one- to two-hour hike and make your way to a lookout for a picnic with views across the Berkshires to five states.

Another way to get the lay of the land is to rent a bike and pedal the paved Ashuwillticook, an 11-mile path between Lanseborough and Adams. It steers you through the Hoosic River Valley, between Mount Greylock and the Hoosac Mountain Ranges. Berkshire Outfitters in Adams is right off the trail and rents bikes and helmets. (413-743-5900).

And golfers, don't miss out on the chance to tee off at the Cranwell Resort, Spa & Golf Club in Lenox. Their Golf Digest School boasts the finest facility in New England: multiple lesson tees with target greens, a 10,000-square-foot indoor hitting barn, computerized analysis systems, and an indoor filming studio. Ever wondered what your game was missing? You'll find out here.

BEST DINING

At GIDEON'S in North Adams it's not unusual for the chef to pay your table a visit. Chef and owner Bill Gideon has whipped up his specialties for presidents and now does the same for his loyal patrons. The welcoming restaurant arranges a mixed menu of pastas, New England dishes, and seafood. Closed on Monday. 34 Holden Street ($10-28; 413-664-9449).

Another good choice based on ambience, good cuisine, and service allowing for easy conversations is the SPICE ROOT MODERN INDIAN CUISINE featuring both vegetarian and non-vegetarian Indian specialties. The tangerine interior and colorful decorations create a warm and welcoming atmosphere. It is located adjacent to the Williams College campus, in the heart of downtown Williamstown. 23 Spring Street ($9-20; 413-458-5200, www.spiceroot.net).

Locals say that the experience of dining at THE TRATTORIA RUSTICA in Pittsfield is like "going to Italy without the jetlag." The authentic interior was built by hand by the owner/chef Davide Manzo, who is a third-generation Napoletana Chef. The tiles, brick, and even the bee-hive wood-burning oven were imported from Italy. You'll appreciate the warm intimate setting and fine cuisine from Southern Italy. 26 McKay Street ($12-28; 413-499-1192, www.trattoria-rustica.com).

In summer you may prefer to dine outdoors in the bistro-style patio, or in cooler months, warm up indoors by the fireplace at the AEGEAN BREEZE, Great Barrington. Authentic Greek and Mediterranean cuisine compliment a very cozy setting. 327 Stockbridge Road ($14-22; 413-528-4001, www.aegean-breeze.com).

SIP AT A WINE BAR

Open every evening, the Brix Wine Bar in Pittsfield, with 40 wines by the glass and 150 on reserve, serves classic bistro meals, European tapas, and desserts. It's a great spot to go to with a group of friends before or after performing arts venues in Pittsfield such as the Colonial Theatre (former Vaudeville stage), Barrington Stage Company's productions, symphony and folk concerts at the First United Methodist Church, or the Berkshire Opera. 40 West Street (413-236-9463, www.brixwinebar.com).

EVENTS TO FLY IN FOR

The juried Berkshire Art Festival takes over Ski Butternut in Great Barrington each July. Hundreds of fine artists turn the mountain resort into a contemporary art museum. Also in Great Barrington, at the Berkshire Crafts Fair in August you can hunt for one-of-a-kind ceramics, textiles, and jewelry. Or plan your visit around Tanglewood's summer concert series in Lenox. Flip to Chapter 2 Spirit Boosters for more on Tanglewood.

WHERE TO STAY

The tranquil 49-room Orchards Hotel in Williamstown, home of the Clark Art Institute, Williams College, and the Williamstown Theatre Festival, often puts together reasonable packages that combine meals, an in-room massage, a round of golf, or tickets to the some of the local festivals and museums. A leading small hotel of the world (starting at $159; 800-225-1517, www.orchardshotel.com).

The Old Inn on the Green, a quintessential New England inn, sits peacefully among meadows with rooms that could make an interior designer drool. Starting at $205. Check online for seasonal packages like the lodging/dining special: Wednesday, Thursday Dinner and a Room, $99 per person (double occupancy). 134 Hartsville, New Marlborough Road, New Marlborough (413-229-7924, www.oldinn.com).

The Wainwright Inn in Great was built in 1766 on the Boston-to-Albany stagecoach route. Some of the rooms have fireplaces and the inn has parlors where the guests meet and share stories. No phones and no TVs in the rooms. 518 South Main Street, Great Barrington (starting at $139; 413-528-2062, www.wainwrightinn.com).

Or if there are just a few of you, you can take over the Hollyhock House in Pittsfield, which keeps up three flowery rooms for guests. Try them for that last-minute weekend or mid-week stay. They don't aggressively advertise, so you might be lucky. 1130 Barker Road, Pittsfield (from $75 off season, $90 peak season, including breakfast; (413-443-6901, www .hollyhockbb.com).

Travel Tip: Summer lures the most visitors, and for good reason—there's Tanglewood, professional theatre county-wide, craft fairs, and the Jacob's Pillow dance festival. Then fall brings leaf peepers en masse. If you'd prefer less hubbub, the first couple of weeks in September may be the sweet spot: Discounted rates, warm days, and fewer fellow shoppers.

ONE CLICK AND YOU'RE OFF: Berkshire Visitors Bureau (800-237-5747, berkshires.org).

Door County

☞ WISCONSIN ☜

In Wisconsin's Door County, you'll arm yourself with an ice cream cone and visit shops on whitewashed, waterfront main streets. Certainly the landlocked Midwest has gotten a terrible rap for lacking a shoreline and is overlooked by vacationers desperate for the ocean. But on a 75-mile peninsula sticking out into Green Bay on the west and Lake Michigan on the east, Door County presents 300 miles of coast with dunes and historic lighthouses, earning it the designation the "Cape Cod of the Midwest." Gulls glide overhead, sailboats cruise offshore, and breezes sweep off the water. And in the delightful towns, simply a ten-minute drive apart, the work of local clothing designers, craftsmen, antique collectors, and painters is showcased in hundreds of shops and galleries. The county is also home to 2,000 acres of cherry orchards, a handful of apple orchards, five wineries, and numerous dairy farms, making for excellent gourmet food shopping. Farm stands and specialty food stores are everywhere; they're great places to pick up gifts and picnic fixings. Most of Door County's visitors arrive between the beginning of May and the end of October. It's truly a marvelous time to visit: The cherry trees normally bloom in mid-to-late May with cherries ready for picking in mid July to early August, and apples are ripe for picking in the fall.

BEST GOURMET FOOD SHOPS

In Fish Creek, the Oilerie's expansive tasting bar lets you sample freshly pressed olive oils in a variety of flavors (garlic is my favorite). Nearby is the Orchard Country Winery and Market, which sells wine from their vineyards and jarred goodies from their orchards. Sister Bay's Topshelf Café and Gourmet carries fancy mustards, jams, marinades, and olives. And in the Door County Gourmet in Sturgeon Bay, you'll find imported and domestic cheeses and wines. Curt's Spice Co. & Oilerie, 4083 Main Street, Highway 42, Fish Creek (920-868-1561). Orchard Country Winery and Market, 9197 State Highway 42, Fish Creek (920-868-3479). Topshelf Café and Gourmet, Country Walk Mall, Sister Bay (920-854-5040). Door County Gourmet, 957 Green Bay Road, Sturgeon Bay (920-743-0969).

BEST ANTIQUING

Nearly every town on the peninsula has its own pocket of antique shops. Among the best, Baileys Barn Antiques and Gifts in Baileys Harbor fills a 5,000-square-foot, 135-year old barn with assorted furniture and gifts; Chelsea Antiques and Blue Window Shops outside of Sister Bay is dedicated to English and French antiques. Baileys Barn Antiques, 10079 Highway 57, Baileys Harbor (920-854-2412). Chelsea Antiques and Blue Window Shops, 10002 Highway 57, Sister Bay (920-854-4828).

BEST ICE CREAM SHOP

Wilson's Ice Cream in Ephraim celebrated its 100th anniversary in 2006. Across from scenic Eagle Harbor, this old-fashioned ice cream parlor scoops creamy homemade goodness. Wait in line to get your cone and join the folks who gather by the water for sunset. Expect applause at the finale (920-854-2041).

BEST PLACE TO BUY PRESERVES

Seaquist Orchard Farm Market, north of Sister Bay, turns their fresh-from-the-tree cherries into mouth-watering jams, jellies, and pies. 1482 Highway 42, Sister Bay (920-854-4199).

TAKE A BREAK

Kayaking is a terrific way to explore the beautiful coastline here. Door County Kayak Tours brings you up close to the lighthouses, caves, and dramatic bluffs along the shore. Sunset cruises with wine and cheese and sailing charters can also be arranged with various outfitters. The peninsula is home to five of Wisconsin's state parks as well. One you certainly shouldn't miss, Peninsula State Park, sticks out into Green Bay; bikers enjoy its Sunset Trail, which runs through marshes and hardwood forests, and hikers are rewarded with views from the bluffs rising high above the shore. Climbing the 109 steps of Eagle Tower gets you a 360-degree panorama view of the park, islands, and the Michigan shore. Door County Kayak Tours (half day starting at $48; 920-854-292, doorcountykayaktours.com).

BEST DINING

A tradition since lumberjacks and Scandinavian settlers populated the area, fish boils are best described as culinary performances. Whitefish from local waters and potatoes are heated in a kettle over a fire. When at a boil, oils rise to the surface. This is when the boilmaster tosses kerosene on the fire, resulting in a brief inferno with 15-foot flames and a perfectly cooked meal that you then slather in butter. Also part of the tradition is the slice of cherry pie that follows. Fish boils are held all over the place in summer. The historic **WHITE GULL INN**, on the water in Fish Creek, hosts fish boils year-round. Arrive 30 minutes prior to your reservation to

PACKING TIP

Shoes are the heaviest items. Three pairs should cover your needs unless you are going on a long cruise or to Las Vegas when you might pack an additional pair of evening shoes to match your evening attire. Wear your walking shoes the day of departure and pack only two additional pairs; one pair for evening and sandals or athletic shoes for sports. If you cannot leave home without a dozen shoes, you need a self-help group for overpackers.

watch the pyrotechnic show with a glass of wine. 4225 Main Street, Fish Creek. (Fish boil $18.75; 888-364-9542, www.whitegullinn.com).

EVENTS TO FLY IN FOR
The third weekend in May, the Festival of Blossoms celebrates the gorgeous apple and cherry blossoms. In addition to the concerts and fish boils, the occasion is also marked with open historic lighthouse tours. And running from June to August, three plays and musicals are staged under the stars in Peninsula State Park by the American Folklore Theater.

WHERE TO STAY
The Chanticleer Guest House, a cute B&B in a former farmhouse and barn, sits among fields of wildflowers north of Sturgeon Bay. And the Landing Resort in Egg Harbor puts guests up in one- to three-bedroom suites with decks and equipped kitchens. Set in the woods, it's still an easy walk to the shops and cafés in town. 4072 Cherry Road, Sturgeon Bay (starting at $117; 866-682-0384, www.chanticleerguesthouse.com).

ONE CLICK AND YOU'RE OFF: Door County Chamber of Commerce (800-527-3529, www.doorcounty.com).

Carmel

❧ CALIFORNIA ❧

Carmel has it all: coastal beauty, inspiring art, invoking theater, great golf, diverse restaurants, indulgent hotels, quaint cobblestone streets, excellent weather, and, of course, fantastic shopping! The community artfully retains its small-town, European feel through banning billboards, house numbers, and neon signs but incorporating such modern attributes like the Fountain of Woof, a permanent drinking fixture for the town's carefully groomed dogs. Photographer Ansel Adams, author Robert Louis Sevenson, and actor Clint Eastwood have all called Carmel home. Carmel is a great place to explore by foot; it's safe and nearly impossible to get lost in and has some of the best, most diverse, and exclusive boutiques in all of California.

BEST LEATHER AND SHOES
Coach at Carmel is a Coach Outlet store, very popular for discounted goods and an extensive selection. If you're a Coach fan then this is your

paradise. Ocean and San Carlos (831-626-1777, www.coach.com). For the finest haute couture leathers go to Augustina Leathers. Not only does it sell one-of-a-kind and custom creations in both leather and fur, all of the designs are hand-beaded, hand-painted, and hand-knitted. San Carlos between 5th and 6th Streets, West Side (831-624-2403, www .augustinaleathers.com). You can find an impressive selection of shoes at Lloyd's Shoes. They work under the motto that they sell "designer shoes from around the world"; a statement that has held true for more than 30 years. Ocean Ave at Dolores Street (831-625-1382, www .lloydsshoes.com).

WEDDING AND SHOWER GIFTS
If it's a wedding or shower gift you're looking for, go no farther than Jan de Luz. It sells the finest of French linens. Dolores between Ocean and Seventh Avenue (831-622-7621, www.jandeluz.com).

SHOPPING VILLAGES
The Crossroads Shopping Village on Highway One has a plethora of individual boutiques and restaurants at 243 Crossroads Boulevard (831-625-4106, www.crossroadsshoppingvillage.com). Another popular yet quaint shopping village is the Barnyard. This brown-shingled building has a vast array of boutiques, restaurants, open-air patios, and mosaic paths that wind around cute ponds. On the way to Carmel Valley at 3618 the Barnyard (831-624-8886, www.thebarnyard.com).

BEST WALKS
Stillwater Cove Beach offers a short, gentle walk along a calm bay. The public entrance to the beach is at the end of the Beach and Tennis Club parking lot. 1576 Cypress Drive, Pebble Beach (831-625-8507, www .pebblebeach.com). Another fantastic walk is Bird Rock. Park at Bird Rock on 17-mile Drive (halfway between Cypress Point Golf Club, 3150 17 Mile Drive, 831-624-2223, www.golflink.com, and The Inn at Spanish Bay, 2700 17 Mile Drive, 831-647-7423, www.pebblebeach.com) and walk north on the dirt path that stretches along the coastline for several miles. This is a great path for dogs and kids; the views along this undeveloped stretch of coastline are gorgeous.

MUST-SEE MUSEUMS
For a look into Carmel's past, go no farther than its peaceful and poetic Mission Basilica. Constructed in 1771, this architectural masterpiece is home to fascinating art, history, and exhibitions. The museum will

intrigue, as will the grounds. 3080 Rio Road, Carmel (831-624-1271, www.carmelmission.org). The Monterey Museum of Art boasts a fine collection of paintings, photography, and sculpture, with a particular slant toward American art from the Monterey Peninsula and West Coast. You'll also find a good selection of Asian art, photography, and contemporary paintings here. Carmelites love Ansel Adams. There are two locations for the museum: The larger site is located on 559 Pacific Street with eight galleries (831-372-5477, www.montereyart.org) and the second, smaller site with four galleries is located on 720 Via Mirada (831-372-3689, www. montereyart.org).

A NIGHT AT THE THEATER
The Forest Theater is one of Carmel's most treasured venues. It plays host to a wide selection of plays and films, performed and shown on its historic outdoor stage. Audiences are kept warm by two large bonfires on either side of the stage. The theater is fast approaching its hundredth birthday. On the corner of Mt. View and Santa Rita (831-626-1681, www .foresttheaterguild.org).

EVENTS TO FLY IN FOR
For lovers of Bach, the Bach Festival is three weeks of bliss encompass-ing performances by international artists, various concerts, lectures, and outreach classes; it is culture personified. The festival takes place in late summer, usually July/August. For more information go to www .bachfestival.org.

TRAVEL TIP

Unless you're driving north from Los Angeles to Carmel, time your departure from San Francisco or San Jose to avoid rush-hour traffic hours. Take the 85 bypass to avoid down-town San Jose. Give yourself 2 full days and nights in Carmel, and half a day to travel to and from San Francisco/San Jose airports. If you take the inland route—from downtown San Francisco—Carmel is a two-hour drive south.

BEST DINING

For some of the best Italian food on the peninsula go to JOE ROMBI; it's a local favorite and the small intimate setting gives the place a quaint, romantic feel. Joe's best dishes include handmade ravioli and mouthwatering meatballs (keep in mind the latter are only served Sunday nights). His strawberry shortcake will melt in your mouth. Reservations are strongly recommended and there's a free parking lot across the street. 208 17th Street, Pacific Grove ($18-25; 831-373-2416, www.joerombi.com). Another local favorite, as well as my own, is CASANOVA, a romantic little restaurant nestled in the palm of downtown. It emphasizes French and Italian cooking with a wine list that complements everything on the menu, and then some. From fresh mussels to veal to crème brûlée, this restaurant is both delicious and charming. It's expensive but worth every penny. 5th Avenue and Mission ($29-53 for dinner entrees; 831-625-0501, www .casanovarestaurant.com).

BREAK THE FAST

The waffles, eggs Benedict, and brioche French toast at KATY'S PLACE will satisfy the hungriest of customers. Come early as Katy's is always crowded. Mission and 6th Avenues ($11-17; 831-624-0199, www.katysplacecarmel.com).

LUNCH ANYONE?

THE COTTAGE isn't pretentious or typical. Instead it feels like a rural English tea room and serves delicious homemade lunches. The artichoke soup is to die for. Lincoln, between Ocean and 7th Avenues ($11-15; 831-625-6260, www.thecottage.com).

SUNSET DRINKS

There's no better place for sunset drinks and bagpipes than the Inn at Spanish Bay. Sitting on the stone terrace as the piper ushers in the setting sun from a nearby beach is unforgettable. 2700 17 Mile Drive, Pebble Beach ($9-16 cocktail prices only; 831-647-7500, www.pebblebeach.com).

WHERE TO STAY

Centrally located, the Cypress Inn is one of Carmel's most popular destinations. Its garden courtyard, marble tile bathrooms, and afternoon tea, serving sandwiches, scones, jam and cream, are a few of the many highlights. There's live entertainment in the hotel's busy bar and a good in-house restaurant. Dogs and cats are welcome here. Doris Day is co-owner of the hotel, the reason for all of the Doris Day memorabilia. Lincoln and 7th Avenues (starting at $150; 831-624-3871, www.cypress-inn.com).

For a grander experience spend the night at the La Playa Hotel. Built in 1905, this Mediterranean-style villa has impressive gardens, courtyards, and private cottages. The location is ideal; both beach and town center are only a few blocks away. Camino Real and 8th Streets (starting at $190; 831-624-6476, www.laplayahotel.com).

AVOID
During school vacations, especially July and August, and when the fog rolls in, the sidewalks in Carmel; can be so crowded you can't walk. Avoid the Classic Car Show week (mid-August) too, unless you get reservations well in advance or you're a classic car fan.

ONE CLICK AND YOU'RE OFF: www.carmelcalifornia.com.

Scottsdale

ꙮ ARIZONA ꙮ

If you're looking to indulge yourself then you couldn't find a better place than Scottsdale; a place where world-class golf courses, luxurious spas, and extravagant hotels coexist alongside majestic mountain ranges, wide open deserts, and a soft setting sun. Today Scottsdale has a polished, pampered vibe but it hasn't always been this way. Initially the area was inhabited by Native Americans until U.S. Army Chaplain Winfield Scott bought the land and called it Orangedale; in 1894 his brother changed the name to Scottsdale. The area was Wild West terrain until the 1950s when factories moved in and began polluting the land and water with toxic chemicals. In the '80s the government decided to clean up the environment and rebuild the area. This cleansing resulted in new parks, golf courses, and restoration projects. Old Town was renovated, an arts center was built, and billboards were restricted in both size and height to retain the city's intimacy. Golf courses and multimillion dollar homes couldn't be built fast enough. Spas popped up alongside high-end shops, galleries, and restaurants. Today Scottsdale remains a coveted place to both live and play. It's where one comes to relax and enjoy; where the sun and stars are always shining.

RETAIL THERAPY
A great way to escape Scottsdale's heat is to shop. Malls and shops are air-conditioned bubbles that protect you from the weather, whatever it is, and

Scottsdale has the cream of the crop. Fashion Square is home to just about every major and minor retail shop under the sun: Ann Taylor, Anthropologie, Betsey Johnson, Coach, Gucci, Jimmy Choo, Louis Vuitton, and Neiman Marcus—to name but a few. There are also 20 restaurants to choose from that range in price, type, and flavor. This mall is enormous! Cambelback Road and Scottsdale Road (480-941-2140, www.fashionsquare.com).

The shops on Fifth Avenue make up three blissful blocks of excellence. Garden cafés break up the lines of shops, restaurants, and theaters. This is the street to be seen on. Fifth Avenue, between Scottsdale Road and Goldwater Boulevard (www.scottsdale5thave.org).

Kierland Commons is a relaxing outdoor shopping experience. Here you'll find all the usual suspects: Bebe, Barnes & Noble, Restoration Hardware, and Banana Republic, along with numerous restaurants (my favorite is P.F. Chang's; the Chinese food is great and the décor authentic), but you'll also cross paths with musicians and a tasteful landscape decorated in flowers and trees. Greenway Parkway and Scottsdale Road (480-348-1577, www.kierlandcommons.com).

If you're itching for an oasis-like market place experience then El Pedregal Festival is perfect. It's got plenty of atmosphere with a great canopy overhead and soft walls that reflect the colors of the surrounding desert. Here you'll find more than 30 shops and restaurants to indulge your shopping desires. Southeast corner of Scottsdale Road and Carefree Highway (480-488-1072, www.elpedregal.com).

BEST OUTLET
If you're looking for bargains then run to Last Chance. Here you'll find a Nordstrom outlet; it's much better than Nordstrom Rack and a great place for treasure hunting. 1919 East Camelback Road, Phoenix (602-248-2843, www.shop.nordstrom.com).

BEST STREET FOR STROLLING WITH SMALL SHOPS
Walk the wooden sidewalks of Old Town where you can't help but peer through the polished windows of shops, art galleries, and restaurants. This is a good place to find art and Southwestern souvenirs. On Thursday evenings don't miss the Art Walk; all of the shops and galleries stay open until 9 p.m. (www.scottsdalegalleries.com).

BEST DAY TRIPS
Carefree and Cave Creek are small towns at the north end of Scottsdale and each offer a variety of shops and restaurants. Carefree is quaint with fun street names like Ho, Hum, Nonchalant Avenue, Lazy Lane, and

Do your homework before you travel. Call or email your destination's Chamber of Commerce or the CVB (Convention and Visitors Bureau) and request visitor information. Your mailbox will soon be filled with a package of brochures and media guides so you can get ideas and feel prepared.

—Marybeth

Rocking Chair Road. The streets downtown are often closed off for art sales. Wine is usually available, so you can wander with a glass in your hand and maybe find just that right piece you have been looking for. Not so long ago Cave Creek was just a dusty cowboy town with dirt roads. The cowboys rode their horses into town, tied up at Harold's Cave Creek Corral (6895 E. Cave Creek Road, 480-488-1906, www.haroldscorral.com) and went in for a drink. Harold's Cave Creek Corral and the Buffalo Chip (6811 E. Cave Creek Road, Cave Creek, 480-488-9118, www.buffalo chipsaloon) still serve up country music and cookin' and give line and round dancing lessons.

BEST WINE BAR
Brix Wine Spot at Stagecoach Village is in Cave Creek. It's a country-and-western wine bar—the dream of the young owners, Brian and Nancy Franks. They have a great wine selection. You never know when someone will come in with a guitar or a fiddle and start playing. 7100 E. Cave Creek Road (480-575-9900, www.brixwinespot.com).

BEST PLACE FOR TEA
The English Rose Tea Room is absolutely jam-packed with all things English and tea-related retail. Lunch and afternoon tea turn into an event. The food is delicious and typical of what you would expect to find in a tea room—cucumber and watercress sandwiches, soups, and scones with clotted cream and jam and of course a huge variety of teas. To make it even more special, there is a bin full of glamorous hats, gloves, and boas to put on and make you feel oh so English and proper! 201 Easy Street, #103, Carefree (480-488-4812, www.carefreetea.com).

EVENTS TO FLY IN FOR
The Scottsdale Arts Festival takes place the third weekend in March and offers an exceptional array of fine arts, performances, and demonstrations.

It's been running since 1971. Center for the Arts (480-874-4686, www .scottsdaleperformingarts.org). Scottsdale Culinary Festival attracts more than 40,000 visitors. This is a one-of-a-kind event with cooking demonstrations from top chefs, benefit dinners, food sampling from more than 50 restaurants, and live entertainment. The event takes place the second weekend in April. Center for the Arts (480-945-7193, www .scottsdaleculinaryfestival.org) ArtFest of Scottsdale, the third weekend of November, brings over 200 artists together for a fabulous festival of art, literature, fashion, and culture. Contemporary Art is a major theme. Scottsdale Civic Center Sculpture Garden (888-278-3378, www.888artfest .com/scottsdale).

BEST RESTAURANTS

BINKLEY'S in Cave Creek is small so you need to reserve a table, sometimes weeks in advance during high season. The portions are reasonable compared to restaurants who feel they have to throw a ton of food at you to keep you happy and coming back. The plates are works of art and there are always little surprises that arrive at your table in between courses; a little taste of this, a spoonful of that. You can choose from dishes like summer truffle polenta, cornbread stuffed quail, mustard crusted monkfish, rack of lamb, and pheasant breast. 6920 East Cave Creek Road; ($38-44; 480-437-1072, www.binkleysrestaurant.com).
RAZZ'S RESTAURANT is a special place. It's been around for years—Razz is the chef and its heart and soul. On the menu you'll find ceviche, sea bass en papillote, chicken scaloppini, and bouillabaisse. The food is distinctive and very flavorful. Sit at the bar and order the small plates.

TRAVEL TIP

The best time to go to Scottsdale is in winter, spring, or fall. Annual temperatures average around 72 degrees Fahrenheit but low humidity in this region makes the summer months uncomfortably hot. It's nearly 19 miles from Phoenix Sky Harbor International Airport to downtown Scottsdale, about 25 minutes driving (without traffic).

Whatever Razz feels like cooking is what you get, and you never know what is coming next. And Razz is the entertainment as he holds court behind the bar. 10315 North Scottsdale Road ($22-30; 408-905-1308, www.razzsrestaurant.com).

WHERE TO STAY

The Fairmont Scottsdale is luxurious. It's a pink palace silhouetted by imposing mountains and the bluest of skies. Here you'll find the Willow Stream Spa—one of the best in North America according to *Condé Nast Traveler*. There are also two 18-hole golf courses, one of which is home to the annual PGA Tour FBR Open. This hotel has over 700 rooms, suites, and casitas. It's a AAA Five Diamond paradise. 7575 East Princess Drive (starting at $219; 480-585-4848, www.fairmont.com/scottsdale). The Royal Palms Resort and Spa is all about peace and tranquility. There are 119 casitas, or guest rooms, as well as a great pool and spa. Camelback Mountain sits patiently in the background. This hotel has been around for a long time and was recently renovated. Within the hotel, T. Cook's restaurant serves fantastic food, especially brunch. The lemon brioche French toast is so good it's dangerous. 5200 E. Camelback Road (starting at $169; 800-672-6011, www.royalpalmshotel.com). The Boulders is a very special place to stay with its flagstone walkways, crackling fireplaces, clear calm pools, and Southwestern architecture. It is tranquility to the highest of levels. Here you can stay in a casita, suite, or villa (one, two, or three bedrooms). The Golden Door Spa will make you feel like water. 34631 N. Tom Darlington Drive (starting at $169; 408-488-9009, www .theboulders.com).

ONE CLICK AND YOU'RE OFF: For up-to-date information on Scottsdale, visit the city's official website: www.scottsdaleaz.gov; or contact the Greater Phoenix Visitors Bureau (602-254-6500, www.visitphoenix.com).

Travel Companies for Women

ADVENTURE WOMEN
15033 Kelly Canyon Rd.
Bozeman, MT 59715
(800-804-8686, www.adventurewomen.com).

THE WOMEN'S TRAVEL CLUB
200 Broadacres Drive
Bloomfield, NJ 07003
(800-480-4448, www.womenstravelclub.com)

CANYON CALLING TOURS
200 Carol Canyon Drive
Sedona, AZ 86336
(800-664-8922, 520-282-0916,
www.canyoncalling.com)

MARIAH WILDERNESS EXPEDITIONS
P.O. Box 70248
Pt. Richmond, CA 94807
(800- 462-7424, www.mariahwe.com)

NORTHWEST WOMEN'S SURF CAMPS & RETREATS
Oregon and Kauai
P.O. Box 425
Seaside, Oregon 97138
(503-440-5782,
www.nwwomenssurfcamps.com)

ADVENTURES IN GOOD COMPANY
5913 Brackenridge Avenue
Baltimore, MD 21212
(877-439-4042,www.adventuresingood
company.com)

WOMAN TOURS (BIKE TOURS)
2340 Elmwood Avenue
Rochester, NY 14618
(800-247-1444, www.womantours.com)

SHERI GRIFFITH EXPEDITIONS
P.O. Box 1324
Moab, UT 84532
(800-332-2439, www.griffithexp.com)

CALL OF THE WILD
2519 Cedar Street
Berkeley, CA 94708
(888-378-1978, www.callwild.com)

THE WOMEN'S TRAVEL NETWORK
8990 Yonge St.
Richmond Hill, On L4C 6Z7
(905-771-8338, 888-419-0118,
womenstravelnetwork.ca)

GUTSY WOMEN TRAVEL
101 Limekiln Pike
Glenside, PA 19038
(866-464-8879, www.gutsywomentravel.com)

CANADIAN WOMAN TRAVELER
758 Bath Road, Kingston
Ontario, CAN K7M 4Y2
(1-888-830-5324, www.cwtraveller.ca)

ADVENTURE ASSOCIATES
P.O. Box 16304
Seattle, WA 98116
(888-532-8352,
www.adventureassociates.net)

WOMEN TRAVELING TOGETHER

1642 Fairhill Drive,
Edgewater, MD 21037
(410-956-5250, www.women-traveling.com)

ADVENTUROUS WENCH

1515 S. Extension Rd., Suite 2015
Mesa, AZ 85210
(866-419-3624,
www.adventurouswench.com)

CHICKS WITH PICKS (WOMEN CLIMBING WITH WOMEN)

Raising money and awareness for local
women's shelters in Colorado and
New Hampshire.
(970-626-4424, www.chickswithpicks.net)

MIND OVER MOUNTAINS

Women's adventure retreats in the
Colorado Rocky Mountains.
(970-626-4424,
www.mindovermountains.com)

BABES IN THE BACKCOUNTRY

Women's outdoor workshops and
adventure trips.
P.O. Box 8227, Breckenridge, CO 80424
(970-453-4060,
www.Babesinthebackcountry.com)

Volunteer Opportunities for 1-2 Weeks

SIERRA CLUB

Service trips, roughly 90 a year.
(415-977-5522, www.sierraclub.org/outings/
national/service.asp)

GLOBAL VOLUNTEERS

Offer service trips in the USA and abroad.
One week.
(800-487-1074, www.globalvolunteers.org)

AMERICAN HIKING SOCIETY VOLUNTEER VACATION

One week. Visit stunning backcountry
locations to construct or rebuild footpaths,
cabins and shelters. From Florida to
California, Maine to Washington State.
The trips are only $130 ($100 for American
Hiking Members)!
(800-972-8608, www.americanhiking.org)

HABITAT FOR HUMANITY

(229-924-6935, ext. 2551 or 2552,
www.habitat.org)

TEACH ENGLISH I-TO-I.COM

(800-985-4852, www.i-to-i.com)

Helpful Travel Websites

GUTSYTRAVELER.COM offers
women travel tips, (solo travel, family
travel, teen travel, serious defense tips,
packing and more), resources for women's
trips, stories about girlfriend weekends,
reunions and more.

TRAVELADVISORS.COM offers
reader's unbiased hotel, restaurant,
destination, and tour company reviews.

BUDGETTRAVEL.COM offers last
minute sales, and special promotions—
all tested and approved by Budget Travel
editors.

WWW.CITYPASS.COM offers a coupon book for major cities which cuts about 50 percent off published prices for major attractions. Available for San Francisco, New York, Philadelphia, Seattle, Toronto, Atlanta, Boston, Chicago, and Hollywood. From $49-63. (888-330-5008)

WWW.CRUISECRITIC.COM is a guide with ship reviews, readers' ship ratings and reviews, news, bargains, tips and message boards.

WWW.THEBATHROOMDI ARIES.COM is for those of you who are sticklers on cleanliness in public restrooms. This site rates more than 9,000 public restrooms worldwide in the areas of safety, hours of operation, aesthetics, handicap accessibility, including talking toilets for the visually impaired with microprocessors and infrared beams which act as an audible landmark, and cost (if there is a charge).

WHICHBUDGET.COM lines up all the discount and nondiscount carriers that cover your chosen airport. Just click the city or airport (worldwide) you want to fly to, or from.

LOWCOSTAIRLINES.ORG offers comprehensive listing of global low-cost airlines, including a list of now defunct carriers. This site does not sell tickets; it is informational.

FLYCHEAPO.COM will search only European budget airlines just like a regular search engine.

WWW.TSA.GOV/PRESS/HAPPEN INGS/THREAT-CHANGE.SHTM gives the latest in security regulations.

WAITTIME.TSA.DHS.GOV/INDEX .HTML provides the wait times for security checkpoints around the country. On the website, indicate what state, airport, day of the week and time you'll be at the airport.

Acknowledgments

My heartfelt thanks to several talented researchers, editors, writers, and marketing gurus: Elizabeth Newhouse, Holly Saunders, Ruth Chamblee, Al Morrow, Bridget A. English, Fiona Parrott, Annalyse Sheppard, and Gwen Kilvert. We share a mission and believe passionately in empowering and inspiring women to travel.

Simply, sincerely, thank-you to all my travel buddies, supportive friends, family, mentors, and role models who have inspired, advised, and encouraged me.

About the Author

Marybeth Bond is the nation's preeminent expert on women's travel. She is the award-winning author-editor of 11 books, including the bestsellers *50 Best Girlfriends Getaways in North America*, *A Woman's World*, and *Gutsy Women*.

Bond has hiked, cycled, climbed, dived, and kayaked her way through more than 70 countries around the world, from the depths of the Flores Sea to the summit of Mount Kilimanjaro. She studied in Paris for four years, earned two degrees, and had a business career in high-tech marketing.

Bond has traveled—along, with her gal pals, daughters, sisters, and mother and husband—researching travel books and articles and for adventure. She reminds us that gal-pal time and getaways are good for women's health.

COURTESY OF THE AUTHOR

She was a featured guest on the *Oprah Winfrey Show*, with her book *Gutsy Women*. As a nationally recognized travel expert and media personality, Bond has appeared on CBS News, CNN, ABC, NBC, National Public Radio, and *National Geographic Weekend*. She was the "Smart Traveler" radio host for the nationally syndicated *Outside Radio* show and the travel expert/columnist for the Travel Channel on ivillage.com, the women's online network. She was also the "travel expert" for CBS's *Evening Magazine*.

Follow along with her at www.gutsytraveler.com.

...blished by the National Geographic Society
...45 17th Street, N.W., Washington, D.C. 20036-4688

Second edition published in 2009

ISBN: 978-1-4262-0460-9

Founded in 1888, the National Geographic Society is one of the largest nonprofit scientific
educational organizations in the world. It reaches more than 285 million people worldwide
month through its official journal, NATIONAL GEOGRAPHIC, and its four other magazines; the Nati...
Geographic Channel; television documentaries; radio programs; films; books; videos and DV...
maps; and interactive media. National Geographic has funded more than 8,000 scientific research projects
supports an education program combating geographic illiteracy.

For more information, please call
1-800-NGS LINE (647-5463)
or write to the following address:

National Geographic Society
1145 17th Street N.W.
Washington, D.C. 20036-4688 U.S.A.

Visit us online at www.nationalgeographic.com

For information about special discounts for bulk purchases, please contact
National Geographic Books Special Sales: ngspecsales@ngs.org

Cover and Interior Design: Peggy Archambault, Cameron Zotter, and Al Morrow
Illustrations: Sheila Aldridge/Swell-Art